MAU MAU INTERROGATOR

by Ken Lees
with Introduction and Afterword by
David Elstein

Mau Mau Interrogator
Published by
Hotham Consultancy Limited,

First published 2019

Reprinted as a paperback 2020

Copyright © 2020 Ken Lees and David Elstein

Cover design by Grace Fussell Studio,
adapted by Abigail Mansion

Typesetting by chandlerbookdesign.com

Printed by CPI Group (UK) Ltd,
Croydon CR0 4YY

ISBN-13: 978-1-5272-7105-0

CONTENTS

INTRODUCTION

T he Mau Mau uprising against British rule in Kenya in the 1950s was bitterly fought: as has been the historical debate about it ever since. Was Mau Mau (a name whose meaning is still disputed) primarily a nationalist movement, calling for "land and freedom"? Or was that political slogan a cover for a power struggle within the Kikuyu tribe (Kenya's largest, constituting 20% of the population), as a generation of landless young men tried to overthrow the rigid age-based hierarchy that prevailed? Was the "moral balance" between Mau Mau and the British weighted to the former, given the heavy casualties suffered by Mau Mau? Or has the extent of Kikuyu casualties at the hands of Mau Mau been understated or suppressed by historians? Was the tough detention regime that at least 80,000 and perhaps more than 100,000 Kikuyu were subjected to, during the 8-year State of Emergency that was declared in 1952, in breach of international law? Or were the atrocities inflicted by Mau Mau on their loyalist fellow Kikuyu such a threat to law and order that the only option was detaining the most dangerous and forcing the rest of the Kikuyu population to live in "protected" villages whilst British forces subdued the armed bands of Mau Mau guerrillas?

In recent years, the argument has been fought out in the British High Court, in the shape of two huge lawsuits. After the first was settled by the British government – paying £20 million in compensation to over 5,000 former Mau Mau who claimed they had been tortured whilst detained – a second, involving over 40,000 claimants, was set in motion.

The claimants were people in their late 70s, 80s and even 90s, nearly all former members of, or supporters of, Mau Mau. As someone who had written a number of articles about Mau Mau, I had been put in contact with Ms Anju Lohia, one of the team of Treasury lawyers who were preparing the Foreign Office defence, to see who could be of assistance in finding evidence or witnesses that might be deployed by the Crown in resisting the claim. In July 2015, I sent an email to Ms Lohia, suggesting that she write to Ken Lees, who lived in Australia, but who had been brought up in England and had served a contract as a police inspector in Kenya during that period, attached to Special Branch. Ken had emailed me, through a friend of his who was helping him write a memoir of the period: they had seen what I had published, and thought I might be interested in what he had to say.

The Foreign Office lawyers duly spoke to Ken, at some length, but decided not to ask him to come to London to give evidence. Possibly, that was because he was well into his 80s, in poor health, and would have had to travel 12,000 miles to attend the High Court. On the other hand, it may have been because the story Ken tells, whilst strongly supportive of the Crown's case, also exposed a sensitive flank of the British government's handling, not just of the crisis in Kenya, but also of those two massive court cases fought out in the Royal Courts of Justice 50 years later.

In the first case, the Crown's defence had been hugely compromised in the middle of legal arguments by the revelation that a large part of the colonial administration's records, thought to have been on public view in the National Archive for many years, had instead been secretly stored in a depository at Hanslope Park, and had only just been re-discovered. As it turned out, these new papers were of only modest support to the claimants, but the embarrassment for the Crown – and the clear displeasure of the trial judge at this belated revelation – forced a tactical retreat, in which fault was admitted, including the use of torture, retribution offered, and finance even provided for the erection of a memorial to Mau Mau in the Kenyan capital, Nairobi.

Just as importantly, the Foreign Secretary, William Hague, included in his statement of apology a version of the level of casualties in the uprising, as between the loss of life among Kikuyu civilians and Mau Mau, which strongly – and wrongly – suggested that the former were much smaller than the latter. Quite why Mr Hague used this formulation – which is drawn from the work of a key American historian who has strongly supported Mau Mau in her published writings and the litigants in their claim for compensation – is hard to judge.

The second case collapsed in the High Court in November 2018, after Mr Justice Stewart rejected the first two of 42 test cases selected from the 40,000 claimants. He declined to over-ride the Act of Limitation, which allowed only exceptional reasons for submitting claims more than three years after the event. In his view, the damage alleged was too limited, and the many decades that had elapsed since the supposed events made it almost impossible for the Crown to find relevant evidence and witnesses, and so mount a defence.

Even though Ken Lees could have covered a good deal of the ground in respect of which the judge expressly regretted the dearth of witnesses, he was not called. I sent the judge a sample of what Ken might have offered in sworn evidence, but he politely informed me that it was entirely up to the Crown, not him, who was called as a witness on its behalf. This book, therefore, fills the gap that the four-and-a-half year court case left: the testimony of a key participant and eye-witness involved in a crucial element of the suppression of Mau Mau as a threat to the Kikuyu tribe.

For more than three years, Ken Lees oversaw the process by which tens of thousands of detainees were allowed their freedom, provided they confessed to the crimes they had committed. Lees had overhauled the Special Branch filing system so that he had multiple accounts of every Mau Mau incident in the Fort Hall area (where he was stationed as a Special Branch inspector): anyone seeking release who offered a false confession would be quickly exposed by Lees' interrogators. Lees handled thousands of interrogations himself. To begin with, he checked the terrible crimes being admitted by exhuming bodies, but he quickly realised that those detainees genuinely seeking release needed to cleanse themselves of their pasts, for their own psychological welfare. The story of Lees' interrogation technique, and the picture of Mau Mau it helped paint, is the core of this book.

Central to his account is his estimate of the number of murderers amongst the Mau Mau detainees – well over 10,000 – and the number of Kikuyu he estimates the Mau Mau murdered – between 20,000 and 30,000, perhaps even more. The scale of slaughter has been largely elided or denied by the dominant school of historians of Kenya of this period. This book sets the story straight.

In my afterword, I explain how the debate over the scale of Kikuyu deaths has developed, and why the revelations from Ken Lees strongly suggest where the truth lies. It is more than sixty years since Ken departed from Kenya, his experiences in the detention camps etched indelibly into his mind. The confessions he heard were deeply disturbing, and for decades he did not talk about them. Now, he tells his story for the first time.

David Elstein
September 2019

PROLOGUE

Stretched out on my bed, in the straw-roofed African hut known as a rondavel, I listened to Max Bruch's violin concerto. It was my favourite way of winding down after an intensive day of interrogating Kikuyu tribesmen who were members of Mau Mau, the terrorist organisation in Kenya that was trying to expel the British from their land. I had taught myself some skills needed to get beneath the skin of the detainees in the camp where I worked, disarming them and making them realise – or believe – I knew more about every detail of their lives than they did themselves. If I could persuade them of this, I could make them also believe that it was in their own interests to forswear the oath of allegiance they had taken to Mau Mau and allow us to release them to go back to their villages, no longer a danger to the government or themselves.

The skills I needed had the nature of a theatrical performance, every move I made planned and rehearsed.

One day, a man turned up, a fellow about 55, with thinning hair, and well made, steel-rimmed spectacles. It was about three o'clock in the afternoon and when the sun sets, it goes down like a stone. You don't get a lot of evening in Kenya.

So this man came in and he didn't sit in the chair although I motioned to him to sit down, but stood up in front of me. That didn't bother me. I didn't show any sign of displeasure. I had to be completely relaxed, even though I did not feel it. We got started, and another man came in, perhaps from Nairobi. I have a feeling he might have been a doctor.

This man sat in the corner behind the translator, and I started the detainee interview in earnest. It lasted for a couple of hours at least. The sun went down, and it got pretty dark in the hut. As I was talking to this man and making the points that I wanted to make, I was leaning across the desk completely absorbed by the fact that this man and I had made contact some way. He sat down first of all, which was one victory for me, then his head dropped, and that was another. I continued in these short sharp sentences, and he then started to lean on his knees, and he eventually ended up with his head between his knees. And I left him like that for a whole two or three minutes. I didn't think about the other man in the corner, he was now in the dark as it were. And then I said to the detainee, 'You've done well. I'll recommend that you'd go to the open camp as soon as possible. Thank you.' and he stood and went out and this fellow in the corner jumped out and started to jump from foot to foot and shouted "You got it! You got it!" and off he went. I have no idea who he was. He was probably from the governor's offices or maybe from the hospital in Nairobi. But whatever it was that I had done, it made a real impression on that man and he had seen me working at my best. The detainee did go to the open camp and he did get released and I never heard of him again and neither did anybody else. He just went back to life as he lived it before. And I was just delighted about the success.

On days like this, where I felt a sense of pride in what I had achieved, I thought back to the strange and wandering path that had led me from a poor childhood in the north of England during the Great Depression to an interrogation hut in the highlands of the British colony of Kenya…

1

OPENING THE TEXTBOOK OF LIFE

The best way to describe my childhood would be to say that it fell into two parts. The first began with my birth in 1931, which was at the height of the Great Depression, to a family that were suffering from the economic situation. It was also at the beginning of my father's illness from rheumatoid arthritis, and he was virtually bedridden when I was born, in Lancaster in the northwest of England.

I was told later by my mother that when I was born my grandmother, my father's mother, said "I don't think he'll last because he's wheezing." But it just shows that people who think they know things are not always right, something I learnt later on, because I'm still around 89 years later.

The second phase of my childhood was when we were moved to another house nearer town, and I remember that it had a downstairs and an upstairs. The bedrooms were upstairs and the kitchen was downstairs with the dining room and lounge, and the toilet was outside. It was at the end of a cul-de-sac, and blocking off the end there was a big stone wall, behind which there was an enormous lake of water which was used for cooling purposes for the weaving mills that were all around. It was all very Dickensian. For instance, the lighting in the house was gas, and I remember my mother lighting these gas mantles at night-time, and also the man who used to come along the street and light the street lamps with a long pole and a flame on the end.

The next thing I remember about that period was when I was two or three. I realised that all the other little boys and girls lived in families where people, grown-ups, came home from work, and played with them and talked to them. But nobody came to talk to me. This didn't bother me too much, but I found out that these other people, these grown-ups, were fathers and brothers, and other close male relatives. Although I had an elder brother, four years older than me, I didn't see much of him because he was at school all day, and I was in bed when he came home at night so I didn't see him then either. So, I knew I had a brother, but only at weekends, as it were.

I clearly remember a scene when I must have asked my mother who and where my father was, and she took me upstairs to a bedroom that I'd never been in. There was a window on the other side of this rather large room, and a bed against the window, and there was a man in the bed with his head turned away from us, and he was looking out of the window towards that big stone wall. And my mother said, 'This is your father, Ken'. And I looked up at her – I remember doing that – and said something like, 'Oh.' We turned around and left. And that was all I remember about that. I next saw my father about four years later.

Another significant memory from that time was of standing on the stairs one morning, and hearing a miaowing at the back door. My mother opened it and a black and white kitten came in which she fed with some milk in a saucer. She said, 'Shall we keep him?' and of course I said, 'Oh, absolutely!' So, we did. And he stayed with us for probably ten years, and we called him Punch, and he was a delight.

I went to the infants' school, which was quite near to where we lived, and my mother took me there on the first day, and every other day, I suppose. I went there for a little while, and then we moved to a new house with electricity and plumbing and a bathroom, and a toilet inside, a semi-detached house, right on the outskirts of Lancaster.

I remember fairly clearly the move to the new house because I'd never been in a motorcar before. My father had two brothers; one of them, Archie, a commando who was to be killed during the Second World War, and another brother, Ron, younger than Archie, who became a builder. Archie had this car, and I remember being driven in it. It was an old, black thing, not very large, and I remember that it rattled.

We were in the last row of houses before the countryside, 23 Beaumont Place, Skerton, Lancaster. In fact, there was a field opposite my house where we played. Mr Askew was the farmer, and we used to see him ploughing and harvesting. I was there from the age of about five or six, and I went to the local junior school, St Luke's. Because my father was a stonemason, there was a dedication stone outside the front door of the school which had been carved by my father, and every morning I would walk past this stone, which had about twenty lines on it, and I used to marvel at the fact that someone could so neatly carve words on to a piece of hard stone. I remember quite clearly thinking – what happens if you make an error and knock a bit off the last word? Do you have to stick it on, which you can't, of course, or do you have to start all over again? And I remember asking my father this question and he said, 'Well, it's quite easy, son,' he said, 'what you do is you knock off what you don't want.' I thought this a rather ambiguous kind of answer…

My father's illness meant that during the time that I was very small he had to take to his bed. In fact, I never ever saw him standing up, and I had no idea how tall he might be. He was always in bed, and he was there until I was seventeen, when he died from cancer.

He was nursed all that time by my mother, which meant that she had something like twenty years of continuous caring for my father, twenty-four hours a day, seven days a week. Because he was unable to hold things and he had difficulty raising his hand to his mouth my mother had the task of feeding him, cutting his food into mouth-size pieces and guiding them into his mouth.   She also took care of his washing but only when Bob and I were out of the way.

There were no holidays for her because there was nobody else to do this work, although when I became old enough, eight or nine, I helped with carrying urine bottles and so on.

I realised quite soon in my life that caring was a thing that had to be done and I got on and did it. Situations like that teach a child responsibility and self- discipline.

After St Luke's, I attended the local higher school, but the lessons were quite boring for me. I was always thinking about something else, and so I never did really well at school. But my father, being bed-ridden and being the sort of man he was, read a lot, non-fiction mainly, and we got into the way of talking about these books and what was in them and what it meant, and so on. It was way above my head when he started, of course, but, being a good teacher he explained things to me simply and I picked up an interest in them. Because he was so interested in books – reading was the only thing he could do – I used to go into town to the library and pick books for him from the non-fiction section, which meant looking over all the non-fiction, which covered ancient history to philosophy to economics to all aspects of knowledge. I would pick up these books and see whether I could understand what was in them and selecting what my father might find interesting.

He was very interested in the way in which language and culture behaved as mirrors of each other. His favourite metaphor was that of a lock and a key, the lock being the culture and language – including words, gestures, drama and song – as the key to opening that culture. I would sit on the floor at the side of his bed whilst we discussed how it could be that this world of "things" had names, sounds, propositions, and meanings and how this garment of interlocking words gave shape to the everyday activities and intentions of people which may differ from group to group. This kind of chatting, usually in the evenings as the light was failing, would lead us from the nature of people to the need for organisation, states, laws, rights and wrongs and how they took shape.

All of this thinking was to be very important to me when I was faced with the problem of communicating with the ever growing population passing through my camps. I am sure that all this debate, to-and-fro, with my father later guided me through these cultural encounters.

Very early on I learned how to look at a book rather quickly by going to the contents page and seeing what it was about, and then having a quick glance at the conclusion and deciding whether to take it or not, because I could only carry about three of four of these heavy tomes.

In this way, my father took on my secondary education and I became his student, and I used to sit by his bedside or lie on the floor with my back against his bed and he would talk and I would listen, and then I would talk and he would listen, and I learned how to discuss things when I was quite young. He taught me about logic and rationality and rhetoric, and what these meant and how they could be used, and how the emotional dimension of what you say is just as important as the actual words that you use.

And all this became so important to me that schoolwork itself became a total bore, and I couldn't wait to get home to my father and discuss what we'd been talking about or reading the week before or the day before, or the previous evening.

My father's bed was in the downstairs lounge, up against the window which faced the back garden, which was abutted by the Manchester/

Kendal canal. And at that time there were barges being pulled by great big shire horses going up and down this canal most of the time, and these barges were floating homes with little chimneys with smoke coming out, and washing on the line on the boat, and the man at the back would be steering this long barge around the bends and under the bridges. Over the years, the boatmen began to realise that there was somebody in this house, confined permanently to bed. They could just see his head and they used to toot their horn and wave. My father couldn't wave back because of this debilitating arthritis, but they knew that they'd made contact. Such a friendly gesture was always well-received by my father.

My father's total incapacity made me aware that the world was larger than 23 Beaumont Place. This was brought home to me during the Second World War. His bed was up against one of the back windows in the lounge overlooking the canal and when the German bombers came over, we could always tell because the engines made a throbbing noise instead of the unbroken roar of any of the other planes I knew. At the beginning of their campaign against the North West of England, Liverpool, Manchester, Salford, Preston and Barrow docks, we thought it best that if they decided to drop one near us we should all go together, so as soon as we heard the throb of the engines we collected together in the lounge. I remember my father telling Bob and me to climb under his bed where we would be safe from flying glass. After a number of raids we became bored with squeezing under Dad's bed; and as the bombers hadn't dropped anything near us, we pleaded with him to let us go upstairs and watch the show from there. So it was that we had a ring-side seat watching the sky light up with the bombs as they dropped on Manchester and Salford. The planes passed over us to get at Barrow docks so we only heard them coming and going. What we didn't know was that our uncle Archie (Dad's brother) was a police officer in the midst of it all in Salford.

Archie had been trained as a cabinet maker at Waring & Gillow in Lancaster, and had made my father a four legged book rest which fitted quite high on his chest, allowing him to reach it with his page-turning fork, which he held in his mouth. Archie joined the police at the outbreak of war. When we were running out of men the police were given the choice of being drafted into the Air Force or the Army. Because of the high rate of casualties in the Air Force at the time Archie chose to go into the Army and was sent into one of the Commando Regiments for training.

As fate would have it, after about six months Archie was killed whilst on a training exercise in Scotland.

The time I spent with my father taught me that there are many ways of looking at an issue, and there are many ways of solving an issue, and that the Aristotelian syllogism – all men are mortal, I am a man, therefore I am mortal – is not necessarily the way in which one should tackle the real world, because of the impact of continuous change on everything. The fact that my education was an oral one rather than a written one gave me a facility with words and an ability to argue. The arguing part was taught to me in a subtle way because my father would ask me a question which was, if you like, a hook, an intellectual hook for me to spear myself with. It became quite a lot of fun between the two of us for me to either get caught or see that it was a hook and wriggle off it.

It was like education in ancient Greece. The people that went to the Stoics, for instance, were educated orally. They were taught the art of rhetoric, the art of winning in discussion and argument, the skill of quickly getting all your ducks in a row, and in the correct row; expressing yourself in the right kind of language with the right kind of pauses, with the right kind of tone, so that you could win the argument. I have read somewhere about "the alchemy of language". You mix together all the different words, length of sentences, tone of voice, emphasis and so on and so forth until you get the right mix, and it either works or it doesn't.

That's how I learned with my father, and we would both find this highly amusing and did it for hours, while my mother went out to work, to try and supplement the family income. All this time we were being paid from the Poor Relief Office, I think it was called.

When I was a little boy, like four, I used to be tidied up and my curly blond hair combed, and I would be trotted off to this office as a kind of mascot. I remember feeling apprehensive before we went into this place. I didn't like the atmosphere, and I was ashamed of the way in which my mother had to behave to get this money from the man who was so important and a big civil servant.

All these visits failed to reveal something which would have helped my mother so much if someone at the Social Security Office had done their homework. Three weeks after we had buried my father, a letter came to advise my mother that, as a full time nurse, she would be paid a weekly amount of money to assist in caring for him. She wrote back saying that it would have been of great help while he was alive, and enclosing his Death Certificate to show that he had just left… As Baroness Von Blixen's manservant said —"the Gods play games with us, memsahib".

My unorthodox education at the feet of my father meant I have never been fazed by people in authority, such as those who were of a higher rank in the army or civil service. I was always able to 'manage' such situations quite well.

And I needed that skill when I was called up for National Service.

I joined the army in August 1949, and I went down south to Princess Elizabeth Barracks in Fleet, Hampshire. I was assigned to the Royal Army Medical Corps which meant that I had to study physiology and first aid and other medical subjects. There was no weapons training, but we did all the other training, including the drill: marching and marching and marching, *ad nauseam*. We also had runs and route marches to improve our fitness.

I finished that about December, 1949, and was so good at the drill – which I actually disliked – that I was asked if I would like to stay at the depot and become a drill instructor. But what I really wanted was to have an adventure somewhere, and I volunteered for a section of the barracks called the Holding and Drafting Company, where people arrived and departed from postings overseas.

I soon learned that the thing to do was always to appear to be busy, and so I got myself the job of mopping out the NAAFI – the dining hall for the troops – after the meals. It took a long time, every day, and I did that for probably a month. I would often see a crowd of soldiers march in under the command of a sergeant major, and they would all be ticked off a list and away they would go. This was the 'holding and drafting' that went on in the Company. These men were the draft, and they were usually going somewhere, Germany or further away.

One day I was busy mopping the floor when in marched another group, about fifty men accompanied by the sergeant major, who started going through the list of people who were supposed to be there and they all bellowed back their name and number. The sergeant major reached a name on the list and got no reply. Then he shouted again and somebody from the back shouted that the missing man, from the Parachute Regiment, had broken both his legs, presumably from a misjudged jump. The sergeant major needed to fill out his form and he obviously didn't enjoy this man being missing. He exclaimed "Shit!" and looked wildly around. Seeing me, he said, "You!", and I tried to hide, and keep mopping, hoping it wasn't directed at me. But he said, "No, you there!" So, I immediately said, "Me, sir?" and he said "Yes, you. Fall in."

And so, I 'fell in' and he bellowed, "What's your number and your name?" and I bellowed back "22165091, Lees, K", and he said, "Lees, you're going to Malaya". Of course, it was my training as a medic that was going to be a lot more important for my army career than any potential as a para.

That was the unorthodox way I suddenly found myself en route for the adventure I had sought.

We started with even more arduous route marches and exercises for a fortnight or so, and then we went by train to Harwich docks, boarded a ferry and set sail for Berghaven in the Hook of Holland. There was a train waiting for us, and we set off across Europe to Trieste. The train turned out to be a bit like the Orient Express. We all had rather luxurious cabins to live in, and stewards who came and served dinner and it was all delightful. We travelled across Holland and through Germany and Austria. Every city we went through was absolutely flattened, and I remember the silence that fell on the cabin as we looked out at this devastation. Sometimes, you couldn't see a house for a mile in any direction; they were all flattened by the bombing. It made quite an impression on us.

I remember once when the train stopped in the middle of nowhere. It was about 11 o'clock at night, and we weren't allowed off the train, but because we had stopped and there was deep snow outside, I just had to go on to the steps of the train and put my foot in the snow. And I looked up and there were some lights, and they seemed to be stars, but I realised after a second or two that they weren't stars at all, they were actually houses, and they were way up in the sky. We were in the Alps, in the middle of a great big valley, called Villach.

Then the train set off and we travelled for perhaps half a day, and arrived at Trieste, and the train drew up on the dockside, and we were transferred from the train to a ship.

Just as we were all collected in the dining car ready to leave the train, one of the young German stewards who had served us during our three-day trip came into the carriage and asked if he could address us before we went on our way. We all agreed but were puzzled and wondered what he was going to say. He started, in very good English, to remind us of the utter defeat suffered by Germany. He went on to tell us that economically things in his country were very bad and that, for instance, the best – perhaps the only – currency was the cigarette. He said that if we were pleased with the service he and his colleagues had given us during our trip perhaps we would show our thanks by giving them any spare cigarettes we might have. We were all quite touched by his request and as we were given fifty Players cigarettes every week, free, we all responded by loading him up with as many as we could find, which was quite a lot. I didn't smoke, for instance, and had three unopened tins in my kit. He got the lot.

The ship waiting for us was called the *Westralia*. She was one of the vessels that used to make trips around the coast of Australia before the roads became passable: routes like Perth to Melbourne, Melbourne to Sydney, Sydney to Brisbane and back. It was a beautiful old ship, all mahogany inside, quite small, only about 10–15,000 tonnes. The crew were all Australians and they were delightful. We were well fed and well looked after. I remember that we were given steak for breakfast.

There were two of us to a cabin, and we had about three weeks sailing. We went down the Adriatic and through the Suez Canal. This was where I first came across Islam; I was standing, looking over the rail of the boat at the sand and so on passing by. A man was on the deck above me and he started to call in Arabic and bow down, obviously saying his evening prayer. I'd never seen that before and it made quite an impression on me. It was my first contact with another religion, and spurred my interest in comparative religion, an interest I have followed all my life. We sailed out into the Red Sea and then across the Indian Ocean, stopping at Colombo and then arriving and disembarking in Singapore.

I remember looking back at the boat and thinking what a wonderful time I had had, because of the calibre of the crew and facilities. It was a small ship and we were quite near the water, and I could stand on the deck and lean over the side of the rail and watch the flying fish go between one wave and another, and the porpoises come flying at the boat, three, four, five of them all in a row. They'd dive underneath the ship, and we would run across the deck and watch them come up the other side, which was great sport.

It was a wonderful experience in itself. I have never forgotten that journey in the *Westralia* and its Australian crew, who were great mates.

Of course, where we were going was no picnic. Malaya was in the throes of countering a guerrilla uprising spearheaded by Chinese communists. The way the British dealt with this insurgency would be studied carefully by those responding to the Mau Mau rebellion in Kenya a couple of years later.

During the voyage, we had talks about the Malayan terrorists and what they did, how to keep your eyes open out in the field, and the dos and don'ts on patrol, and so on. We also had sessions on medical topics: how to deal with bullet wounds and broken legs and other injuries.

When we got to Singapore we were transferred to Nee Soon barracks, a great big block of about five floors. There were three buildings shaped like a horseshoe, and we were in the middle block.

I was desperate for the toilet and I ran up to the floor that I was supposed to be in, dropped my kit on the bed and flew into the toilet, slamming the door, and quickly sitting down. On the door right in front of my face was a spider about the size of a dinner plate. It was a bird-eating spider, and every time I put my boot out and kicked the door it would dive at my foot. Eventually, after sitting there for ten minutes or so in absolute terror, I managed to grab the door, and slam it as I flew out. I thought, 'well this is terrific, I've only been here for about three hours and here I am already being terrified by the local fauna.'

When we'd been there a day we were told that the communist terrorists did not follow the Geneva Convention as it applied to medical personnel, and so we had to learn how to use small arms. We had three weeks of learning how to load, fire, clean and strip down weapons like the new .303 short-barrel Lee Enfield, which had a rubber cushion on the butt, because it kicked like a mule. We spent a week at least, firing these things incessantly; learning about the Sten gun, and the Bren gun, the light machine-gun that we used in the British Army. We also learned how to use the pistol, the Smith & Wesson 38, how to fire it and how to take it to bits. This is how my real National Service started.

When we'd been in Nee Soon for about two weeks, we were told that we were being posted to Kuala Lumpur, which was up north in Malaya, across the causeway which joins Malaya and Singapore. For our train journey, we were issued with a .303 rifle, ten rounds of ammunition and a bayonet, and we were told to load our weapons, take the cover off the bayonet, and stick the whole thing out of the window of the train. Since the train had no windows, only blinds made of bamboo, which you pushed up and down to keep the draught out, this was easy. It was an armoured train and as we went across the causeway very slowly, the first thing that came into view was the Juhor Bahru station, which had been burned down by the terrorists the week before. We went very slowly for the whole of the night, until we got to Kuala Lumpur itself, which had the most gorgeous railway station, all Islamic turrets and beautiful architecture.

2

CULTURE CLASH

From Kuala Lumpur we were sent off to various regiments. My group of about thirty were sent to the Sixteenth Field Ambulance, which was stationed about half an hour outside Kuala Lumpur in a camp at a big tin mine. The camp was shared with the Suffolk regiment. This was our headquarters where I stayed for four or five months, training in the art of jungle warfare. At least that was the intention. But I acquired an additional job when someone discovered that, before I joined the army, I had been articled to a chartered accountant and had sat some exams. This was enough to get me appointed as pay corporal, so I did the payroll for the men for about three months, even though it was not really my sort of thing. I didn't go there to do accountancy, I went there to have an adventure, and so I made it quite clear that I'd rather be doing something else.

To my surprise, shortly after arriving in the camp I was sent for by the regimental sergeant major, a man called Joe Heeney. Why? I wondered. All sorts of things ran through my mind but none of them approached the real reason he wanted to see me.

"Lees," he said, "I'm glad you've come here."

"Yes sir?", I said, and he said, "Because I know your mother!"

In the middle of Malaya in 1950 I didn't expect to meet an old flame of my mother's but here he was.

"Your mother was my girlfriend for quite some time before she met your father. Now, I'm going to look after you and make sure you won't come to any harm, is that clear?"

"Yes sir" I said.

"Well, dismissed," he said. And that was it.

I thought this was rather promising. I was reminded of the World War II song "Kiss me goodnight, sergeant major," but was soon disabused of the idea that I would get special treatment when RSM Heeney sent us all, including me, down to the railway station to shift a few tonnes of coal on to lorries

However, when I had done my time as a pay corporal, I was posted to the 1/10th Gurkha rifles at Bentong, up country in the Pahang state. This part of Malaya is covered with very deep and dense jungle, and very hard to fight in. As newly arrived recruits we knew we would be required to face a much more experienced enemy, people who were experts in jungle warfare. They had got together to fight the Japanese during the Second World War, so they had had some eight years' practice and we'd just arrived off a boat, and could hardly compete with them.

So while we were out scouring the jungle looking for them, we rather hoped that they wouldn't be looking for us.

Thankfully we were with the Gurkhas, and I was sent to a place called Kuala Padah, about an hour's drive out of Bentong, at the end of a road that ran past all the rubber plantations. We were in what was called a 'defended camp', put together by General Templar to prevent the terrorists getting food from the Chinese rubber tappers, by concentrating everybody in a number of camps around the place. It was a strategy that really worked.

Our job would be to patrol the camp wire fence, and I of course had to supply medical aid when necessary. In fact my medical training was called for on the first day I was there. I arrived at about ten o'clock at night, and took my kit into my bed space in a big room which I had to myself in an old Chinese school. The bed was known as a char-poi, made up of rope slung together on a frame, and from time to time you have to tighten the ropes, which means you have to untie the knots and redo it all, a bit like restringing a guitar. But they were comfortable enough.

I had just deposited my kit and was putting my things together when a police Land Rover sped into the parade ground with a wounded policeman in the back. He had been shot in the back but he was lucky because the bullets had hit his scapula and had spread out across his back. Nevertheless, it was quite clear that I couldn't do anything about him there and then; he'd have to go somewhere where they could carry out surgery and put him right. We radioed for support and eventually two armoured cars turned up from the Guards regiment with an ambulance. I gave the policeman morphine and we got him into the ambulance and he went to sleep. It was pitch dark in the ambulance and as we set off I was prepared for anything to happen. I sat there with my Sten gun, and we drove for about an hour and a half to a medical facility. After the doctors came and examined the man, we were relieved of duty and set off back.

While on our way in convoy, we came on a big fire, which was about a mile off the road, so the armoured cars went off to find out what was up, and we were left in the ambulance, in the middle of the night. The driver and I jumped out and slid into a ditch by the side of the road. I remember feeling for the magazine on my Sten gun, and discovering that it had been knocked off as I was getting out of the ambulance. So I sat there with this useless Sten gun waiting for the armoured cars to return, which they did eventually and we got safely back to base. That was my first day there and I thought, 'Well this is a fine start, what next?'

Our camp was only about fifty yards from the jungle edge and we were well within range of enemy fire. This could lead to the occasional disruption to our routine. Because I was a European in the midst of Gurkhas, they'd organised for me to have a cook who would cook European food in my room. This had gone quite well for about a month, and then one day, all of a sudden I heard a hell of a clang across the room. I got up to investigate and was confronted with the cook holding a flattened 9-mm round which had hit his frying pan. Thinking about it later I realised that the frying pan might have saved my life because I was in direct line of fire and if the round hadn't hit the frying pan it would have gone right through my bed space.

The cook was absolutely terrified, and he said something in Chinese and kept waving the squashed bullet about. After I took it off him, he jumped on his bike and flew off down the road and I never saw him again.

I went to see the captain, and told him what had happened, and he said, "Well, you'll have to mess with the men." From that point on, I ate the same rations as the Gurkhas: dal and different curries, which was fine. I got to know the Gurkha soldiers very well. They used to teach me Gurkha songs, none of them actually printable.

One Gurkha custom I learned about occurred in the aftermath of a tragic event which happened when I was in a truck with ten men, on a road where we should really have been accompanied by two other vehicles and more men, because of the poor quality of the road. I was in the back, with a sergeant major on one side and me on the other and the men between, and the driver and a Bren gunner were in the front. Suddenly, because we were going too fast, the vehicle skidded on the wet road, hit a rock, flew through the air, and turned over. All I remember is flying through the air under the vehicle with this black shape above me. The next thing I remember was waking up under the truck.

I was lucky to land feet first and came to right side up, arms outstretched, in an unknown depth of thick evil smelling mud. I still had my sten gun in my hand though. Glancing round I saw two or three others on their backs face up, pinned down at their chests by the side of the truck. I started for the fast-closing gap between mud and the tail-gate whilst they were gradually sinking into the mud head first.

As I looked round, the one nearest me said, "Don't leave us, John" (everyone was 'John', to the Gurkhas) and I said "No, I'll be back, I'll be back". But I had to get myself out first. I think I'd been hit on the head when the vehicle came down and pushed into the swamp rather like a nail into a piece of wood. I waded, and pushed, and shoved, and managed to get out as the vehicle was sinking. I could see the space decreasing quite swiftly, and I managed to get out by putting my head down and pushing it into the mud and coming up the other side. I looked round, and there were men lying groaning on the road, or on the bank at the side. Some of them were badly injured but there was nothing I could do because there were too many and I was stunned myself by the experience.

I got up to the road and, amazingly, there was a car coming along, an open car with two Asians in it. I waved them to stop, and jumped in and said, "Drive me to the police station", which I knew was about four or five miles up the road. We hadn't been driving for more than five minutes before I saw coming towards us about six police Land Rovers, bristling with policemen armed to the teeth. They weren't coming to look for us, but were just on patrol. I stopped them and explained to the European police inspector what had happened. We got back to where my truck had overturned, and I leaped out and ran down the hill, got hold of the side of the truck and started to bellow "Come on, you Gurkhas, push this blasted truck off these men!" I remember screeching at the top of my voice to get all these people up to help, and a lot of them did. Eventually, with the help of about twenty or thirty police, we started to lift the truck up. We just got it to the point where it was going to flip, when we heard the most awful gurgling, and everybody stopped. There was a split second where we could either let it come back, or push it further, and I had to decide which it was going to be. I decided we should keep pushing so I shouted louder, "Push, push, push, push, push" at the top of my voice. And so we did, and it flipped over and that was it. I just collapsed on the bank, and then as I was watching the hole in the mud where we'd been, a body floated up, one of the Gurkha soldiers, and he was obviously dead.

I felt a hand on my shoulder and it was my C.O., Dr Ball, and he said "You've done all you can, Lees." And I just sat there while he talked to me, and then he attended to everybody and the ambulances came and took us all off to Bentong. When I got to the hospital to help with the injured, I didn't realise that Dr Ball was unaware that I'd been in the truck. He'd thought that I'd come with the police afterwards. We sorted out the people who'd been trapped, and then I started to feel a lot of pain in my legs, and he said, "What's the matter?" I said, "Well, I was in the truck when it overturned. I was underneath it –". He looked astonished and said "You were in the truck?" and I said "Yes, I was underneath the damn thing!" He lifted me onto the examination stretcher and at that point, in walked an Asian man from the first car I'd met on the road. He was Indian and he came said to Dr Ball, "This man gave great service today, great service!" I was very grateful that at that time of night he had searched the hospital to find me.

After four days in Bentong Hospital, I returned to Kuala Padah and the Gurkhas. When I came out I got a message from the C.O.'s office. The adjutant of the Gurkhas wanted to see me, and because I was absolutely filthy I had to borrow a pair of shiny boots and a clean uniform. I went into his office and he looked up at me and he said, "Well, Lees, I've been going through your records, and I see that you put down to go to university when you leave the army. Unfortunately," he went on, "the rules are that you have to be at university before you join up in order to go when you come out, otherwise you've got to pass all the exams again."

This seemed a surprisingly irrelevant thing to summon me to talk about at the time, and I think it was just an excuse to see who it was who had helped at the scene of the accident, rather than anything to do with me going to university. I was a bit taken aback and just said "Not to worry, Sir," and dismissed myself and left.

The next morning the whole squad arrived at my bed space in an excited state. They insisted that I go with them, because the Captain (who was a Gurkha himself) wanted to see us all. We formed-up as usual, and the Captain stood on a box and said that he wanted to draw attention to my behaviour at the crash site. Even though we had lost fellow soldiers, he wanted to thank me for the part I had played in saving the others. Everybody clapped and at that point the corporal stepped forward and said "We would like Private Lees to be able to wear a Kukri [Gurkha knife] and belt because he saved lives, Sir!" The Captain looked into the distance for about twenty seconds and then said "Can`t be done, unfortunately!" There was a groan of disappointment from everybody, but that was that. I, of course, was really chuffed about the whole thing.

These men wanted me to have a sign that I had passed their test, as far as being a soldier was concerned, and they wanted to give their symbol, their kukri, to me. I was really touched by that, of course and we were all very disappointed by the captain's refusal. What I learned about the Gurkhas from that was that they were very generous towards people from another culture, provided that they performed as they themselves expected a Gurkha to perform. This insight, applied to other cultures, became quite useful to me in Kenya.

I was beginning to see the value of looking at other cultures in a different way, but it wasn't always possible to understand them, particularly if they resisted any form of communication.

For example, one day, when I was with the Gurkhas, three Aceh natives came along. They were from the north end of Sumatra, the large island to the southwest of Malaya. These Aceh people are all head-hunters, and they were sent over to Malaya to be trackers. I tried to get some kind of conversation going with them, but it proved to be completely impossible. We did have an interpreter, and through him I learnt that the Aceh didn't want to talk about what they thought, or what they did, or how they lived, which was quite surprising.

Another group of people who aroused my curiosity were the Saki. We were so far into what we called the deep jungle that from time to time we'd find an aboriginal forest-dweller from this tribe standing and watching what we were doing, and I often wondered what their lives were like. They weren't as small as the pygmy people I saw in the Ituru forest some years later, but they were about five feet tall, and they all had bigger heads than the bodies really warranted. Occasionally they came into contact with our soldiers, but I never had the chance to find out more about them.

Eventually, the Gurkhas were withdrawn from that posting and replaced by the 4th Malay regiment which I transferred to. When I'd been with them for about five or six days, I experienced something surprising about the cultural differences between us.

It was evening time, after dinner, and I was in the bed-space that I had. A 4th Malay sergeant came in and said, "We'd like to talk to you." And so I said, "Oh, fine." There was a table-tennis table in the main body of this room, which they used to play on from time to time. So I sat on that, in front of all these guys, and the sergeant began to ask me questions about myself.

I thought, 'this is very strange, what's he driving at?' It went on for possibly ten minutes, and there were questions which were circling round an issue, but which I only understood towards the end of his questioning. It was about my sexuality. From my scant knowledge of Islam, I knew that homosexuality is seen as a sin, and their questions showed that they found some aspects of my behaviour puzzling. The sergeant would ask me questions like "We've noticed that you don't go down to the village," which is code for 'You don't go looking for a woman' or something of that kind. And when I'd convinced them that it wasn't because I didn't need women or anything like that, but just because I had made the choice not to bother, they were all highly pleased, and they thanked me and dispersed.

It crossed my mind that, had I actually been gay, this might have been so abhorrent to them that I wouldn't have been the first European officer to be shot in the back of the head on a patrol for reasons other than being a bad officer.

I needed that kind of insight if I was to have to go out in the jungle with them in situations where misunderstandings could increase the danger.

I remember one day we were out practising firing the three-inch mortar. This is like a piece of drainpipe about two yards long, and you put a bomb in one end and it fires out of the other. It's a very powerful weapon with a very long range, and the effect of the mortar shells when they land is quite horrific. We fired about four of these at a big white tree that was at the top of a hill, probably five or six miles away. We didn't hit the tree, but it gave the guys practice in trying to. But when we came to the next round and they pushed it down the pipe, it went 'pop' and flew out of the end, and then it hung for a moment in the air about thirty feet up, and then just fell, 'clomp' onto the ground in front of us, on its belly. And we all stood there, frozen, waiting for it to go off, but it didn't. Then we had to think, what the hell are we going to do now? So we got a stretcher and we pulled out one of the poles from one side to use to roll the bomb on to the stretcher. We then put the pole back, and I volunteered to be one of those carrying the bomb, without dropping it, out of the camp and up the hill and depositing it in a deep pool, tail first so that it wouldn't go off as we put it in. And then we retreated fast.

After I'd finished with the 4th Malay I moved again, this time to the Scots Guards.

Going out with the Scots Guards, people of my own culture, was a shock in reverse, because I wasn't in charge any more, as I had been with the previous two groups. Now, the sergeant major was in charge. One day, we were out in a rubber plantation, the sort of place you got bitten to death by mosquitoes, and it was terribly hot, and it went on for ever and ever, and there seemed to be no end to the trees. I had been taught by Dr Ball that heat exhaustion in Malaya was in some ways a bigger hazard than getting shot. You can't carry a lot of water and you've only got one water bottle, and so to prevent heat exhaustion you have to have fairly frequent mouthfuls, just one, and never ever drink a lot. So you wet your mouth and swallow, and that's it.

I had acquired this habit and while I was in the middle of this patrol, we stopped, and I pulled my water bottle out and took a quick mouthful, but the sergeant major came roaring up and bellowed at me and said "You will drink water when I say, not when you feel thirsty!" and of course I was chastised appropriately, and said "Absolutely, sergeant major." I knew very well that he was wrong, but that's not the point. The point was that he had the rank.

On another occasion, we had intelligence that there was a gang who had moved into a village on the road between us and the headquarters at Kuala Kubu Bharu, which was quite a drive away. And the day that we were to go out, the C.O. sent for me for some medical attention. He had a quite a bad ulcer on his leg, because he had been wearing jungle boots for long periods, including overnight – it was just one of those things you have to do – and he said, "Can you do something with this, corporal?" I looked at the ulcer and I put some penicillin powder on it and a dressing, and stuck waterproofing round it so he could get his boots on and it wouldn't get wet again. And as I was doing that he was talking to the lieutenant colonel who was in the same tent as he was. They were discussing what they were going to do, and I couldn't help hearing that they'd got intelligence of some sort, but they didn't say what it was. Later in the day I was called to parade with the men and we went off in our trucks, down the road to the village, and the guardsmen ran into the village, and out the other end ran eight men, running fast up a hill. You can't hear much noise in the interior, not even gunshots, because of the thickness of the jungle, but it seems that the three Bren gunners opened up on these people, and they killed all of them bar one, who was badly wounded. I was standing by the ambulance as they carried all these people back. Most of them were Chinese, but one of them was an Indian, and I said to the guardsman who was escorting the other two, "What happened?" And he said, "Well, this guy was lying on the ground groaning and the sergeant came up and just fired half a magazine, into his back, and sure enough he was nearly cut in half." He was certainly very dead. They just put him in the ambulance and the sergeant major came to see what had happened. We went out again the following day and got the last of the terrorists. He'd decided not to run on the first day but he did on the second and didn't get very far. And so the Guards got nine in two days, which I think was a record of some sort.

There was yet another change when the Guards were withdrawn and replaced by the Royal West Kent Regiment, who were new to Malaya at the time. When I was on patrol with them we were somewhere in the jungle near Kuala Kubu Baru, a place we called K.K.B. About four of us were quietly talking, squatting next to a large tree with deep cover all around, when there was a burst of fire from close by. (You couldn't hear the shots if they come from any distance over twenty yards). The tree shattered just above our heads and fragments flew everywhere. We all froze as we were for perhaps ten minutes, during which I felt the bridge of my nose bleeding and I could taste blood dripping into my mouth. Nothing further happened, so we crawled away into cover and kept very quiet until we decided we were clear. I had sustained a close encounter with something sharp which had skinned my nose but nothing more. The skin has never grown back properly and from time to time I will rub my nose and re-skin it. Other than walking into one of my own punjy sticks (sharp pointed bamboo sticks around the camp to protect it) I survived Malaya intact.

I have to say I felt there was a slackness about the West Kents and my impression was confirmed in a tragic way. I was later sent down to Singapore to finish my time in the Army and caught a boat called the *Empire Orwell*, formerly the liner *Bremen* which had been captured and turned into a hospital ship. It was full of people from Korea and I learnt from somebody who'd been listening to the news that the Royal West Kents had been caught in an ambush and eight of them had been killed. I wasn't really all that surprised, but I did think that they might have shared some of the blame for the tragedy.

These were terrible things for a young man of my age to experience for the first time. But the major thing about my time in Malaya was a personal recognition of the fact that terrorism must be terrible. I mean that terrorism, to work, to be terror, must be terrible. This is something Lenin said. Half-hearted terrorism won't be terrorism. It's got to be full-on.

I had one experience which hammered this home. It was the middle of the day and there was a local bus for the people in the village to get to Bentong for supplies and it would return about two or three o'clock in the afternoon. We got information that the bus had been hijacked down the road and we all jumped in our American troop-carrier, and we set off at a great rate, armed to the teeth, down this winding road, following the path of the river. We came around the corner and saw the bus stopped about a hundred and fifty yards in front of us. In front of the bus there were about twenty-five local people all squatting down.

There were three people in some kind of uniform, one of whom was pointing a tommy-gun at the head of a young man. And as we came around the corner and stopped, it was quite clear that we couldn't fire because we might hit the local people who were between us and the terrorists. But as we stopped and gaped at the situation, this terrorist blew the face off the young man that he was holding. Blood flew all over the place and he fell in a big bloody heap on the ground. And this terrorist turned around, grinned at us, and the three of them disappeared into the jungle.

We started to trail them but they could have been ten yards into the jungle and hiding and you would have walked right past them. It is the best cover ever and they were absolute experts at it. So, there was this young man with half a face, lying on the ground dead. His colleague was kneeling on the ground by his side in total shock, as were all the other people. I tried to talk to this man, to get him to say something, but he couldn't speak, his mouth opened but nothing came out; his eyes were staring and he just couldn't take in what had happened. So I and another soldier got hold of the dead man and dragged him into the bus so he was out of sight of the other people. And we waited there for our men to return. When the police arrived, and we went back to camp, that was the end of my first serious experience of terrorism.

Otherwise, our encounters were confined to exchanging fire, or trying to. Usually, the jungle was so dense that when we were fired on, we couldn't see the shooter and just fired back in the general direction of where we thought he was.

Thinking back, I was fortunate to come through unscathed. I lost several colleagues and friends, not always through terrorist action.

There was a man called Summers, Private Summers. He was carrying a sten gun and riding shotgun in an ambulance on a road which was a bit dangerous. He was sitting in the front passenger seat and he put the gun under his chin and was leaning his head on his hands, which were covering the end of the barrel of his Sten gun. The ambulance went over a bump and the gun went off and shot him through the head, an outcome which was hardly unforeseeable.

Another one of my friends who was killed was called Shufflebottom. We used to joke with him that he would be safe from terrorists because they'd never fit his name on a bullet. One day, he and a man called Shirley were in the back of a truck coming down the Bentong Pass, which was always a difficult and dangerous road, and the terrorists opened fire on them and Shufflebottom was shot. While he was rolling around in the bottom of the truck, according to Shirley, they fired again and hit him and killed him. Fortunately for Shirley, they turned a corner and were out of the line of fire. Poor Shirley just sat there in the truck with the dead body of someone he had known for a year, until they got back to Kuala Lumpur, about two hours later.

The third death occurred when a group of men were out practising how to get a critically injured man across a river. One of the men had volunteered to be the patient, and they had constructed a stretcher and raft out of bamboo, and they bound him as if he had broken legs and broken arms and other injuries, and they had him half way across this river and the stretcher that they'd just constructed fell to bits, and the 'patient' sank like a stone and disappeared beneath the surface. He was unable to move because of the bandages and one of the people in the group was a very good swimmer, but it took him about half an hour, diving down into the river, before he found the body of the young man on a ledge and he brought him up. I remember seeing them taking the body of this man along the side of the parade ground to the Medical Inspection room, with the captain looking very dejected.

Of course, although I survived I was often terrified by the situations we were in. But I immediately had to re-channel that terror into some kind of action. I knew that standing there with my mouth open wouldn't save lives. When under fire, you either go and stand like a tree so that they don't see you moving, because that's the only way they can't see you, or you fight back. The emotions are absolutely immediate, and rational decision-making is a poor second. The rational part of you is slower than the emotional part of you.

My training in accounting had taught me the importance of details. The area of Malaya we worked in was all jungle. This was what you walked into and it's like walking into a thick London fog, except that it's all green, and you can't see a damn thing. There were two ways of making progress in this jungle: one of them was along a dried-up river bed, the grooves that water had worn down the valley. You can walk through those because all the trees have been washed away. It's a bit dangerous to do that because obviously the communists knew that we would be doing it but if we'd stayed among the trees we would have had to chop our way through and the enemy would have heard us. At least we were reasonably quiet walking along these dry river beds. One major problem with them was that if it rained heavily, which it did every day, you couldn't hear it falling because of the canopy high above you. Down at ground level it was as silent as a tomb. But rainwater deposited miles away might all come rushing down your particular river bed and you would suddenly hear the roar the water as it approached and you'd just leap out of the way as quickly as possible otherwise you got swept away.

The other way through the jungle was using what I call pig runs. Pahang was an area of very thick jungle which was about 150,000 square miles. The whole place was infested with pigs, big boars with tusks and their sows, and there are hundreds of them. They made tunnels through the jungle and we would sometimes get about using them as paths. They were quite wide but they weren't very big or very high, so we had to double up to go down them, and there were branches all over the place. The big problem was that you might meet a boar coming full tilt the other way. This would be highly dangerous because some of them were the size of a man, with huge tusks. Fortunately, I never did meet one although the danger was there. I think they may have been more frightened of us than we were of them.

My time in Malaya was an intensive learning experience, both in developing flexibility in judging and assessing people from very different cultures and in dealing constructively with fear rather than letting it overwhelm me.

You have to redirect that fear into action, and not just any action, but action with a purpose and as quickly as you can. Bear in mind that all these basic emotions are instantaneous because they are biologically wired into our brains and we fear immediately, without thinking. When thought follows fear an instant later, we make a decision, which might be to run – although that immediately draws attention and the attackers see you and you'd be dead. You have to redirect that fear immediately into some other kind of action and the fear will dissipate and free you to think about what you should do. If you don't act, the fear will just make you freeze to the spot.

My medical skills turned out to provide a learning experience with much wider scope than just how to deal with medical emergencies. Every emergency is different and dealing with it requires a unique set of decisions, so you learn decision-making skills that can generalise to all sorts of other situations.

I was once faced with people who were drowning in a river, thrown from an upturned vehicle. I was looking down from a bridge, and knowing that all rivers flow in one direction, I looked in the direction of the flow. A bit further down the river I could see a boy about eight or nine struggling in the thick reeds at the side of the river, and about to be swept away. I shouted to my driver to go and get this young boy, because I knew that he could do that while I went down to the truck with a colleague. We both dived into the river and got inside the back of the truck, and pulled out the remaining passenger, a young woman, but she was unfortunately in a very bad way by the time we got her out onto the bank, so there wasn't a lot we could do about her, but at least we saved the young boy.

I remember, as we were doing CPR on this young woman, I looked up and there was this young lad standing with an Asian man who was obviously his father, and I felt good that at least, we'd saved his son. I was commended for that rescue and that felt good too.

My time in Malaya and the range of different people I worked with formed a good introduction to cultural relativity, and established in me a mindset which was to be invaluable later in my career. I realised that you had to know three major things about whoever it was you were working with. Because they weren't European, and they didn't want to be, they had little conception of the way in which Europeans approach everything from a kind of rational/objective point of view. You have to discover what it is the other group sees as 'manners': how you say things to people; how you approach people; what body language you use. I learnt that language itself is more than one thing. In fact there are three facets which make up the alchemy of language. There is the language that you speak, the sound; there is the language that the emotions speak, the way you sound; and there is also the language that your body speaks – you can say things, but if you don't mean them, your body and your emotions and the tone will tell anybody who's looking for the signs that you actually don't mean it.

You also have to understand the customs: what it is they think is of value; what they think is not; what is the right thing to do; what is bad, what is good. I came to see that in every culture you'll find subtle differences, and you will be really in trouble if you don't understand that. You must also understand what it is they believe in. Of course, other people's beliefs can be very different from ours. But whatever it is they believe in, they believe it. And however different – perhaps even nonsensical – their beliefs seem to us, we have to start with respect for what it is they believe.

The value of this approach is that if you don't adopt it, your life can be in danger. Every time you go out on a patrol you're on your own with six or more people, and you're putting your life on the line. When things happen, you have to know what it is the others will do and why they'll do it.

These lessons are not a luxury, but a vital part of the job. You have to learn that other people do not approach reality – whatever that is – with the objective mental tools that you do. Life in the West is based on objectivity and rationality, but many other cultures have a very different approach to living in this world. You have to find out sensitively what it is they actually value, what they consider to be virtues, and what their cultural ambitions might be. I learned in my dealings with the Gurkhas and the indigenous Malayans that you have to change your methodology according to the

culture that you are facing, otherwise there is no communication and you
run into problems.

My first real contact with the Gurkhas, before I joined the 1/10th
Gurkha Rifles, was as part of a medical training exercise. The captain said
to me one day that they were getting a platoon of Gurkhas in, and he asked
me to help with their training. He said, "If you're agreeable, what we're
going to do show them what a compound fracture of the leg looks like,
and what you do about it."

A compound fracture is where the bones have broken in such a way
that they're very sharp and they penetrate the skin and stick out of the leg
with the possibility of infection, especially if you're nowhere near a hospital.
So we had to find a way to show them what it looked like and what to do
about it. And I had the job of being a guinea pig.

We mixed plaster of Paris, and stuck it round my left leg, and then stuck
broken bones in the plaster of Paris to imitate what a compound fracture
would look like, with these sharp bones sticking out at odd angles and the
whole lot painted bright red to simulate the bleeding. You couldn't see the
'fracture' when I put my long trousers on and my jungle boots because it
was designed to look normal, and the idea was that I would walk along as
if I was on a patrol and I would pretend to trip and I fall down and start to
groan and roll about, as people do if they get shot in the leg. The captain
would take my boot off quickly and cut my trousers up so that the plaster
of Paris and the bones sticking out would be clearly visible to these Gurkha
soldiers who were all stood round.

When I fell over they all thought this was a joke at first and started to
laugh. But when they saw what was happening they took it seriously and
their captain told them that this was an important training session and so
they all became quite serious and they listened carefully to was said about
how to stop bleeding and immobilise the bones, and get the wounded man
on a stretcher, and how you then get that stretcher to an ambulance. And
I did this for every day for a week or so.

When they were on parade, every morning and every night, I used to
watch them, and I felt that they were the smartest young men that I think
I'd ever seen. So I was really pleased when the sergeant major said that I
would be going to the 1/10th Gurkhas, because the excellent character and
calibre of these men had been shown in the way that they responded to
the training that I'd helped to organise.

The big lesson of my time in Malaya, which was to serve me well when I went to Kenya, was to do with the nature of terrorism and the importance of the right emotional attitude to it.

I've seen a lot of dead bodies, but until I went to Malaya I'd never seen anyone get his face blown off in front of me, and so I'd been able to come to terms with the fact that people can do terrible things to other people and not turn a hair, especially if it's politically motivated. The impact that the Malayan communist terrorists had on me was quite profound. I learnt how to respond to a terrorist act effectively, which was quite useful later in my interrogations, because anything that the perpetrators might tell me didn't anger me, and I deliberately didn't show if I was disgusted. I also discovered how important it was during my interrogations to engender an emotional response in these people in some way. If you can generate an emotional response, perhaps by yourself becoming emotionally aroused, those emotions can be infectious, perhaps transmitted by the way you speak, what you say, how you say it, the words you use, the silences that you observe and perhaps pretending to be interested and demonstrating this interest.

So my time in Malaya taught me a whole range of lessons which I could never have learnt in a classroom, or vicariously through the experience of other people. And this was to be crucial in the next stage of my career.

When I finished my time in Malaya, I continued my service back in the UK on a part-time basis, for three and a half years. Every Thursday night I paraded in uniform, on one weekend a month I did gun-drill, and I practiced live fire for two weeks full-time every year. In many ways this restricted the kind of 'day jobs' that you could do. Under the rules, your original employer had to take you back, and since I had worked at a local accountant between leaving school and being called up, I went back to this job, and soldiered on at a desk for the three and a half years of part-time army service. But as soon as I was discharged from the army, I got a different job, the first one that I could find, which was selling photocopiers. I did this reasonably well, and it was good fun, meeting new people and trying to sell them something. But I missed the sense of adventure and so when I saw an advertisement for a position of Police Inspector in Kenya in mid-1955, I applied, and got the job.

3

INTO AFRICA

B y the time I arrived in Nairobi, the Emergency was well into its
third year, having been declared in October 1952, after many months
of murder and mayhem committed by a Kikuyu movement that
called itself (or was called by others) Mau Mau. The name, as I discovered,
deliberately had no meaning, in order to be more mysterious and so more
powerful, like JuJu in the Cameroons (where I served after my stint in Kenya).
Most people in the UK knew little about the conflict other than what could
be read in newspapers, where Mau Mau was depicted as a depraved terrorist
group, held together by fearsome oaths. As it happens, by the time of my
arrival, the military campaign against Mau Mau had been largely successful,
and the real battleground was in the detention camps in which tens of
thousands of Kikuyu were held, and who could not be released unless the
authorities could be confident they would do no further harm.

Soon I would be plunged fully into that world, but to begin with my
knowledge of Kenya was virtually zero. The only research I did before I
left England was to go to the cinema to see a film called *Simba,* starring
Dirk Bogarde, about a British family living in East Africa, who become
embroiled in the Mau Mau uprising. It was the usual Hollywood movie
treatment: 90% imagination. They were the bad guys and we were the
good guys and that was it. This was the sum total of my understanding of
what Mau Mau might be before I went to Kenya.

I remember looking out of the airplane window as we came into
Nairobi, and I thought, 'Good God, these roads are absolutely terrible!

They're only mud tracks!".

But my first impressions were largely positive. It seemed a fairly sleepy place to me when I first arrived. I went to a hotel in Nairobi to recover from the flight and the jabs, and got kitted out and was sent up to the police training college at Kiganjo. I was there for about two weeks.

I remember I went out of the college one weekend for some recreation, and when I had to get back, I knew there'd be traffic on this road, so I stood by the side of the road, hoping to hitch a ride. And a police Land Rover drew up, and I jumped in, and they were talking about which place had the best shrimps in England, which was an odd thing to be talking about there, at that time. And it turned out that the man that I sat next to, called Bill, came, strangely enough, from Morecambe, which is just down the road from where I was born, in Lancaster. He was at the training college as well.

Bill did his time in Kenya, and while he was in the police he was in charge of a station which covered part of the territory between Kilimanjaro and the Kenyan border, looking for cattle thieves. When Bill left the police he became a white hunter, and had an unfortunate encounter with a buffalo that he was supposed to be helping an American tourist to shoot. The tourist didn't shoot when Bill told him to, and the beast kept rushing at them, so Bill had to shoot it and because of its momentum, it ended up running into them both. Bill was trapped underneath and the American thought he would do the right thing and shoot the buffalo because it was struggling, and he fired into it and unfortunately hit Bill in the leg.

Kenya seemed a very quiet sort of place in those days. After training I was posted to Kisumu county, to a station called Miwani. I was in uniform at the time but not qualified in any way, and did odd jobs around the place. Miwani was underneath the Nandi Escarpment, which is about two thousand feet straight up, and it's the border between the Nandi and the Luo.

President Obama's father was a Luo. One of the things about Luo which interested me is that their method of selecting leaders is to get little boys of six or seven to stand up and give speeches in the circle of elders, and they judge their capacity by what they say, and how they do this. And you can see it in Obama, it's genetic, I think; the way he speaks is absolutely the same as Tom Mboya who was another Luo, or Oginga Odinga whom I met in Kisumu. Odinga was a typical Luo, fairly tall, broad, and with a very loud voice and could talk the hind leg off a donkey. All Luo male names begin with the letter "O" – Odinga and Obama and so on.

Miwani was at the bottom of the Nandi Escarpment. The Nandi are Bantu and are brown and thinnish and reasonably tall, while the Luo are all very broad, and black, with flat noses, and they eat a lot of fish caught in Lake Victoria, Africa's largest lake.

As well as being physically different, the Nandi and the Luo are also different mentally. They have a completely differently view of life, and it's odd that one should live on the top of this escarpment and the other one should live just at the bottom. Spatially they're separated by about six feet horizontally, but by about two thousand feet vertically, and that made all the difference.

I thought Miwani was a beautiful place. It was alive at night with animals like hyena. If you went out at night you took a torch and you could see them running across the road, like a small donkey with stripes on. And they're all at the front and nothing behind, most ungainly, but they can go like the wind if they want to. They are also the raw garbage collectors of Africa, with a lot of carcasses to dispose of. One of the reasons why it has been so difficult to track the number of Kikuyu who died at the hands of Mau Mau has been the efficiency of these scavengers. It is unlikely that anyone killed in the evening would be missed by these "garbage-men" by morning. Everything eatable was gone by then.

One day, the police commissioner in the area had to make a tour of police stations and he chose me to accompany him. I think he wanted somebody to talk to on the long trip. He had been there for about twenty-five years and his conversation, no matter where it started, would end up with him talking about how he would be glad to retire to a cottage in Devon. We didn't get back until about eight o'clock at night, and because we were so late his wife had put his dinner in the oven. As she didn't expect two of us, there was only enough for one, but he insisted that I should have it because the mess at the station had shut. His wife was upset about this but he was only trying to be kind. Perhaps he had enjoyed our conversations as much as I did.

One of the differences between Malaya and Kenya I noticed when I arrived was the lack of temples and places of worship. In Malaya you can't walk more than half a mile before you find yourself confronted by a roadside shrine or some other tribute to one of their gods. These are nearly always Chinese and are to be found everywhere. Then there were the mosques and temples, including a large minaret in Kuala Lumpur itself which was really beautiful. It was built in the middle of the commercial district as a reminder to everyone of the power of the Gods. These places of worship reminded me of a Longfellow poem my father used to quote:

"In the elder days of Art,
Builders wrought with greatest care
Each minute and unseen part;
For the Gods see everywhere."

Longfellow's verse seemed to apply very much in Malaya, but I saw nothing of the sort in Kenya.

There were no signs of the local people's worship at all. There were the Christian churches, of course, in Nairobi, but there were no Kenyan places of worship similar to the Chinese shrines in Malaya.

Spending time with other African peoples later, I found a different picture. When I went to run a plebiscite in the Cameroons I was struck by the existence of Juju huts and the gargoyles that surrounded their doors, the beautiful carvings they made of images of spirits and demons and so on. In fact, I used to have to visit these villages and some of them were quite isolated, and in every village that was some distance away so I had to stay the night, I was always billeted in the Juju hut, among the drums and sheep's heads and old snakes and that sort of thing. This was because nobody from the village would ever come in, and so my boy, Wenceslas, would set up my camp bed and my mosquito net and leave me a Tilley lamp, and I would turn it down and in the light of this Tilley lamp, I would be able to see all the way around this building which was made of very, very thick bamboo pieces. There were little spaces between each of the bamboo poles that held up the walls and you could see the eyes of these little children of various heights staring in the dark as they looked in at this strange creature going to bed underneath his mosquito net. And I was completely safe. I was unarmed, but they presented no threat whatsoever.

At that time and at my age, I had not developed any strong views about British colonial control of Kenya and the other African colonies. I knew that I was there to do the best job I could for the police in Kenya and the people of Kenya. I suppose if I thought about it at all, it was along the lines of the grand Marxist view of the evils of capitalism and its need to have colonies to take its excess produce, and I didn't have any ambivalence towards it. I just accepted what I saw for what it was and thought that if we didn't do it, someone else would, America or China, or even Russia.

But over the years, and following what I saw and experienced while I was working there, I came to see the colonial situation in Kenya as to be untenable. In fact, I only realised what my own views were and how strong they were as a result of a conversation with a good friend, Sean McHenry.

One day I was walking back to the officers' mess for lunch when I bumped into Sean and his wife, Patsy, whom he'd married in Ireland and brought out to Kenya. They were well settled into their married quarters and I used to see them going off on trips in Sean's motor car, to see the game, and explore some of the beautiful sites in Kenya. We chatted for a while and then, out of the blue, Sean said to me, "Ken, how long do you think this thing's going to last?" and I realised that he was talking about the colonial situation. It turned out that he was thinking about signing a permanent contract with the Kenya police. He'd been a medical student, was an educated man, really good at writing forensic reports, and was highly regarded by his superiors. All of a sudden I realised that he was thinking of signing up permanently and looking ahead to a career of, say, 25 years or so.

Now, Sean and I had shared accommodation for quite some time when we first arrived, and we knew each other quite well, so I felt I had a duty to Sean to tell him what I really thought. At this stage, I hadn't really even admitted it to myself. But as soon as I was put on the spot, I knew.

And so when he said, "How long do you think it will last?", by which, of course, he meant the European domination of Kenya, I thought to myself, 'Now, do I tell him?' Because I hadn't told anybody else because nobody else had asked me. But I thought about it for a moment or two, and I remember looking down at the ground and drawing circles in the dust with my boot, as I thought 'Now shall I say what I think, or should I say what he thinks I should say?'

And I thought 'I owe Sean more than I owe anybody else here', so I said to him, "Five years."

That was in February 1958, and independence was declared in 1963, so I was absolutely right. It was a wild guess, but somehow or other I knew that the situation there was not tenable. I'm glad I did say it, because Sean didn't sign and went back to Ireland and became one of Ireland's most successful businessmen.

There were of course many 'colonisers' there, and the ones I met were actually delightful people, in the main. Usually I got to know them on official business. I might arrive at an isolated farm and then I would be expected to stay the night. I was invited to sit at table and entertain the guests with stories from my working life, playing the role of a fully-functioning part of the society that they'd developed out there. They hadn't seen anybody for perhaps three weeks, and they were very glad to see me and they insisted that I stayed and performed at dinner, and told them funny stories, which was rather nice. In fact, generally speaking, I rather liked them.

As time went on and I was in a better position to understand how they were placed, one of the colonial European settlers that I got to know was Michael Blundell, who was a minister in the Government. The first time I met him I was called to the DC's office, and introduced to him. He was thick-set; not too tall; a well-built fellow; about 55, and the D.C. said, "This is Minister Blundell. I want you to take him round the camps and show him what he wants to see." Which I did, and that was the first time that I knew Sir Michael, as he became.

He would turn up with his Land Rover and driver at odd times, and talk to me about what I was doing in this camp, or that camp, or what the situation was with regard to the villagisation program. I remember one day we'd been to Kamaguta, and we were on the way back through Kigumo, and I knew the rondavels, the round houses we lived in, and the one where the district officer for Kigumo lived. It was up a fairly steep rise, and part of an African village. And I said to Michael Blundell, "Would you like to talk to this D.O.?" He said, "Oh, yes, that might be useful", so we stopped.

I jumped out of the Land Rover and ran up the hill and banged on this fellow's door, and opened it and there he was, lying on his bed. I said, "I've got the Minister outside, he wants to have a word, quick; he doesn't have a lot of time." And this man decided that he had to start to put his uniform on, with his funny hat. And I said, "Come on, for God's sake, just come as you are." But he insisted on getting his jacket with the brass buttons on and so on, and he was trying to put his trousers on. So, I left, went back down, and said to Minister Blundell that he'd be down in a minute or two. We sat there for about five minutes, then Michael said, "Oh we haven't got time to wait for him to come." and we set off. So he never did meet the D.O. of Kigumo, but it was the man's own fault.

My view of European settlers was coloured quite a lot by the attitude of hope and confidence that Blundell displayed every time I met him, on perhaps a dozen occasions. He would just turn up, and have some specific

issue that he wanted to talk about. Perhaps it would be how many people
we'd managed to get through the camps during the month, or whether we
had had any people revert to criminal activities? Or what was happening
with regard to the villagisation program, and did I think that they were
settling in?

After I had settled in to my police role in Kenya, I was assigned to Special
Branch, to work in detention camps at Fort Hall, one of the Kenyan districts
and the heartland of the Kikuyu. I had to learn all I could about this tribe
and the way in which the Mau Mau organisation tried to control Kikuyu
tribespeople to achieve its aims.

Once I familiarised myself with the camp's routines, and the policies
applied to former and current Mau Mau detainees I realised that I needed
to upgrade the database that was being used by the detention system, and
more importantly to make a deeper connection with the detainees than
simply interrogating them. In trying to understand the Kikuyu people, my
experience in Malaya and the way in which I'd been educated convinced
me that it was a matter of understanding the manners, the customs, and the
beliefs of the people. These include the values they hold to, which ones they
consider to be important; their ambitions, that is where they think they're
going; and the cultural mythology, which is best approached through things
like proverbs, which are a staple part of the Kikuyu language.

What this understanding can achieve is a level of trust with the people.
You do that by demonstrating truth, keeping your word and showing that
you are keeping your word. With regard to the Kikuyu you also have to
bear in mind that there is an age-grade system, the *riika* system as it's called,
where newer age groups owe respect to the older ones, through forms of
speech that they use for that.

One big issue was, how do you form a contract in an illiterate society?
This was one of their major problems, and they solved it by designing their
contracts around the taking of an oath.

Now, the breaking of an oath in the old days used to result in public
shaming and possibly even physical violence. A contract could not be
repudiated once an oath had been sworn, other than through a public
demonstration that you were actually trying to deceive somebody else, in
which case your ability to make contracts with other people disappears.

It's rather like being refused a credit card in the West, forever. So there's
the oathing and the contract part of it, then you've got to bear in mind

the rituals that they follow. They have rituals like everybody else. We have rituals of saying 'hello', shaking hands and so on; they have similar rituals and they're all appropriate to the kinship organisation that they follow. In the west, of course, to make a contract you have to provide what is called 'a consideration'. Even if it's just one pound, it has important legal significance. Well, in many ways the oath takes the place of a consideration amongst the Kikuyu, in that everybody is taken at face value, and if they take an oath with regard to ownership of some particular land, or whatever, that is taken as being the same as a consideration in our way of law.

You also have to bear in mind that they don't reason as we do. An Aristotelian syllogism is something that they would probably find hilarious. In their thinking, their myths and language and ideologies come into play, and so their reasoning is sometimes very difficult to follow unless you understand what their mythic background is. Their assumptions are not necessarily those which a European would make in the same situation. I often felt that I lived in a parallel universe to the Kikuyu.

In order to immerse myself in Kikuyu society, which I was going to have to do to understand the people I would be interrogating, I tried to memorise as many as I could of their sayings. There are a couple that come to mind: 'Haraka haraka haina baraka', which means 'rushing doesn't help in the end' – literally 'hurry, hurry has no blessing'. Another one that I remember was 'Haba na haba, hujaza kibaba', which means 'little by little fills the cup'.

I also tried to find out what made them happy, what made them laugh, that kind of thing. How they reasoned things out when they were talking, which is very hard to do because you don't have the common assumptions that they have, but a set of completely different but possibly parallel ones from the west, which you can't use.

It was particularly important to recognise that the Kikuyu and most of the other tribes, particularly the Luo, are past masters at the art of persuasion using designed speech or rhetoric. They've got all their relevant facts, as they see them, marshalled before they start to speak and it was really good to listen to them as they were really terrific at it. But you have to recognise that what they're saying to you may be interpreted in a different way in your own society.

Within about three months of my arrival in Kenya I had begun to grasp some of the key issues at play between Kikuyu tribal customs and the settlers' efforts to manage the Kenyan economy. It didn't take me long to realise that any society that shares out land equally to all the male children, rather as the French used to do, eventually ends up with very small patches of land scattered around all over the place. And while this system may be economically sufficient for the feeding of a family, it hardly produces a surplus that can be exchanged for cash on the market, so that the ability of that particular country to exist in the modern world is virtually zero. And I could see the clash between the settlers trying to manage large areas of land so that the productivity could go up, and the Kikuyu trying to get hold of the same land and divide it up so that everybody got some, with the productivity of that land going down to virtually zero as far as surpluses for the market were concerned.

But it was this Kikuyu approach to tribal land which was at the heart of the claims made by the Mau Mau against the British colonisers. When I was talking to the people in the camps, I used to say to them 'What were you promised by Mau Mau?' and they would say, 'We were promised freedom and land by our leaders.'

Freedom I could see simply meant to them the removal of the Europeans and the transfer of power to Africans (led by the dominant tribe, the Kikuyu). But land? I remember saying to the young men 'how much land do you think you would get? How many acres would it be?' 'Enough for the family' would be the reply. So I said, 'You mean so that all the families had enough and they would all be able to feed themselves?' 'Yes, that would be right, that's what we want.' And I would tell them, 'But unfortunately it might be that if you all produced just enough for the family there would be nothing to sell to anybody else to bring new ideas, machinery, or whatever it might be, from abroad.' 'Well, do we need it? Do we need that sort of thing?' And that was the place where we would reach an impasse. On the one hand they saw the Mau Mau promise as being land for everybody; on the other hand they could see that that in itself wouldn't be an economic solution for the country as a whole. But then they didn't care about that anyway. In fact, that whole concept was not part of their world view, only of the West's.

In a sense, their view had a sort of legitimacy, provided that the aim was that the entire country would stay completely tribalised *and* that you could get the other tribes to agree to do the same thing. That would, in fact, have been a big stumbling block to the sharing out of land because the other tribes might wish to have as much land as the Kikuyu, and so conflict would result, and you would end up as you always ended up: in a sort of fluid stand-off at the tribal borders, effectively the status quo. Of course, that meant that you'd continue to live as you do now, or go backwards in terms of technology, and so on. They didn't really seem to bother about that. All they really saw was the fact that they could have land, feed the family, have children, and they were the key issues.

So the conflict had a genuine root in Kikuyu society. Their land use was intimately linked with the use of memory in their culture. Jomo Kenyatta, in his book *Facing Mount Kenya*, explains the method that they use to improve the spatial memory of children, similar to what we call photographic memory. Most of them, especially the girls, seem to have a spatial memory which is nearly faultless.

Later on, when we were investigating Mau Mau murders, I discovered that the Kikuyu had an unfailing memory for where bodies had been buried, in the middle of nowhere, with no obvious signs or marks, but they knew exactly where at the side of the path we should dig. And we dug, and there was a skeleton.

They saw the world in spatial terms. It always had been that way, and they could see no good reason to change it because they didn't realise the way in which the modern world was trying to change – and, the argument went, improve – societies that lived at subsistence levels. I tried to suggest to them that they wouldn't always be happy with their current way of life as the world changed, but they were reluctant to accept the argument.

Some people saw the Mau Mau as an evil cult. They were evil, certainly, but I don't think they fitted the definition of a cult. In fact, they were a political movement, which used terror to try to achieve their aims, including obtaining hegemony over the other forty-one tribes in Kenya. If you look at the positions in the new administration in the government of Kenya you'll find that most of them are Kikuyu. To a certain extent, that is an accident of history. The railway line bringing missionaries and others to the area stopped in a Kikuyu-dominated area. It couldn't get past the swamp called Nairobi. Consequently, the people who came up the line, the original missionaries, stopped there as well, and founded the first schools in that area. So the people who benefited from education were the Kikuyu – Jomo Kenyatta himself went to a mission school and the Kikuyu became highly educated, building on their natural intelligence, which was considerable. It is more than a coincidence that they occupy most of the senior positions in Kenya. It's an accident of fate, perhaps, partly, but it's also due to the fact that they are what they are.

The Luo too are exceedingly intelligent, but the railway line didn't get as far as them. Nevertheless, President Obama's Luo father was one of the best economists that Kenya has probably ever produced. But describing Mau Mau as a cult is misleading, as it implies that it was a kind of religion, rather than an ideology that fitted tribal thinking and needs. One of the mistakes that many of those responsible for rehabilitation of detainees in the early days made was that Mau Mau oaths fulfilled some spiritual need, which – when rejected, after much persuasion by the rehabilitators – required replacement by Christianity. This rarely worked. Oaths were a deeply traditional part of Kikuyu society, and the more serious the oath, the more compelling was the obligation to observe it, come what may. Yes, Mau Mau followers sang songs to Jomo Kenyatta, but these were not Christian-style hymns, even if they sometimes used hymn melodies borrowed from the churches. My experience was that the Kikuyu sang at every opportunity, not least in the detention camps, or when they were working at some task. The more tedious the task, the more attractive the option of everyone singing, in a form of chant and response – and the wittier the words chosen by the lead singer, the more enjoyable the whole experience.

4

GETTING TO WORK

When I started work, I was an Inspector of Police, my contract was for three years, which was then extended for six months by Bill Pollok-Morris, the Assistant District Commissioner (in the end, only three of those months were needed for me to wrap up my work at Fort Hall before returning to Nairobi). He and I got on very well.

One incident in particular might have helped to consolidate my direct line to Bill Pollok-Morris. I was rostered for night duty on a regular basis, as well as working with detainees during the day. It was tough to do both, but I accepted my share of the workload. Night duty involved leading a patrol of policemen and checking on the banks and the businesses and residences in the town. I used to go into the bars that the people used to see what was going on, and have a laugh, and share jokes with them, and then move on to the next. I walked into one of them one night, about 11 or 12 o'clock at night, and there was a chap of about fifty-five or sixty, wearing a rather expensive gown. He was leaning on a table, and talking to two young men who were eating their dinner. When I walked in, he half-turned round and saw me. He said goodbye to these men he'd been talking to and slowly walked off. It came into my head that he didn't fit. His gown was far too expensive and he wasn't the sort of person you would expect to see in a dive like that late at night. As I talked to some of the other people in the bar, I kept one eye on this chap, and he seemed to be pretending to be looking for a table to sit at, running a finger along the table tops as he passed. All the time he was getting nearer and nearer to the door and as he walked his gown lifted and I could see that he wore expensive shoes with a perfect pair of unworn heels, gleaming with polish. I knew that nobody in Fort Hall owned a pair of brown shoes that were polished and had a perfect pair of heels, so he was obviously from outside Fort Hall. And I let him continue until he was very near the door, and I shouted to the policemen with me "Arrest that man!"

Now, I didn't actually have a reason for arresting him, but at the same time I felt that there was something very odd about his being there, and I didn't know what he was doing talking to the two young men.

I continued my patrol and then returned to the police station early in the morning, about quarter to seven. I was walking across the yard towards the steps which led up to the office where the charge people lived or worked, and a man called Hill, in charge of Special Branch in the area, came out of the door. He was rubbing his hands in glee, with a great grin on his face, after talking to the man I had had arrested. As he approached me, he said, "Excellent work, Lees. They're forming a new organisation. It's called the Kiama Kia Muingi, the KKM." He was really pleased because he'd now be able to report that he had uncovered this new organisation, which presumably was connected in some way with the Mau Mau, and it would be an unlawful assembly under the Emergency regulations.

Shortly afterwards, and rather oddly, I was no longer rostered to do night patrol duty. This was very gratifying but I could discover no reason for it. I can only guess that when the Assistant DC, Bill Pollok-Morris, was told of the discovery and that I had suspected the man on a night patrol, he asked "What the hell is Lees doing walking around all night and then trying to do all this work with the detainees all day?" Whatever the explanation, I was never rostered for patrols again.

It was fairly obvious when I went to Fort Hall that the people who were supposed to understand what they were trying to do with the detainees hadn't really got any plan. They didn't know how to organise an intelligence system that would open the doors to the conversion of all these people away from Mau Mau because they didn't really understand the cultural problems that they were going to face. I'd already faced these sorts of things with the Gurkhas and with the Malay Regiment, and I knew that in the Kenya situation we had not only to understand the cultural differences but also to find ways use to use that understanding to achieve our aims.

When I arrived at the Fort Hall camp, I was introduced to the screening system that they used there on detainees from the Fort Hall area. The first step was to ascertain whether they had been involved in Mau Mau or not and note the kind of responses that they gave. They were then interviewed by local chiefs from each of the districts who would probably know them because the Kikuyu have fantastic memories, and can remember who's who, whose father someone was or whose son, how many brothers and sisters he had and so on.

I then went to see the chiefs in the separate districts and talked to them about how they would function if we returned detainees to them: how they would keep these people under their wing for six months, which was the rule, so that if they behaved properly and followed all the rules of the families and the chief and the police that they would then be struck off the roll and be able to do exactly what they wanted to do.

In that way, I familiarised myself with the process outside the office that John M ran, under my control. I then spent a day or so being shown the files – how they were, and what was in them – and it was apparent that they were growing at a fair rate and that we couldn't continue to just work by filling in forms, filling in these foolscap pieces of paper and filling files with information about what they'd done or not done, who had done what, and who else did they know was Mau Mau, and so on.

The question arose as to whether the District Commissioners of different areas should be responsible for a large number of prisoners who had been rounded up by Operation Anvil in 1954, which removed about 30,000 Mau Mau from Nairobi, or whether they should hand the task over to the prison service.

Fort Hall was the only area where the District Commissioner had wanted to keep control of the detainees rather than handing them over to the prison service. John Pinney, the D.C. at the time of this decision, was assisted by Bill Pollok-Morris and because he and I got on well, I found myself embarking on the next stage of my career – devising techniques to ensure the safe release of detainees back into their villages.

You have to remember that at every stage in my career so far, most of my training had taken place on the job. And indeed, many of the situations I found myself in had no textbooks to tell you how to deal with them. I was also sure enough of my own native intelligence to avoid doing this in a particular way, just because that's the way it had always been done.

At Fort Hall, I and my immediate boss, Group Captain Tiger Shaw, could have decided to do what we knew was done in the prison service – monitor and record data about detainees on four-inch by two-inch record cards. Now, you cannot get an awful lot of information on a four by two card and so the amount of information people gathered in the prison service about an individual was limited by the size of the card, not by the amount of information that the prisoner conveyed. At Fort Hall there was a different system which was based on a foolscap piece of paper which went in a file, and some files contained a number of foolscap pieces of paper, and each of these sheets could contain much more information in foolscap format, and the files themselves could contain much more than a four by two card. The problem was that it was information that wasn't collated in the right way; it wasn't cross-referenced. To cross-reference it meant that you had to take information from one file and stick it in another file. The result of that was that some files became thinner and thinner, and other files became thicker and thicker, which meant that the amount of information in the thick file was of importance to me. The person that this thick file was about had done, or been responsible for, or organised, all the things that the others had reported.

Now, for the two years before I joined the Police, I'd been working in a factory accounting office where we used a data management system where we had a large database of performance of machines and we had to determine statistically which of these machines and which of the processes were the most effective and efficient in terms of the total cost. The costs that we were calculating included a whole range of factors such as labour, including materials and so on, the share that the machine bore of the depreciation of the factory and even things like the insurance that the company paid. Every machine had to be assessed with an element of that in its total cost.

I thought of that experience when I looked at the mass of foolscap files of varying thicknesses, and began to dip in and see all the different types of characteristics of each man that led to a report or a comment being written in the file. I could see that if we could get assigned to the office some extra staff, clerks who could be trained to retrieve, assess and weigh the information, we might be able to find the detainees who needed much closer attention, and separate them from those who would most likely do no harm to anyone in the future. In this way, some files would grow larger and larger while the majority of files grew thinner and thinner, so that it became obvious who had been the instigators of particular incidents and I could target my activities on those people and authorise the release of others.

Over the years, although many thousands of detainees passed through our hands, I was to interrogate in detail only about 4000 of them, much fewer than ten percent, the ones with the thickest files. In this way I came to know more about the possible leaders of the Mau Mau within my Central Province area than anybody else did. With the right approach, I could try to 'turn' one of them, and perhaps turn all the people who were controlled by him, so that they were no longer a threat.

I explained these ideas in an early meeting with Bill Pollok-Morris, in order to get him to agree to find more people to do the clipping and sticking and cross-referencing that would make the files more useful. I explained to him that we had all this information in these files about all these people, and it was useless to us because it wasn't collated in the right way.

You will remember that I mentioned that my father and I used to play at rhetorical games, and the issue with rhetoric is that it is in fact a methodology of persuasion. As such it has two major dimensions. One of them is the logical or rational one, which is the chain of statements which follow one from the other, and the other dimension is the emotional one, where the individual statements are given an emotional weighting. These two aspects of rhetoric, or persuasion, are absolutely vital for barristers, for instance, and people in politics. And because of the years of playing at this game with my father, it became natural to me to just do that, unconsciously – break these things down. I wanted to get Bill to give me those clerks, and so I had the reasons why and I made it as emotional as possible by explaining the consequences and the results, and the value that there would be in having those extra people doing this particular sort of work. And that of course reinforced his confidence in my ability to do what I had to do next, whatever that might be. The extra staff arrived, and we got on with it, and it worked. And once we had made the breakthrough, so it went on for the whole time I was working at Fort Hall.

The two key individuals working with me were John M, the chief clerk, and my driver, Muli.

John organised the clerks into a team that was expert in noting the similarities between the statements made by X and Y and putting comments about the actions of X or Y into one or two files which eventually became quite thick. It meant that the vast majority of files were slimmed down because the paper they were written on was cut out and stuck into these other major files. So I could see straight away from the thickness of the files who to get hold of, wherever they were, and talk to at great length. This is why I didn't have to see every one of the tens of thousands (nearly 70,000 detainees and perhaps 20,000 "repatriates" and time-served convicts returning to the Reserve from where they had been working or serving a sentence) who passed through the system before the end of 1958. I only needed to interview personally the people with the thick files.

John M masterminded a lot of the micro-systems that were used in the fairly large metal building that his clerks and all the files were in. He was a first-class chief clerk. I thought he was completely straightforward and honest. The only thing I couldn't get him to tell me was what it was that he'd had to do when he was forcibly oathed. I politely allowed him not to tell me, ever, although he did admit that he had been forced to take the oath, as had just about everybody on the team at some point. It was life-saving if you did. It was certainly life-curtailing if you didn't. So their motivation for doing so wasn't political, it was simply to save their necks, which is understandable in the circumstances.

My driver, Muli, was a Special Branch senior constable, and his role was to talk to the camp guards and get a feeling for the conditions in the camp, and the mood of the detainees – whether they felt that they were going to be there for ever, whether they were happy to go to screening and go home; whether they wanted to stick to Mau Mau, and so on – any sort of emotional vibe he could pick up, and just tell me about as we were driving along. He might have had another job, of course, which was to watch what I was doing, but if so, I had no idea he was doing that.

Then there was the fact that in each of the districts, the local chiefs had their own screening teams which carried out the periodic reassessment of people as these ex-detainees learned how to fit back into the society and what the effect of their internment had been, and so forth. Whilst I didn't have direct contact with all of them all the time, they were an arm of the resources that were at my disposal should I want to use them, to go and see one of the chiefs about how things were going in his particular neck of the woods or about a particular person whose name had come up and I'd wanted to talk to him, and so on and so forth.

At one time, Bill Pollok-Morris asked me to go up to see a senior Mau Mau detainee called George Koinange, who was in a remote camp in the middle of the desert. There was no perimeter wire or any other security because it was simply a landing strip, with about four huts. One of them was for the prison officer and the rest were for the detainees, no more than twenty to fifty, a small number anyway. I talked to Koinange for two days, and at the end of that time I remember saying to him that I thought they had won the propaganda battle, with regard to detention, and what he should do is, instead of telling the people to stay in detention and thereby incurring all the expense of their incarceration for years and years, it would be far better if he told them all to be screened, cleared of any crimes, and go home. The continuing detention of thousands of young men cost the government enormous amounts of money and was draining the treasury, and if independence came there would be no money left for them to use for the new nation.

I came back and said to Bill Pollok-Morris that I didn't get anywhere with George, which was true, I got no information from him, but I didn't mention that I'd actually told him that they had won this battle and they ought therefore to call a halt to the whole damn thing and all go home.

For a while, the rate of release stayed more or less as it had always been for about two months after I saw George. But then it started to increase quite rapidly. And by the end of 1958 the rate of increase had gone up by a good fifty percent on the previous years. And I think that George had done what I had asked him to do and that he had let it be known that these people should go home and save the money. And we were reaping the benefits of it.

From what I've described, you can see that nobody actually said to me, a junior Special Branch Inspector, "Your job is to organise detainees' release in the best possible way." I saw what was needed, and nobody stopped me getting down to work in a way which proved over time to be extremely effective, because of John and the new team, and because of Bill Pollok-Morris's trust in the way in which I would use that information discreetly, and intelligently, and – very important – following the rules of Kikuyu custom.

Part of the whole process was gaining the trust of the Kikuyu, and there was one formative incident early on in my time at Fort Hall, which, I'm convinced, achieved that trust at one fell swoop.

One day, John walked in to my office and he stood two or three yards away from my desk, which was odd. I'd become aware of the body-language dimension of the Kikuyu. When John spoke to me he usually came and stood in front of my desk and said what he needed to say, quite close, but this day he stood as far away from me as he could get in the room, and it was quite clear that he was going to say something very important. And I said, "John, what is it?" and he said, "Did you know that the people are coming from Manyani in chains and they are treated like criminals? They're not criminals, they are detainees, but they still come all the way from Manyani in chains." And I was appalled. I did not know how detainees arrived at Fort Hall reception and I'd never been told that they came in chains. I said, "John, I'll go and talk to Bill Pollok-Morris about that, and so I went to him and said, "Sir, did you know that the people who come up from Manyani come up in chains?" and he said, "No". And I said, "This presents us with an opportunity to build enormous trust with our detainees, because they don't see themselves as criminals, they see themselves as warriors, if anything. They don't see that they ought to be sent up in chains." And he agreed to issue an order that they should be sent up to Fort Hall without any chains. I went back to my office and I said to John, "They won't come up in chains any further," and John was very pleased.

I knew that John had a direct line to Manyani and I said to him before he left, "John, it's obvious that if these people are not chained and there is the slightest trouble from them when they come up I will not be able to help them again. Do you understand that?" He said, "I do." I knew for a fact that within a day the people in Manyani knew that the next batch of people to come to Fort Hall would come without chains.

So it was arranged that I and Group Captain Tiger Shaw would be down at the railway station with the trucks ready to take the detainees to Fort Hall, to meet the train. Just the two of us; no army, no police, no nothing.

The success of my efforts to release detainees safely back to their villages was noted by other camps. I was asked to go up to Nyeri, for example, and help them improve their methods but because they used a card index system, there was nothing I could do. Each 4 by 2 card recorded a minimum amount of information – name, village of origin and so on. That was no use to me, having established the need to separate the big fish from the small fry. For that you needed much more data, cross-referenced. The 4 by 2 cards might be OK if you're running a prison, but it's absolutely useless if you're trying to gather enough personal information about individual relationships or hidden tribal connections to convince detainees over a period of time to repudiate the whole idea of Mau Mau, because they understand that it is not to their benefit in any way, and that the whole thing is designed to be for the benefit of a certain small group of people that were politically aware and understand the politics of Marxism and revolution and terror.

5

SCREENING AND INTERROGATION

Much of the success of the screening and interrogation programme at Fort Hall depended on understanding the Kikuyu mindset and its origins. To start with, like most people, they had an origins myth: They believed that in the beginning of time there was a female called Moombi, and she had nine daughters, fathered by a man that she had found called Gikuyu. They were the Adam and Eve of the Kikuyu nation, Moombi and Gikuyu. Moombi went in search of husbands for these daughters and found nine young men, and they started their families. The family unit is called *mbari*. It is the fundamental unit of the Kikuyu tribe. Now, the families could be grouped into clans, nine families making a *moherega*.

So the family is the basic unit, and the clan is the next large unit.

Something which it became very important to understand is the *riika*, the age grading that is totally binding on Kikuyu males. You can think of it in terms of an isosceles triangle with sides that are like the sides of a ladder, and rungs of the ladder decreasing size as you go up, but equally spaced.

The rungs in the ladder are age grades. Each one of them represents a date of birth, and the recognition of hierarchy based on this ladder underlies all the relationships between Kikuyu males. The younger males pay respect to the elders in the family, and the younger brothers address the older brothers in a way which demonstrates their active obedience all the time. It's a system of respect, duty and obedience paid by the younger ones to the elders. Of course, to justify this respect the elder has to display wisdom, and responsibility and he must exercise his age grade authority wisely.

Over time the two sides of the 'ladder' come closer together because people die and you end up with fewer people at the top. The performance of these people near the top in their *barazas*, their meetings, is monitored quite closely by everybody else. The young men through time progress from the bottom to the top if they survive, and if they've survived and performed adequately or effectively in the meetings, they achieve chiefhood and become the leaders. And when the time comes for the appointment of a chief, it's fairly obvious to everybody who is the most capable and the most charismatic of the people that they have and consequently they get to be the chief.

For instance, I met senior chief Njiri a couple of times and he was extremely intelligent, a very, very shrewd old guy. And I think that the system worked for these people extremely well.

Another important aspect of Kikuyu culture was that a man can marry more than one wife. In fact, he has to in many ways because he's not allowed to have intercourse with his wife for two years after she has given birth. So if he is wealthy enough and has enough goats or cows, he goes and he buys a girl from some other family within the age grade that is appropriate. Each wife will have her own individual hut. These are laid out in the form of horseshoe, quite close, but not too close. And the wife rules that particular house, everything in it is hers, and her children live with her in that house.

The horseshoe formation of the houses is called the 'fire group'. Everybody has their own fire in their own hut for cooking and there are no chimneys in these huts, so the smoke just rises towards the roof and stays there. They are not healthy places.

If the fire in one of these places goes out, it's the duty for somebody from one of the other huts, the rondavels, where the fire is still going, to carry some embers to the hut which has lost its fire and restart the fire in that hut. So that was a way of always providing for fire in any fire group, as it's called.

Kikuyu society has a belief in wizards, known as *mundo mugo*, someone who has got secret magical powers. There are two types of *mundo mugo* – those who practice white magic, which is beneficial, and the ones that practice black magic, which is harmful. The black magic people were always secret, and they used to use the 'evil eye'. If one of these people gave you the evil eye, something dreadful would happen, for example your animals would die or even you yourself could die.

Kikuyu society as a whole did not like the black magic wizards, and they had a ceremony where, if they discovered one, they would execute him. The people would all gather together, and tie the offending wizard to a post or tree. Everyone brought a dry banana tree leaf and the executioner would build a pile of these leaves around the wizard. Then at the time of execution the assembled tribe would turn their backs on the scene and the executioner would light the fire and keep it burning until the person on the middle was consumed.

The Kikuyu believed that there was an entity that created their world and he was called *Ngai,* who lived at the top of Kirinyaga or Mount Kenya, and whose name means the mountain of mysteries. *Ngai* is supposed to have pointed to a particularly fertile batch of fig trees which are now considered to be sacred trees, and some Kikuyu pray to them.

Now, all these things that I've talked about are necessary to understand my approach to screening and interrogation. We needed a very good handle on what sort of a world they lived in. This was not a world of the west, of rationality and technology and so on. It was also a world that the Mau Mau movement, the largely Kikuyu-based anti-British rebel group, understood and were able to exploit.

The power the Mau Mau held over the Kikuyu was very strong, as a result of the horrifying psychological and physical elements of the oathing process, and the implied consequences if a Kikuyu subsequently broke his oath.

The first Kikuyu to get a university degree, R. Mugu Gatheru, wrote a book called *The Child of Two Worlds,* in which he described the role of oaths in Kikuyu society:

> First of all, the taking of oaths was not new to the Kikuyu. It was an integral and powerful part of our society as in most societies at one time or another in their development. The variety of oaths was large to suit the many serious occasions of life. A binding force providing an important moral sanction of society. They were an essential part of tribal law, like the ordeals of fire and water of early English society. Basically, the oaths fell into two categories — major and minor. If a man denied responsibility for the pregnancy of a girl, the council of elders would administer a minor oath to test his innocence. If the man lied, the punishment which he himself had invoked would fall on him between seven days and seven months from the oath. His body might erupt with boils, his animals, his wealth or even he himself might die. Whatever its form, the punishment was inevitable.

The major oath was used to settle land disputes, allegations of larceny and other criminal offences, and to test witch doctors suspected of using black magic to poison others on their own account or hired to do so. Again, the Council of Elders, having failed to solve the problem by arbitration, would administer the oath. However, the major oath had such terrible consequences, involving the man's family and even his entire clan, that he had to obtain their permission before submitting to it. The punishment to follow a major oath dishonestly sworn will fall three and a half years after the oath ... and would be incalculable in its effects. The psychological effect of the oath was literally terrifying to the Kikuyu. If a man lied, he lied not only to society but also to the ancestors' spirits who we have seen could cause great suffering if displeased and still more, he lied to the Creator, Ngai himself. Once taken, it followed that an oath was irrevocable. There was no possibility of mental reservation or de-oathing.

Elspeth Huxley quoted the above in her book, *Nine Faces of Kenya* and she also quoted the account of the experience of one oath-taker, Karari Njama:

By the light of a hurricane lamp, I could see the furious guards who stood armed with pangas and simis. Right in front of us stood an arch of banana and maize stalks and sugar cane stems tied by a forest creeping and climbing plant. We were harassed to take out our coats, money, watches, shoes and any other European metal we had in our possession. Then the oath administrator, Githinji Mwarari – who had painted his fat face with white chalk – put a band of raw goat's skin on the right hand wrist of each one of the seven persons who were to be initiated.

We were then surrounded (bound together) by goats' small intestines on our shoulders and feet. Another person then sprayed us with some beer from his mouth as a blessing at the same time throwing a mixture of the finger millet with other cereals on us. Then Githinji pricked our right hand middle finger with a needle until it bled. He then brought the chest of a billy goat and its heart still attached to the lungs and smeared them with our blood. He then took a Kikuyu gourd containing blood and with it made a cross on our foreheads and on all important joints saying, "May this blood mark the faithful and brave members of the Gikuyu and Mumbi Unity; may this same blood warn you that if you betray our secrets or violate the oath, our members will come and cut you into pieces at the joints marked by this blood".

We were then asked to lick each others' blood from our middle fingers and vowed after the administrator: "If I reveal this secret of Gikuyu and Mumbi to a person not a member, may this blood kill me. If I violate any of the rules of the oath may this blood kill me. If I lie, may this blood kill me".

We were then ordered to hold each other's right hand and in that position, making a line, passed through the arch seven times. Each time the oath administrator cut off a piece of a piece of the goat's small intestine, breaking it into pieces, while all the rest in the hut repeated a curse on us: "Slash! You may be cut like this! Let the oath kill he who lies!"

We were made to stand facing Mount Kenya, encircled by intestines, and given two dampened soil balls and ordered to hold the left hand soil ball against our navels. We then swore: "I, (Karari Njama), swear before God and before all the people present here that ..."

We repeated the oath while pricking the eye of a goat with a kei-apple thorn seven times and then ended the vows by pricking seven times some seven sodom apples. To end the ceremony, blood mixed with some good-smelling oil was used to make a cross on our foreheads indicating our reception as members of Gikuyu and Mumbi while warning us: "Forward ever and backward never!"

We were then allowed to take our belongings, put on our coats and shoes and were welcomed to stay. We paid 2.50 shillings each for registration. During the course of our initiation, one person refused to take the oath and was mercilessly beaten. Two guards were crying out seeking permission from their chief leader to kill the man. The man learnt that death was approaching him and he quickly changed his mind and took the oath.

This was the basis of the mindset of the people who came into our camps in their thousands. Some of them took the oath but did not go on to carry out the hideous crimes that were associated with Mau Mau. We were interested in the ones who played a much more active role – their thick files showed who they were. If they still considered themselves bound by the power of these oaths, very little would change. We had to find a way to free the worst of the detainees from that power in a believable way.

For a detainee to secure his release from detention he had to agree to meet a screening team and make his confession. The team would judge from his file and from conversations with him, whether it was safe to send him back to his village, cleansed of any obligation to Mau Mau which might lead to further criminal behaviour. Often, we already knew everything we needed to know about their association with Mau Mau from our cross-referencing system, but we had to hear it from their own lips. After a period of time cross-checking the records the amount of information we had was enormous. The Kikuyu members of the screening team had phenomenal memories and were able to recognise the activities of people either from the files or from the statements that had been heard. To check that the screening system worked, back in the villages the chief ran a team which, over a period of six months after release would talk to former detainees and assess whether they had decided to reject the whole thing and get on with their lives, which was the purpose of the system.

Nobody was forced to be screened; people were being released on a daily basis, and the others knew that if they wanted to go, all they had to do was to approach the screening team, and be completely honest, knowing that the screening team were already in possession of a lot of information about their activities. In fact, that's one of the reasons why they called me *Bwana Kihara*, which, whilst it means 'old baldie' – I was losing my hair at the time – also means 'he that knows' or understands. They thought that somehow or other I had some odd power which provided all this information that I could trot out in front of them. They had no idea how I got it, which of course was a great lever for me. Most of the work was done by the screening teams, but I selected a targeted group of detainees to interview personally, based partly on the size of their files. I selected those files and interviewed those people and it was a matter of deciding whether I could turn that man or not, knowing very well that he was some kind of leader. I was looking to chop the head off the snake, that's what that was about.

But you've got to bear in mind one thing: that not everybody who was detained was an active Mau Mau. There were only probably at the most 20% of the total who were really active. The rest of them were either innocent Kikuyu who had been forced to take the oath and couldn't wait to get out, or people that had just been caught up in Operation Anvil or other general sweeps of the population.

The 20% were the ones that were being difficult, by refusing to present themselves for screening, say, or were people who I knew were deeply involved in violence and probably felt that they would be punished if we found out about it. But eventually they realised that there was a general amnesty and the government meant it, so they could say quite freely whatever it was that they had done. All we would do is write it down, but no action would be taken – that was the whole point. So they secured release by deserving release and when they achieved that, they went as quickly as possible, after a period of rehabilitation.

This started by deciding who were the leaders, and turning them. The others simply followed. And as soon as you got rid of the leaders the rest of them flooded in to get clear of the oath, and confess what they had done, which was usually little or nothing. The work in the camp was simply to keep them occupied and to avoid boredom. In fact, it was not really work, just something like taking them outside the camp, getting them to build a wall, or cut back some brush that needed cutting back, a job for a couple of hours, and then back in the truck and back to the camp. It was a taste of the outside, designed to re-introduce them to their own home reserve more than anything.

Elsewhere in Kenya, the camps were run on different lines. And, indeed, the Emergency reached such a peak that the government had to call a general amnesty for people accused of Mau Mau crimes. A camp like Manyani had a crowd control problem. It was where Josiah Mwangi Kariuki launched a propaganda campaign of letter-writing to British newspapers which had more influence on the outcome of the Emergency than all the bombs and troops you might poke a stick at. At the Mwea camps they used what they called a 'dilution technique' which was simply a fancy name for splitting up the people into manageable lumps, instead of having them all in one great crowd when they would have had the power to overcome the guards at any time, if they'd wished. Then the ones keenest to get home would harangue the hard core and urge them to co-operate.

The security arrangements at Fort Hall were actually very light, because the problem was not to keep the detainees in but to get them to go home. We even had some "scroungers" who were quite happy to eat the food provided, at no charge, do light work, and take their time before making their way home.

Continued detention was an enormous problem for the political parties in the UK. The longer the detainees stayed there, the greater the problem became in the British parliament, and the more letters that Josiah Mwangi Kariuki wrote, the hotter the fire became. And yet these people were not in prison. They were not contained in any way. The gates of the camps were usually open most of the time. If they'd wanted to escape they would have escaped when we took them out – which we did, frequently, every day, on work parties, and there would be twenty people scattered around doing various tasks. They could have made a bolt for it at any time; there were only three or four guards. I used to go myself, quite frequently, in the truck with the detainees, and they'd all jump out, do the job, and sing and carry on, have a good chat, all jump back in again and we'd be back for lunch. That was the day's work. They were quite happy with that. They could have escaped at any time; I couldn't have stopped them; the guards couldn't have stopped them if they'd all run in different directions, but they didn't.

At the heart of our information-gathering techniques was the interrogation. Of course, our cross-referencing of the files was important, for ensuring that we could identify the individuals to interrogate, and not waste time on people who played no active part in Mau Mau. It was also the case that in the 'thick files' of the detainees we interrogated, there was a lot of information they didn't know we had, which made it possible to knock them off balance when they were trying to pull the wool over our eyes.

I actually developed my interrogation technique by making mistakes and correcting them. And the first mistake was to consider interrogating in Kiswahili, a delightful and complex language, but of which my knowledge was quite primitive. I had been in the country probably no more than six or seven months, and I spoke a fairly fluent form of what is known as 'kitchen Swahili'. Now, it's also the case that most of the people that I was talking to spoke the same sort of kitchen Swahili but that is not a medium for the expression of emotion, or what I would consider to be important issues. I realised that there are more dimensions to the spoken word than the word itself – all words are either loaded words emotionally, or neutral words emotionally. And I also realized the body language of the spoken form was nearly as important as the words you used. The body language and the facial expressions which accompany loaded words or emotional words communicate more than the words that you use.

But much of this was unavailable to me because I was having to concentrate on choosing the words to use in Kiswahili. I was neglecting to notice the changes in body and facial expression which were absolutely vital to follow, so I decided to speak in English through an interpreter.

I organized the setting of the interview in such a way that the light was behind me, and the person I was interviewing was either standing or sitting in front of me. There was also a chair that was available for other people to sit on the other side of my desk, and my screener or interpreter was on my left facing the detainee. So the detainee had to move his head – every time I spoke he looked at me, every time the screener spoke he looked at the screener and I could see the front of his face and the left side of his face, as he turned back and forth. I could also see what he was doing if he was standing, what he did with his hands, what he did with his legs, if he stood still, if he moved, how he moved, whether his head was down or up, whether he was nervous, whether he was relaxed, what happens to his breathing, all the kinds of things that are visible representations of the mental state of a person. All these subtle clues come and go in an instant, and unless you're absolutely aware of what you're doing you will not succeed in screening people effectively, properly and fairly.

And so I developed my interrogation technique bit by bit over a period of months, and saw the value of dispensing with questioning in Swahili. There were a number of extremely effective and efficient instant translators and if I used short but pointed, organized sentences, they would translate them immediately to the detainee. Now, a lot of the detainees understood some English. They heard the tone of my voice. They noticed the pauses that I made and these were transmitted by the translator to the detainee in his own language. I realized that the instant translation into the birth language of the person I was talking to would trigger the emotions carried by the words that were used, and I would see what the emotions were, and what the response was.

I knew that the Kikuyu are very dramatic people. They love the drama that surrounds debate, and they delight in the context of rhetorical skills set one against the other. And so I tried to make each of the interviews that I held into a dramatic event for the person that came in the door. If you were to categorize them, there were some interrogations that were very short. I would start as far away from the issue that I really wanted to talk about as possible and after the first two or three questions, if their response to those questions was aggressive or antagonistic, it might be that I would terminate that interview and say, 'well, you're obviously not in the right mood to talk to me today, so come back some other time', which meant that he had to wait until either his turn came around again or he went to see the screeners and said, 'Can I go and see Mr Lees?' So it meant that none of the time that I was screening was wasted: it was either determining who I should talk to again, or talking to the people I could talk to and should talk to at length, because they were important, judging by the size of the file and the information in it.

Every interrogation was different, but I was always talking to an individual who was in stress. Consequently, the one way to relieve some of that stress was to provoke an emotional response. So all my interrogations were micro- or macro-emotional contests, trying to get them to face up to the fact that they had taken the Mau Mau oath.

Why was it so difficult for detainees to admit having taken the oath? It was difficult because it was a tribal method of justice and a binding contract consummated by the rituals that surrounded its utterance. Those rituals were quite ancient, and the significance to the Kikuyu person taking it was enormous. It was a thing which was full of *fingo*. *Fingo* is a spell, so the people who administered the oath were casting a spell on the person. This was nothing that a rational Westerner could pin down. It's not possible to understand the power of a *fingo* and the magic and ritual unless you have been born into a world which consists of nothing else. Their world consisted of nothing else.

So it was difficult for detainees to admit having taken the Mau Mau oath because they were under a spell not to do so. They were under oath.

Now, we have oaths in the West. When we go to court we swear an oath by putting our hand on a holy book of one sort or another, and saying that you swear to tell the truth, the whole truth and nothing but the truth. Now that in itself is not far away from the *Fingo* that the Kikuyu have when they have to pass through the secret archway seven times. We would have a long discussion about the consequences of the contract into which they had entered. For their services to Mau Mau they were promised *wiathi na ithaka*, freedom and land. And I would discuss with them what they meant by freedom. For them it was just 'let's get rid of the pass system, let's have fewer regulations, get rid of the District Commissioner because all he ever does is get new cars and we pay for it,' and all sorts of things that have nothing to do with 'freedom' that we talk about in the West.

And *ithaka* is land, a fundamental economic resource of the Kikuyu and it has been for many centuries. If you don't have land you don't eat. They thought that if they got freedom the result would be that the land that they thought had been appropriated by whites would be divided up amongst themselves. They had no idea what would happen with regard to the Kamba, the Luo, the Nandi, and the other 41 tribes that live in Kenya. Would they allow the Kikuyu simply to appropriate land in an indiscriminate way? Or would the Luo decide that they weren't going to have that and they would have a war about it? They never thought about anything like that. They would go silent and puzzled when I said to them, 'what will happen to the Luo? What will happen to the other tribes? Will they agree to the fact that you can have land?' And so they began to think about the impossibility of the contract being consummated. They had given their time by being detained to provide the people who were in charge of the Mau Mau, whoever they were, the opportunity to gain leverage with regards to independence which they really didn't talk about. They didn't realize that independence for Kenya was already pencilled in somewhere and it wasn't far off.

This was the end point I wanted to reach with each interrogation. But I didn't approach it directly.

If you imagine a spiral, like a spring in a watch, I started on the outside of that spiral by trying to get the detainee to be relaxed as far as possible. And that meant encouraging him to sit down in the chair that we provide instead of standing up. I wanted him to start talking. I wanted to hear the sound of his voice and I wanted him to hear the sound of my voice. So I would ask him questions which were miles away from the crucial issues of any violence he might have committed.

So I would say, 'Tell me Wangu, is your village near to this camp, can you see it from where we are in the camp, or which direction is it?' This question had nothing to do with what he might have thought he was going to be asked, which was exactly what I wanted. I wanted him to say, 'well, yes, I can, it's over there and it's called such and such.' Then I would say, 'is it a big village or a small village?' And he would tell me whether it was big or small. And I'd say, 'who is the chief there? who is the headman there? do you like the headman? when you left did you like him or will he have changed?', things of that sort.

And what I was trying to do is simply engage him in conversation about things which had nothing to do with the Mau Mau. I'd ask him how many cows or goats or his father had, how many wives did he have, did he have a lot of brothers? If he's got a lot of goats, did he think that they were being looked after properly.

He would talk about these things more easily than he would if I just fired at him the first question, 'did you take the Mau Mau oath?' or 'did you kill?' – that would get me nowhere.

I wanted him to get used to the sound of my voice and I wanted to get used to the sound of his voice because the tone and the way in which people speak is a fair indication of their psychological state – whether they're frightened or not, whether they're relaxed or whether they're anxious and so on.

So the first five to ten minutes of any interrogation would be spent trying to get the detainee into a state where he was used to talking to me and answering in a positive way. I wanted to get positive answers from him, before I moved on to anything that might involve Mau Mau. And I would broach that topic by talking about the people that he might have been associated with. Remember that I had a file on all the people who had actually committed crimes and there were the names of people he might be connected with in a gang or people who were behind an event, or an attack.

When he was quite relaxed and had been talking to me for ten minutes or so, I would then say, 'do you know this fellow?' and wait. Now, because he was relaxed and because he had been saying yes, he was more likely to admit that he did know this chap, but he wouldn't know why I was asking him this. And then if he said yes, I would say, 'do you know this other fellow?', someone else who was mentioned in the file.

My whole strategy was to get these people relaxed and in a mood of agreeing, so that they were not frightened or anxious in any way, and decided that I was fairly reasonable, and they could talk to me.

And so I would move on from that kind of questioning to the issues that I really wanted to get at. And I would talk possibly for half an hour or maybe longer about the things that that had happened and how he was a witness to this or a witness to that or he knew this fellow and he knew the other fellow. And gradually we would reach the centre of the spiral and the story of that man's involvement with Mau Mau would come out, and be acknowledged by him.

Now, it wasn't so much a confession that I was trying to get, as repudiation of the oath, the contract. After I'd seen George Koinange in that remote desert and told him that he should tell all the detainees to go home, a month or two later, people started to come forward in quite noticeably increased numbers. Emotionally it was easier for them once they realized that they had been 'had', and that they themselves would not be given acres of land.

But it took time, and it took compassion and it took ability with words, and I became as emotionally involved with the turmoil as they were themselves. If it were done properly it was very exhausting, and I tried very hard to do it properly. I paid them the respect of being intelligent human beings and they did the same with me. And we talked man to man through our interpreter, and my interpreters were absolutely magnificent. They translated my language in tone and content immediately. And I could read the impact of what I said on the detainee's attitude, his face, the sound of his voice, the way he sat, the way that perhaps he started to crumple.

I should say that, to begin with, like everybody else involved with detention, I had no real idea of how to proceed. In fact, I had a feeling of dread whenever I set foot in the camp to start a day's struggle. I became confused and depressed: I had drawn the short straw! I used to wander around the various camps in my jumping suit, sitting and watching, and waiting to be asked questions, such as "who are you?" and "where is your uniform?", at which point I would try and engage in neutral conversation, using my basic Kiswahili. The main idea was to get everyone used to seeing me around, and as no threat to them. But it was never going to be the way to make a significant breakthrough.

Then one day in Kandara I had the moment of inspiration: stop being rational and only speak to their emotional engagement with Mau Mau. It was not the "individual" but the "crowd" – the tribe, the family – I had to address. That is when I began to ask questions which touched upon personal feelings: about cattle, family, children, land. Once I had obtained my first "yes" in response, I kept going until I received a string of "yeses". As I became more emotional, so too did the man being questioned. And that degree of involvement I managed to inject into the formal interrogations, where again I needed a string of "yeses". Eventually, a torrent of words would pour out, and the detainee would finally throw off the burden of fear and guilt and uncleanness he had been bearing for so long. It was an exhausting process for all involved. But the emotional commitment required, coupled with the nature of the crimes being confessed, drained my emotional energy to just above zero by the end of the day.

The interrogations were as difficult for me as for the detainees. And they left me emotionally exhausted because I had recognized years before that emotions, if you can transmit them, are infectious. And the key to my interrogation technique was to engage the emotions of the detainee. And I would go from issue to issue, from turn to turn, from method to method until such time as I managed to capture his emotional attention. And then I would open that up as far as I possibly could and this was enthusiastically endorsed by my interpreter screeners because they knew what I was doing. And they knew that I could do it. And together we did it.

I interrogated only a small percentage of the detainees, the 'hard cases' if you like. They might have been a minority but they were the most important. Now, to get that quite clear. I might have only seen a minority numerically but in terms of power they were the powerhouse and I saw and battled with them.

The other releases were managed by the screening teams and the headmen and the chiefs. I would see the detainees very briefly when the chiefs and the screening teams were satisfied that they had fully repudiated their oath and any allegiance to Mau Mau, and they went home.

My personal interrogations were perhaps only two a day, because they were hard, intense work, sometimes going on for hours. I was not running to any timetable. I just wanted to do the best job, however long it took. There was nothing else I had to do. I knew that when I finished and walked out of the place, Muli would be waiting for me with a Land Rover and we'd be off back, whatever time of the day, to the mess in Fort Hall and I would go and lie on my bed and listen to music, and he would go and wash the Land Rover.

It wasn't easy to unwind at the end of some days, because I was wound up like a tight spring. I couldn't stop being emotionally involved with the people that I was responsible for. Their futures depended on me and it was a heavy load to carry. Everybody knew that I came back exhausted and I was allowed to ventilate with my friend Sean. If he was in the rondavel, he would say, "How did it go? I will go and have a beer or two while you unwind."

And he would leave the rondeval to me and I would put my record player on and lie on the bed and listen to Max Bruch's Violin Concerto and imagine myself as a violin having a battle with the orchestra, and the music would soothe me and I would relax a little bit and in the end the violin wins, or at least is equal to the orchestra. And I felt that I was at least equal to the job.

When I had got to the point where I was relaxed a little, I used to have a shower and go down to Mr Filo's Bar in the town and it would be filled with people, like an English pub. There would be a couple of doctors from the hospital, three or four policemen, businessmen, white hunters passing through, film technicians on location, and so on. Naughty jokes, gossip and tall stories abounded – all very normal! Sometimes, members of the mess would try to beat each other at 24 Aces, where colleagues choose six drinks from the shelf and you have to drink the mixture, which went on until someone fell off their bar stool or fled for the loo. We also played squash against each other: another of my regular squash partners was Jane Arthur, a nursing sister at the Fort Hall Hospital. We met at the mess film shows (which I organised) and at the Sunday tiffin parties which were occasionally the beneficiary of a curried chicken donation from a grateful local businessman, whose son I had helped save from drowning. I also saw Jane at the hospital if I was following up on a sick detainee. We were young, had fun, but it was never serious.

One of the married women – whose husband, an accountant, was often away from Fort Hall – once made clear she was "ready for love", but I ducked that proposition. More enticing was a woman I met in Nairobi who worked for Alitalia. With long black hair and the looks of Italian film star Gina Lollobrigida, she was obviously in some demand, but we enjoyed each other's company, which took us all the way to the steps of my plane home, where she left me with a good-bye kiss.

Our so called 'prison camp' was unusual in that, as I've explained, the detainees were free to leave at any time if they agreed to repudiate their Mau Mau contract. We were faced with a people whose hostility to their colonisers was based on a struggle for independence when, in fact, Britain was withdrawing from all its colonies anyway and Kenya was firmly on the list. But they didn't know that and, in an official sense, neither did Bill Pollok-Morris, although that was my informal view of the situation. While I was focussed on the screening and interrogation of a small proportion of detainees, the rest of the staff had to ensure that the others led some kind of everyday life.

We didn't want the detainees who were waiting to go through the screening process to be twiddling their thumbs all day, so we put them to work. This was not arduous stuff, but simply something to get these people out of the camp into the countryside and to do something for an hour or two so that they felt an atmosphere of freedom and breathed the air of the villages where they lived. It was an operation designed to relocate them from the camp to the countryside but we had to imagine what these people could do in the countryside that would be of value and also take a couple of hours. It wasn't like forced labour. None of them did any actual digging or very hard work. Sometimes they were in the quarry and broke large stones into smaller stones, for an hour or two every day, but they sang while they did the work.

On some days I went out with the trucks and we might go off to get some sand or cement to build a wall. So we would drive for an hour to a place that one of the detainees knew, where there was some good sand and fill bags and bags with sand and then take them back. And we did build the wall – it was a bit of a dam really – in the river at the bottom of the quarry so that the water would be deep enough for them to swim in. I don't know if anybody ever did it but there was certainly enough depth to bathe in. The only problem with the water was it was very cold. It came from the snows of Mount Kenya, so it was not a place for a leisurely swim, more of a quick in and out.

These sorts of things kept the detainees occupied and were better than them sitting around and becoming terribly bored.

Recent historians have published allegations of unfair and excessive punishment of detainees. I can only speak for Fort Hall but I never used harsh punishments. If I had, I would have lost the trust that I was desperately trying to engender with these people. Punishments and violence were not part of the Fort Hall curriculum. What problems of discipline there were arose in the larger camps, like Manyani and Mackinnon Road, which held up to 10,000 young men.

At Fort Hall I didn't have big crowds. The whole of my system in Fort Hall probably held no more than 3,500–4,000 at any one time. And so we would have 200–300 at most of the camps, while Fort Hall reception might have up to 500.

I made sure I knew what was going on at all times, and was always out and about in the camps, taking part in conversations with the detainees. But I had to respect the manners and customs and beliefs of the society.

First of all, I never initiated the conversation. I tried to make it that it was always the detainee who would approach and begin the conversation and I would give the impression that I wasn't bothered about what he said. In fact, I really didn't care. I told them many times that their sojourn in my camp was their own choice. It wasn't mine. It wasn't ours. It was theirs and that they had could choose to stay there or come to talk and we would help them rid themselves of the Mau Mau by repudiating the oaths they had contracted with Mau Mau. And we would explain why the contract needed to be repudiated.

Of course, there were Mau Mau leaders among the detainees and they would obviously try to prevent repudiation. But in the camps that we controlled, there were only a hundred or so, so that the Mau Mau leadership was reasonably visible, to me and to my screeners and crew and therefore at first we focused on them to get them to talk and to turn them, which we for the most part did. Once we had turned the leaders, the followers would do what they always did and follow. But the key was, they all had to repudiate the contract between themselves and the Mau Mau. They had to recognize that they are confessing and that taking the oath, which is binding in tribal law, had been violated by the Mau Mau. First of all, it was taken in circumstances which were illegal under tribal law, and secondly they had been forced to do it by Mau Mau terror techniques, which removed the binding nature of the oath.

Once a detainee had shown us that he had chosen to do what was necessary to obtain his release, we agreed that he could leave. It was his decision, which we just accepted. Our aim then was, as quickly possible, to get him out and home and back to his village, under the control of his chief where he had been all his life. To get him back to his family, to get him surrounded by the normal everyday Kikuyu life, that's what it was about.

I estimated that under our programme and using our methods, we released nearly 70,000 detainees back into their villages. The official figure was a little higher (including repatriates and released convicts passing through Fort Hall on their way home, it actually came to nearly 89,000) and my preference for my own figure may seem excessively pernickety, but I know the figure to be correct. I was trained as an accountant and one of the things that I started doing when I was 14 or 15 was adding up numbers accurately. We had no adding machines in those days, and so I had to add up long columns of pounds, shillings and pence. And to this day I have this extra facility for dealing with numbers and additions and subtractions and so on.

And my figures were backed up. All the movements and the arrangements for rationing, equipment, blankets, and so on were organised by Group Captain Tiger Shaw. His job was to make sure that no matter what happened, the people that came to the camps would be adequately resourced throughout their movements from the reception camp to the works camps and until such time as they left the work camps. Tiger Shaw and I worked reasonably closely together and my numbers matched his numbers, on a daily basis.

There were others also trying to do the same calculation with different methods, and arriving at different answers, but I was very confident that my figures were accurate. I got into trouble once because I knew how many had gone and it appeared that a man called Hill, who was actually my boss, had a number for the releases which he reported to special branch headquarters which was less than the number that Bill Pollok-Morris and I had.

So we were visited by the Senior Superintendent of Special Branch and I was trotted in by Chief Inspectors into his presence. This man sat behind the desk and was quite pleasant and introduced himself. And I said to him "I believe that the numbers of releases that you are being given are not quite accurate." This seemed to produce an electric effect on the two other men who got me by the arms, one either side, and took me outside and said, "You shouldn't do that. Oh, my God, you shouldn't contradict the official reports!" and I said, "Well, I *know* how many had been released. I don't know where the other number comes from but it's wrong."

6

AFTERMATH

I served about three and a quarter years at Fort Hall, and I knew that at some point I'd have to make a decision about my future. Apart from anything else, as I have said, I was convinced that independence for Kenya could not be long delayed. But also, I could not have gone on doing that job for much longer. To see so many people in distress, not caused by themselves but as a political manoeuvre by people who were never ever in detention of that sort themselves for any period, was heart-rending. Part of the task of getting them out of the camp as quickly as possible was to convince them that they were being used as a tool by the leadership of this organisation called Mau Mau to ensure the future prosperity of the lesser leaders, with no regard whatsoever for the prosperity or otherwise of those people that were in detention.

I experienced daily emotional battles as I fought to persuade these young men that they were being deceived. I would see their sons and grandsons for instance, getting drunk on a toxic type of moonshine, known as Kill Me Quick – and it sometimes did – desperate for the economic situation to improve, living out their days hoping for the 'freedom and land' they had been promised by Mau Mau which never appeared. My failure to convince many of them of the futility of holding to their oaths, and my failed attempts to tell them what would actually happen to their country, had a lasting impact on me.

When I had been at Fort Hall about nine months or a year, I contracted pneumonia, which laid me out for a while. And then, perhaps as a result of the accumulated stresses and strains, I felt really bad one day and got Muli to take me to the casualty department at the hospital. Now that I'm old, in the last two years I've had pneumonia three times and sepsis once, a massive heart attack and pneumonia again. The professor of infectious diseases tells me that it's some kind of a bug that he's not really come across before. It's definitely pneumonia but he put me on an antiviral and I recovered. So I'm all right at the moment, but we'll get this book done and then we'll see how we go. Other than the pneumonia, I remember one day when I was talking to John, I didn't feel very well. In fact, I felt really ill, perhaps because of the accumulated stresses and strains and so I just spoke to the hospital and then asked Muli to drive me there. We just turned up at casualty and I said that I didn't feel well and so they got a doctor. He took my blood pressure and clearly felt it was a lot higher than it should be, which he put down to the work that I was doing. The treatment for that was to be ordered to spend a week in the beautiful resort of Mombasa,

I also suffered stress-related effects not just from Fort Hall, but also from my time in the army in Malaya. The incident when I was trapped under a truck had lasting effects. It made me susceptible to claustrophobia in certain situations. For quite some time in later years I had great difficulty in riding on buses. In fact I used to flatly refuse to get on a bus because I felt that that I couldn't control it when it stopped. As soon as the door closed I used to feel very strange.

So the time came when, in spite of my successes, I became exhausted and somewhat dispirited about what we were doing in Kenya. One evening in Nairobi, with a friend, Bob Murray, on the way to a restaurant for dinner, we came upon a couple of night watchmen and one of them was in some distress as we walked past. And this man said to us, 'one of the Scottish soldiers has just urinated in my cooking bowl, what am I to do?' I couldn't believe my ears. Knowing that Bob had a much better grasp of Kiswahili, I asked him to confirm what the guy said. 'He said that somebody pissed in his cooking bowl,' Bob said.

'What kind of soldier was he?' I asked. He said, 'he's a Scottish soldier.' How do you know?' I said, and he said, 'well, he had that the funny badge.' I assumed he was referring to the Black Watch, but that regiment had already left Kenya. There was no sign of any soldiers by then, so we tried to console him and Bob gave him twenty shillings to buy a new cooking pot. But it was the sort of thing that depressed the hell out of me, the fact that people could treat other human beings like that.

So when the topic of my future came up in a discussion with the Assistant DC, Bill Pollok-Morris, who had in his mind that the camps would be cleared soon, and I would be out if a job anyway, I was receptive to the idea of moving on. But where? Out of the blue, I found myself asking him 'How do you get into the administration?'

"Now you're talking," he said, "it will be much better for you to do that, because you'll know where you are in the future." I went along with his enthusiasm for a while and the next thing that happened was that that I was invited to dinner with Bill Pollok-Morris and his family. There were five or six of us at the table and we had a very pleasant dinner and I told a few good stories and we all laughed, and the atmosphere was very pleasant and positive. In fact, I was invited a second time so I must have used the right fork or tucked the napkin into my shirt properly.

I then got a letter to go to headquarters for an interview, but as I considered the matter I began to have second thoughts. In fact, as I've described, I believed, in a way that Bill obviously didn't, that independence was just round the corner, and the idea of a long future in the administration didn't strike me as feasible. Why was I even considering a job like a District Officer, which I might have to give up in five years' time, and I'd be five years older in the employment market?

But I turned up to the interview and I knew that because of Bill's support, I didn't have to try hard to impress them. And when I went in, there was this appointments board with a chairman, an older man from the administration, and he said "Good afternoon, Mr. Lees, you've come in with the very best recommendation we've had, so there is no need for a lot of the questions we would normally ask – all we have left is just to confirm your education."

I must admit that my heart sank because I realised that Bill had written me a reference which was better than anybody else's, and he expected me to do my bit and dazzle them with my educational attainments.

So I thought, 'well, the only thing I can do is screw up that part and hope that nothing happens' because I didn't want to join the administration, and in fact I really didn't want to stay in Kenya because I thought it would be a pointless decision: I knew that in my heart that independence would come and all these positions in the administration would be handed over to Africans.

So in answer to the question about my education, I emphasised my grandfather's deep involvement in the labour movement and the general left-wing tenor of the autodidactic sessions with my father, and before I knew it I was out of the door and convinced, correctly as it turned out, that I'd managed to avoid getting the job.

When I told Bill, he was so angry that he really couldn't say much. But we parted friends even though I suppose I made him look a bit of a chump.

About a week later I was summarily called to Morris Joplin's office and was told that I would be going to Traffic in Nairobi. I was given the job of a charge officer in traffic, which is where everybody comes when they've been given a ticket, and you have to get the name and address and all that sort of thing. And they go in front of a magistrate and they're either fined or given a caution. But it's a straightforward job and you meet a lot of people.

One day, this elderly chap came in, not very tall, a bit scruffy with a green trilby on over his eyes. I said, "Sit down, sir", and he sat down. And I said, "You know, the constable found that you parked your car illegally." And he said, "Yes, I did." I said, "Well, could you give me your name please?" And he said, "Oh, certainly, I'm Lord Delamere," which took me aback, because I hadn't recognised the unofficial leader of the European settlers, a farmer who had lived in Kenya since 1901 and was an important member of the so-called Happy Valley set, who passed their time drug-taking and wife-swapping.

I got his address and he was very charming, and he went before the magistrate and got convicted and paid his fine.

On another occasion, a very attractive young lady walked in. She was about 28, beautifully turned out, wearing lots of diamonds and had the carriage of somebody rather important. So I asked her to sit and said, "Madam, you parked your Rolls-Royce illegally." And she said, "Yes, I did." So I said, "Could you give me your name please?"

And she leaned forward, giving me a glimpse of things I shouldn't really have glimpsed, and said, "Yes, I'm Baroness von Thyssen."

This was her married name, but she was also one of the leading models of the world, Fiona Campbell-Walter. She said that she would send her lawyer to talk to me because she didn't feel that she ought to be penalised because of a parking offence.

Sure enough, the following day her lawyer turned up and he went through all the motions and I went through all the motions and we argued the law, but the traffic offence was quite straight forward, and he eventually decided he couldn't get her off and he had to abandon the attempt.

Sometimes I had to perform weekend duty. There was an air show in Nairobi and I was on duty at the security gate to the airport. And my instructions were that only people with the necessary invitation of a certain colour were to be allowed through the gate into the air show pavilion. Lots of people turned up, and they all had the tickets, and then another guy in his civilian dress came up with his wife. And I knew immediately who it was. It was a fellow called Senior Superintendent Pridgen and he didn't have a ticket. And so I said, "I'm terribly sorry, sir, but you can't go in. My instructions are that only those people with a ticket can go in." And he said, "You know who I am."

And I did, because of a strange incident when I was first at Fort Hall. He used to do night duty in the operations room and had to call all the police stations every hour or so to see everything was all right. And one morning he came in very early about four o'clock in the morning and called up one of the police stations. He said that he was expecting two people to be brought into the station, and wanted to check that they were all right. These were both Mau Mau people whom he had just captured. Unfortunately, they were being looked after by Kikuyu policemen, which was not a good idea for the hapless prisoners.

Pridgen was told that the men had asked to go to the toilet and after their handcuffs were taken off they had run away, and the police had fired after them. "Are they all right?" Pridgen said, and the man on the other end of the phone said "No, they're both dead" whereupon Pridgen put his head on the table and just moaned. After a minute he got up and he said, "Well, bring the bodies to the hospital and we'll see what the situation is." Of course, many a Mau Mau suspect suffered a similar fate in the early days of the Emergency, when taking prisoners was less satisfying – and safe – than eliminating enemies who had possibly massacred friends and family of loyalist members of the security forces. To see Pridgen again after some years had passed, and brutal civil war had been succeeded by civilian normality, was quite sobering.

My final weeks in Kenya were an anti-climax after my time in Fort Hall, and I applied for a UN job as part of a team running a plebiscite in the Southern Cameroon.

When I went for the interview for this job, I saw that there were twenty or thirty people in the waiting room. And each one was called in there for quarter of an hour, twenty minutes, half an hour, while I sat there waiting my turn, and I was the last to be seen. Then I was called and went in and there were must have been thirty people sitting around, and one of them was an

Ken Lees after finishing jungle warfare training,
Malaya, March 1950

Ken Lees, second left, with platoon of 4th Malay regiment soldiers,
September 1950

Ken Lees, far left, with colleagues at Kiganjo
Police Training School officers' mess, 1956

Ken Lees visiting Kigumo protected village, 1956

Telegraphic address: "Administer"
Telephone No.: 24221
When replying please quote

No. H.A.2/1/2/15
and date

KENYA

OFFICE OF THE CHIEF SECRETARY,
P.O. Box No. 30050
NAIROBI, KENYA

........28th April, 195...8

Sir,

      I have the honour to inform you that the Royal Humane Society has awarded you the Society's Testimonial in Vellum for the efficient and brave part you played when on the 26th September, 1957, you found Inspector Crowe rescuing eight persons trapped in a vehicle that had plunged 16 feet into the river over the Maragua Bridge four miles south of Fort Hall and which had not only overturned but was fast becoming submerged. Five lives were saved and it is said that your strenuous effort for over an hour to restore respiration in three of those released should have proved unsuccessful.

      I am writing to congratulate you most heartily on behalf of the Government to express my own appreciation of your courageous action and my satisfaction that the Royal Humane Society has awarded you their Testimonial in Vellum.

      Arrangements are being made for the presentation to you of this Testimonial on an appropriate occasion, the date and time of which will be conveyed to you in due course.

              I have the honour to be,
                  Sir,
              Your obedient servant,

              CHIEF SECRETARY.

Inspector Kenneth Lees,
Kenya Police,
Colony Police Headquarters,
NAIROBI.

*A river rescue by Ken Lees led to an award from
the Royal Humane Society*

COLONIAL OFFICE

GREAT SMITH STREET, LONDON S.W.I

Telephone: Abbey 1266 Ext.

July, 1960

Dear Mr. Lees,

I am very glad to tell you that you have been selected for one of the posts of Plebiscite Supervisory Officer, and allocated to the Southern Cameroons.

A formal offer of appointment will be sent to you as soon as possible. Pending the preparation of this, I should be grateful if you would arrange to have a medical examination. The necessary forms are enclosed, and you should make your own arrangements for an appointment with the Consulting Physician.

Yours truly,

(F. L. Greenland)

*Letter of appointment for Ken Lees as Plebiscite Supervisory Officer,
Southern Cameroons, July 1960*

*Ken Lees with the son of the Fon (chief) of Oku,
Southern Cameroons, 1960*

older man from the Colonial Office or somewhere similar, and he looked like a man who had had a lot of lot of experience. He didn't say anything, but the chairman started off and asked what I'd done in the UK. My interview must have been the shortest on record because I only got to explain what I'd been doing before my Kenya posting, which was trying to sell photocopiers by going round to industrial sites and knocking on doors asking to see the company's Managing Director, and then demonstrating this product that I was trying to sell. And this old chappie that sat there, who was obviously the key man, interjected, and said "Yes, Mr Lees, but you just want to go back to Africa don't you?" And I was so relieved. I remember saying, "Oh I do sir!" And he said, "Thank you, thank you," and he looked at the man who was running it and nodded and this chap said, "Well, that will do then, Mr. Lees."

About two weeks later I got a letter saying that I'd been appointed. I had no idea why I was one of the seven. Many of those who applied seemed to have been from Oxford or Cambridge. But I was chosen and I was given what was supposed to be the hardest area to deal with, the territory of the Fon of Nsaw, a ruler who had the reputation of being extremely difficult because he was addicted to drinking beer. He was also a very emotional and bad tempered little fellow, but he had enormous power in that part of the world. He was the Fon and he made everybody know it.

When I first went to see him I turned up and did everything correctly with regard to greetings and so on, but the first thing that happened was that he marched me off into this big crowd of about five hundred warriors, and in the middle there were three fully armed warriors, all dressed up in their war stuff. And these guys charged from about twenty yards away with the spears in their throwing position, shields up and their eyes wide and their mouths going and they're shouting and screaming and they charged at me. The Fon was standing next to me, and in Malaya I had learnt that fear had to be re-channelled into activity, instead of showing that you are frightened, which I was. I reached for a cigar case that was in my breast pocket, pulled it out slowly and took out one of the little cheroots. The warriors were now within a yard or two of us and they were leaping up and down and screaming to make me frightened. I casually lit the cheroot and blew the smoke at the warriors, and it was interesting to see their reaction which was to slow down to look at me. They were stunned to some extent by my response. I was supposed to do something other than casually getting a cigar out. And obviously they just stopped and I said to the Fon "that was really, really

Findakly Nga Laurence
One Kamerun (O.K.)
Local Branch – Banso
Bamenda
18th February, 1961

Congratulation

I feel I shall not be doing justice to myself and my Movement if I fail to congratulate one of your brilliant workers even though their nature is against us.

At the start of Mr Lease –Plebiscite Sup. Officer Banso, people were confused as every side looked for cooperation and sometimes might not have been happy in the end.

I must confess that having watcted keenly at this man's exude work in Banso, though an Englishman, I opted to give the devil its due. This man was very liberal and as harmless as a babe. He was as honest as a mirror in his duty as P.S.O. I find him not an Englishman in the way he went round the country skelling the heights explaining the Two Alternatives involed in the Plebiscite. If there had been a man neutral then this was neutrality in itself.

To begin with this man had one of the largest areas and hilly to tour, and yet he was as hard working as an ant. There is no village he has not visited and there is no gainsay or complain from any of these villages of his ever refraining from neutrality; of cause you are aware of our watch dogs all over the country. He went as silent has though, when confronted with politics.

As you must have known, our movement the One Kameun is the only national and anti-colonialism in the Southern Cameroons. As such this placed us at the hill tops to watch especially where we were conscious of an Englishmans' presence.

In the class room during the training of officers for the polling in the plebiscite, he taught honesty in the way that led to the honesty in the plebiscite of this District; this remains indelible in Banso. Very impartial a man. As kind as the sun. Many of your officers may not be free in their minds as they go back but I think that although Mr Lease not be happy with the result of this Plebiscite, but he is free on his mind. If all the workers under your scope were like this man, I think no man will desociate himself from this congratulations.

Lastly but not all I have to thank you for the role you have played in this part of the Cameroons, and pray your good offices to take a keen interest in the partiality and manoeuvres of Britain and Nigeria in the Plebiscite in the Northern Cameroons. You no doubt is aware that these people were not given freedom to express their wishes taking into consideration constant arrests all over there. All the irregularities and the threats of Nigerians there will no doubt nullify that Plebiscite. The world is looking up to your judgement.

Goodbye and bon voyage
Yours faithfully
Findakly Nga Laurence

Ken Lees' conduct during the Southern Cameroons plebiscite resulted in an unusual letter of commendation from a staunch anti-colonialist

impressive" and he told them to go away and we got on with our negotiations with regard to how I would see all villages and so on and so forth.

I retired when I was 60, and lived in Australia, and because I will never stop educating myself, in addition to doing consultancy work with three large companies I kept up my voracious reading habit. I also started to lecture for the University of the Third Age and we had a room at the Australia National University and I used to choose for my lectures each year something that I didn't know a lot about on the grounds that I would have to read up on it in order to stand up in front of 40 people and entertain them for two hours every Thursday. My first adventure was, Why are the Japanese Japanese? That was based on my experience of being the boss of Fujitsu in Australia and talking to Japanese executives when they came over to see what we were up to and what was happening, and realizing that their culture was entirely different from anything that I had ever come across before.

And it was while I was thinking about new courses to teach and browsing in the university bookshop in Canberra that I came across a book which purported to be about Kenya and covered the years I spent there, which made me roll up my sleeves and delve into my memory to try to set the record right. And that's how this book was born.

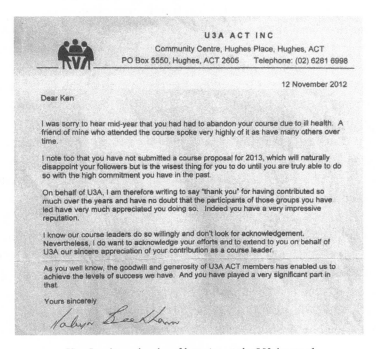

Ken Lees' two decades of lecturing at the U3A earned
him another warm letter of thanks

7
HOW MANY DEATHS?

I am not a professional historian, but as I sat down and read what recent professional historians have written about the Mau Mau period in Kenya, it seemed to me that my experiences at the time provided more valuable insight into history than the second- and third-hand views of people who were not even born at the time the British government was trying to handle an increasingly serious and complex problem.

The first book I came across in the bookshop was called *Imperial Reckoning: The Untold Story of Britain's Gulag in Kenya*, by Caroline Elkins, an academic at Harvard. As I flicked through the book I thought, 'this isn't the Kenya that I knew, nor is it anything like the situation I had in my camps'. I didn't buy the book but put it back on the shelf because I thought it was a piece of what I can only describe as 'journalism'.

But that book, and similar ones published in the 21st century, had more far-reaching effects than the average academic disagreement between historians. The accounts given by Elkins and others of the events I witnessed in Kenya bore no relationship to what I know was the case, in two particular areas.

First, I believe they minimised the number of murders and maimings by the Mau Mau, and second, I believe they exaggerated the number of incidents of torture and deaths caused by the British who were trying to quell the rebellion and deal with the perpetrators of crimes.

In a sense the two go together. If Mau Mau murders were 'only' a couple of thousand, the immense efforts made by me and my many colleagues to capture, detain and rehabilitate the criminals might seem to be overkill, and perhaps even punishing innocent people.

For Caroline Elkins, 1800 or so Kikuyu were killed by Mau Mau, way below the figure I know to be correct, at least 20-30,000, possibly as many as 60,000 or so. She is following the Corfield Report, an official document published by the British government in 1959, in quoting that number but Corfield himself did not offer 1,800 as the last word. He wrote: "Some 1,800 are known to have died, but the true number will never be known."

I made a great effort to use all possible sources of information to assess accurately the number of deaths at the hands of Mau Mau. Of course, among the European population and the administrators, the deaths which had the most impact were those of white settlers, of which there were really only a handful, but a very gruesome and heartrending handful.

I estimated the Kikuyu civilian deaths in the Fort Hall district alone as about 10,000 and it included babies. In the 1950s babies in Kikuyuland were not significant until they got to the time of their first ceremonial induction to the tribe. In any Kikuyu village there are a lot of babies. Now, we would count the babies and to say there were no babies at all killed in Kikuyuland could only appear in a text by an American historian and bears no relationship to reality whatsoever.

In a village of a hundred, there would be twenty to thirty babies and if the Mau Mau wiped out the village, they wiped out the babies. If you read Elspeth Huxley's book, *The Nine Faces of Kenya*, you will read that in the old days the Kikuyu method of disposing of the dead was not burying people but putting them in the bush and the hyenas took the bodies, and this applied to the babies of course. The infant mortality rate before we arrived in Kenya was something like 80% and so the number of new-borns that died after a week or a fortnight was extremely high.

This rate was so high because, as one of the Kikuyu doctors told me, the Kikuyu huts have a fire inside but no chimney, so the Kikuyu home environment is full of smoke. It is as if you were in a bar in America and there were twenty people in the bar and they were all smoking cigars and the doors and windows were closed so that the young lungs didn't stand that too well. So the incidence of lung problems in little ones was extremely high and the way in which they dealt with that was to wrap the baby in a warm blanket and put him outside the hut so that he stopped coughing. But unfortunately, if that was in the middle of the night the temperature there can drop to freezing and by the time they went to pick up the baby in the morning at 5 o'clock or 6 o'clock when the sun came up, the child had died.

Although the bodies of babies killed by Mau Mau would also be left in the bush and therefore uncountable, it is certainly the case that in any village devastated by the Mau Mau the numbers of adults killed would be only a proportion of total deaths.

In addition, unlike historians fifty years later, I often saw dead bodies and was able to count them and extrapolate to get more global figures for the district.

One day, for example, I sat in my office and across the road was a parking space, where some trees had been cleared. I saw a long wheelbase Land Rover draw up with an open back and the driver got out and went into the police station. The next thing I saw was that a man who worked for the CID walked across to this open-back truck and looked into the back when he was about a yard or so away and blanched at what he saw.

In the back were the slashed bodies of six or seven children. Why had they been killed? I have no idea. We had to bear in mind in those days that dying and death were part of Kikuyu society all the time. When we bury somebody, we say that in life we are in the presence of death, as if it's to remind us that we are only here hanging by a hair. But the Kikuyu knew that, and they operated with that knowledge. For them it was a very short step from being alive to being dead.

So my estimates of how many were killed in Fort Hall differ from nearly everybody else's, firstly because I was there and I counted the deaths as they came past my desk, and secondly because I included all the children, which they didn't. And, of course, I listened to thousands of confessions involving multiple killings.

The number of dead that were reported were those remaining at the site of the event, but this figure excluded those who were likely to have been badly injured. These people would manage to escape, but maybe collapse in the bush some hundred or two hundred yards away, and would be taken by wild animals. There would be a lot of them but nobody knows how many, but that is not a reason for excluding them entirely. Now, this is no trivial issue. It probably doubles or trebles the number of people who were actually found at the site. It's a very difficult thing

for people who don't know the actual circumstances to deal with and
report accurately, especially decades later and with no direct knowledge
of what happened.

A measure of the difficulty later researchers find themselves in is that
they can't even agree among themselves. Corfield's 1,800 is dwarfed by
Fazan's 3,000. Then a demographer, John Blacker, has calculated from the
census numbers that the "excess Kikuyu deaths" could be anything up to
50,000 or even 60,000. That figure is not far off what I've calculated based
on reports from Fort Hall, which is one of seven different locations.

Each of the parliamentary delegations that came, when they wrote
their report for parliament included at least one description of an event of
violence by the Mau Mau, whatever it was. But they could never convey
the full picture from such impressionistic details.

I had no doubts about my own estimates but it was nevertheless
encouraging to come across someone with similar experiences who shared
my own estimates. Hugh Mathison had been a captain in the Black Watch,
one of the regiments that were sent to Kenya. He mentioned to me that in
his view, shared by his fellow soldiers, there must have been at least 30,000
civilians of one sort or another killed in the Emergency.

Another way of looking at the 'numbers issue' is through the knowledge
we acquired of how many of the detainees had themselves murdered people.
Clearly, if my estimate of tens of thousands is correct, they could not have
all been carried out by a handful of men.

Of the men who passed through Fort Hall, 20% of 69,000 detainees had
been involved in some kind of violent activity. So the number of murders
committed by them in the Fort Hall district or elsewhere might be between
zero to 20% of 69,000, and if we take a figure somewhere in the middle
we get several thousand. And there would also be murderers amongst the
thousands of detainees released through other centres, such as Nyeri. It's not
so easy to get at the figure the other way: knowing how many killers, can
we work out the number of victims? These people often worked in gangs,
and several men would all slash the same victim, so who actually caused the
death? But it was unlikely that, having sworn their oath, members of the
Mau Mau were only ever called upon to take part in one attack.

If you look at just one massacre, the village of Lari, there were only
97 actual bodies found, but from my own experience, in a collection of
homesteads of that size, there would probably be at least 50 or 60 babies

or toddlers who were locked into their houses, because the Mau Mau ran round them with a rope and set them on fire, and they would be incinerated inside that building. So you have to add to the 97 probably another 100 before you could arrive at anything that's a reasonable number for people killed at a place like Lari.

The one thing that is clear is that the official number which is based on the investigations that the police made is a gross underestimate of the number of casualties.

Clearly, our figures were not based on our own counts of bodies retrieved, as I've explained. We had to extrapolate, and one basis for that extrapolation was the stories we were told during interrogations. But were we right to believe what we were being told?

I'll describe one story which put that question to the test.

It so happened that I was interviewing a young woman who had been caught carrying supplies of ammunition into the forest, and during our conversation she told us about one of the Mau Mau meetings where there was a Christian who refused to be oathed and so he was killed. She knew that the body had been recovered by some Christians who had actually been frightened into taking the oath and they buried him in a maize plantation in the district of Kigumo. It occurred to me that I could check her story, and by implication the stories of other detainees, by going to the alleged burial site and checking for a body.

Now, in all of these districts there is a police station with an inspector whose permission I would need to carry out the search. I turned up at the police station at Kigumo and there was an old Humber car outside and one of the badges on the mudguard at the front was the Windermere Car Club. Now, I lived in the northwest of England and Windermere is about twenty miles from where I lived, and because of this connection I knew the owner who was the local police inspector. It was easy to get his permission to go off and find the place described very accurately by the detainee. The body was there – my informant wasn't a yard out.

I probably used this approach about twenty times, completely at random, and it was a check on two things – on the methodology that I was using and also on whether these people were telling me the truth. It was quite amazing how unfailingly they remembered exactly where bodies had been buried, in the middle of nowhere, with no obvious signs or markings, telling us where beside the path to dig – and there was the body or skeleton.

Of course, I would ask myself, what it must have been like for a young girl, forced by Mau Mau gangsters under fear of suffering the same fate herself, to help slash a family member or clan member to death, and then years later take me back to the place of burial and watch me exhume the victim from the shallow grave she had identified. It was terrible for her, and terrible for me, but after conducting 20 or 30 of these exhumations, not only was I satisfied that confessions were truthful, and my interrogation processes fruitful, but my reputation amongst detainees for being "all-knowing" soared.

In all of this, we should remember that few bodies would actually be buried. It was quite normal for Kikuyu dead to be left to be eaten by wild animals, as the important part of the victim – his or her spirit – would survive that. The number of recovered bodies and skeletons were therefore only a small fraction of the likely number of dead.

It might be asked why no other veteran of the detainee release system has come forward to dispute the low figures given by the historians. In fact, there were no other veterans who had spent as much time as I did in one area and with as thorough knowledge as I have. I spent three years in charge of several camps, while most others were in charge of the camps for a short while, three months or so, and then moved on.

But historians like what they believe to be objective facts rather than personal opinions, even though, in the end, even the figures quoted by the historians came from individuals making estimates, using assumptions, based on a mixture of data, opinions, prejudices and guesswork. But of course, for people some of whom weren't even born at the time of Mau Mau, this is what they chose to go with, and the same sources crop up time and again, such as the Corfield Report and the work of Sydney Fazan.

Corfield says 1800 known dead (that is, excluding all those killed out of sight of the authorities, in effect, the vast majority) and Fazan who would have had the same information decided it was more like 3000 and that is what he wrote in his account of the Emergency.

Historians look at documents. They were not on site actually doing the work – that's a big difference. And it is not just the knowledge of facts like numbers of bodies that is lacking in the later accounts. What is also absent is any understanding at a deeper level of what led to the murders – the culture that bred Mau Mau, the ingrained beliefs in every Kikuyu that could be exploited by Mau Mau to turn ordinary people into killers, the information I and my colleagues gathered during interrogations that fed into our understanding of the whole situation.

The information recording system I described earlier was like no other system in use in Kenya at the time, and was far more sophisticated than the four by two inch cards used in other camps. I'll give you an example of why it was so useful. John came into my office in Fort Hall one day and he had two sheets of paper in his hand. They described the sourcing of an ingredient for the oath ceremony's obligatory drink. What it said was that this particular gang had twenty-seven young women and they collected the menstrual bleeding to mix it with a drink as part of the oathing ceremony, so the people who had to drink this stuff would be quite sure that if they betrayed the oath that they had been forced to take, they would die. There is no room for that kind of telling detail on a four by two.

So you have these poor devils who believed what they have always been taught and on the other hand we expect them to learn our rational ways of doing things, which is something that they find highly hilarious. They can actually do it, but they think it's some kind of a game. However, they can play all these games extremely well, better than a lot of the Europeans, I might add. So scholars like Caroline Elkins, who are so ready, eager in fact, to believe everything that the Kikuyu tell them, seem not to realise that dissembling and playing the game of innuendo is a tribal delight. They do this not to deceive you – it isn't malicious – it's simply that they enjoy the repartee and the winning of arguments by any means possible.

I think that Mau Mau was designed to do exactly what it did and it was highly intelligently done. The use of terror to be effective has to be widespread, random and fatal. Mau Mau leaders like Jomo Kenyatta who had been educated in the Soviet Union followed the model of Lenin and the Bolsheviks, and achieved what they set out to achieve, the Kikuyu domination of that fictitious place called Kenya. Fictitious, like so many colonial territories, because it was simply lines drawn on a map in the late 1800s. It had no reality other than the fact that somebody decided to draw it that way.

The impact of Mau Mau on Kikuyu society was exactly what the Mau Mau leaders organised the movement to do. During his incarceration by the British, Jomo Kenyatta spent his time studying politics and government, and it's quite clear that he was persuaded that he was going to have the responsibility for all the people of Kenya at the time that independence would come and that independence would come sooner than any of the European farmers thought it might do.

But Mau Mau, although a Kikuyu phenomenon, had an impact on Kenya as a whole because it locked in place the dominance of the Kikuyu over the other tribes of Kenya after independence, particular the Luo, a highly intelligent tribe who could have contributed much more to the governance of the new state. Tom Mboya, a Luo and the most serious possible rival to Kenyatta, was shot by an assassin, I presume Kikuyu, who was never found.

In a sense, however, we can't give Mau Mau all the credit for the British departure from Kenya. The campaigns of violence and terror and the propaganda were followed by the result that was already written in pencil by the British authorities with regard to freedom or independence. Independence for Kenya was never at the highest level in any doubt. We only have to look at India and Singapore and the other former colonies which gained their independence from us. The Mau Mau and all its evils were knocking at a half-opened door. And while Mau Mau achieved its own objectives, including dominance of the new state, the thousands of Kikuyu who had been promised 'freedom and land' got little freedom and the people who organised the rebellion got the land.

Little of the cultural background to Mau Mau and the Kikuyu is really understood, at least in the personal way that I understood it, by the younger historians and so they fall back on what they find on paper, in government records and so on, which, as it happens, were probably inaccurate or not carefully compiled for one other reason or another. In the political environment of the late 1950s it had been decided that independence would come in three or four years and compiling accurate figures somehow didn't seem as important as it later became. What you don't know, you can't write about, can you? What you haven't done, you can't describe, can you? What you haven't experienced is going to be forgotten unless you do what I am now doing, and that is talking about it.

AFTERWORD

How many Kikuyu died during the Mau Mau uprising: and who killed them?

The testimony from Ken Lees, after all these years, provides new insight into the late stages of the interrogation process during the Mau Mau Emergency. That in itself is reason enough to want to hear from him, however belatedly. As John Lonsdale, the most eminent of historians of the period, puts it: Ken Lees is entitled to his say.

Unfortunately, one key aspect of the conclusions he drew from his three years of interrogation runs clean against what is currently accepted wisdom: the extent of deaths inflicted by Mau Mau on fellow Kikuyu, either because they refused to swear the oaths Mau Mau demanded, or because they were loyal to the colonial regime. Most of the present generation of historians of Mau Mau put a much lower figure on that toll than Ken Lees calculated from the thousands of interrogations he conducted or supervised at Fort Hall. This question cuts across many other disputed areas of Kenyan historiography: the way in which Britain responded to the Mau Mau uprising, the nature and legality of British counter-measures, the extent and stresses of the detention system, the challenges of rehabilitation, the regime at the Mwea detention camps, the causes and consequences of the massacre at Hola detention camp, and the question of what messages can be drawn from the surviving archives of the colonial regime in Kenya.

In conducting my own extensive research into those archives, I have arrived at certain conclusions informed by the many revelatory documents now available for public scrutiny. I have also tried in this Afterword to place all these contentious questions within the frame of the two massive court cases in recent years, in which thousands of elderly Kikuyu, mostly former Mau Mau, have sought compensation from the British government for the ill-treatment they claim to have suffered during the Emergency. The second case concluded only in November 2018, with more than 40,000 such claims rejected because of the lateness with which they were lodged. Remarkably, the judge in the second case chose to cite verbatim the apology issued by the British Foreign Secretary, William Hague, after the first case was settled by the British government: a statement entirely at odds with the historical evidence, and originating with one of the most partisan of historians of Mau Mau. Why the judge should have done this is the last of the issues I will try and address in this chapter, which also draws on my personal experience of engaging with some of the protagonists in this hotly disputed academic debate.

1. The court cases

In the last two decades, much of the writing about the history of Kenya during the Mau Mau uprising has emphasised the abuse and ill-treatment of Mau Mau detainees by the British colonial administration. In a rare instance of historical research triggering present-day action fifty years after the events themselves, two major lawsuits were launched against the Foreign and Commonwealth Office (FCO) by those who claimed to have suffered at the hands of loyalist chiefs and headmen, soldiers and policemen, prison and rehabilitation officers, and those running the detention camps. This abuse of detainees, they said, was part of a deliberate policy to suppress Mau Mau, following the success of the military campaign against the armed guerrillas, which had eliminated any direct threat from Mau Mau. One historian has even compared British policy to genocide of the Kikuyu.

Detention without trial was a key element in the State of Emergency that was declared in October 1952 by the new Governor of Kenya, Sir Evelyn Baring, almost immediately after he assumed office. He had arrived after a lengthy hiatus ("can we wait till the school holidays are over?" asked the unsuspecting Baring of his predecessor), following the departure

of Sir Philip Mitchell many months earlier. Mitchell and his most senior
minister, Attorney-General John Whyatt (who also served as the Member
for Law and Order in the Executive), had been dismissive of the growing
alarm amongst more junior officials and police commanders in the areas
dominated by the Kikuyu tribe – Kenya's largest, constituting 20% of
the population. These "men on the spot" reported that the tribe was
being terrorised and radicalised by a secret campaign of oath-taking. This
campaign was in support of a movement called Mau Mau (the origins of
the name are still disputed), committed to overthrowing both the traditional
tribal leadership and colonial rule, in pursuit of "land and freedom". The
(unpublished) verdict of the man who wrote the official report on the
origins of Mau Mau, with regard to Mitchell and – even more so – Whyatt,
was: "complacent self-deception".

A rapid increase in population, combined with a partial replacement
of small-scale Kikuyu farmers, using traditional methods, by well-funded
European immigrants in some of the land areas best suited to large-scale
agriculture, had left a generation of young male Kikuyus landless and
rootless, gravitating to the urban employment opportunities of the capital,
Nairobi, and the influence of leaders standing outside the age-group-related
tribal structure. A commission of inquiry in the late 1930s had tried to
address the grievances of those claiming to have been displaced; but had
left a residue of resentment and mistrust for Mau Mau to exploit, linking
tribal issues to larger political ambitions, directed at displacing the colonial
government itself.

Notably, less than three dozen European civilians were killed by Mau
Mau: the real battle was between Kikuyu and Kikuyu. That is why the
colonial government introduced another key policy: "villagisation",
whereby nearly all Kikuyu were persuaded or forced to live in fortified
villages, guarded day and night in order to ensure that Mau Mau guerrillas,
once they had been driven back to bases in the forests and mountains, were
cut off from food and other supplies. Villagisation was bitterly resented by
Mau Mau sympathisers, and itself provoked thousands of complaints of
ill-treatment.

The primary trigger of the claims for compensation, decades after
the State of Emergency ended, was the publication – in the same week
in February 2005 – of two books: "Britain's Gulag", by Harvard scholar
Caroline Elkins ("Imperial Reckoning" was the US title), based on her

doctoral thesis, researched over a period of several years, and for which she was awarded a Pulitzer prize, followed by appointment to a tenured professorship; and "Histories of the Hanged", by David Anderson, at that time a research fellow at St Antony's, Oxford, later a professor at Oxford and now a professor at Warwick University. As well as a common publication week, the two authors shared a common intellectual debt. Anderson had studied under John Lonsdale, the UK's leading authority in this field; in her acknowledgements, Elkins paid tribute to Lonsdale as "the most gifted scholar I know", combining "brilliance with consummate good grace".

The publicity surrounding the publication of these books encouraged the Kenya Human Rights Commission and the Mau Mau Veterans Association to turn up the heat on a long-simmering campaign to seek compensation from the British government for alleged abuses during the Emergency. The two authors played an important and active role – along with a third historian, Dr Huw Bennett – in providing powerful and persuasive academic underpinning for what might otherwise have been seen as simply the latest propaganda battle between Mau Mau and Britain.

The legal campaigns were mounted under contingency fee arrangements, by two law practices specialising in compensation cases. The first, organised by the Leigh Day firm of solicitors, assembled 5,228 claims, of which five test cases, alleging torture and other ill-treatment, came to the High Court in 2011. One case was withdrawn and another was rejected by the judge, Mr Justice McCombe, before a startling revelation threw the Crown defence case into disarray.

It transpired that the records of the colonial administration, available for public and academic scrutiny at the National Archive at Kew, telling the official story of Kenya's progression to independence in 1963, had not included thousands of documents which – along with similar collections of files from other former colonial territories – had been stored at another, non-public, archive, in Hanslope Park; and then, so the FCO claimed, forgotten about. Even though it was a Foreign Office official, Edward Inglett, who eventually tracked down this undeclared archive, that the FCO was forced to admit its existence in open court left the government exposed to charges of bad faith and concealment.

Mr Justice McCombe did little to disguise his irritation at this turn of events, but before he proceeded to a verdict on the remaining three test cases (collectively referred to as the "Mutua" litigation), the British government offered a settlement: nearly £20 million in cash, funding for a memorial statue to Mau Mau to be erected in Kenya's capital, Nairobi, and a fulsome apology for the suffering endured by the claimants, including torture. The statue joined other tributes to Mau Mau, including a commemoration of its most notorious (or famous, depending on your viewpoint) military leader, Dedan Kimathi: it so happened that the first named litigant in the second court case was a Mrs Eloise Kimathi – hence the legal labelling of the second case as "Kimathi v FCO".

The government's climb-down opened the door to a further trawl for litigants, this time organised by the Manchester-based solicitors, Tandem Law, deploying scores of legal and support staff in Kenya, using questionnaires to check dates, locations and alleged injuries, and thumb prints to confirm statements. The number of claimants climbed to over 40,000 and on March 14th 2014 the first case management hearing took place. Detailed proceedings in Kimathi v FCO commenced in the High Court on May 23rd 2016, and occupied 223 hearing days (230 by another estimate) before Mr Justice Stewart arrived at his first verdict in August 2018. 45,000 documents were presented in court, and 70 witnesses testified.

There was a key difference between the two cases: in "Mutua", the government conceded that torture had taken place, seemingly accepting the weight of anecdotal evidence presented by the plaintiffs' lawyers and by historians such as Elkins, along with archival evidence analysed by Anderson (it should be noted that these two authors operate independently: although Anderson has been careful not to say a word about Elkins publicly, it is widely believed that he is not an unqualified admirer of her book). There were certainly hundreds of documented incidents of illegal treatment, including beatings, torture and even murder: we know that from all the prosecutions of policemen, soldiers and auxiliaries undertaken by the colonial authorities, often leading to convictions, though rarely to lengthy prison sentences; and also from outspoken court and appeal court judgments, where the behaviour of those in authority was forcefully condemned. A UK parliamentary delegation in 1954, citing 159 prosecutions for violence and corruption, concluded that "brutality and malpractices by the police were on a scale which threatened public confidence in the forces of law and order".

The colonial files also display much agonising over reported ill-treatment, which led to repeated public admonitions against such behaviour from the

Governor: itself perhaps an indication of a lack of necessary controls, but also – it has been claimed – that abuse was contrary to official policy, rather than part of it. Against this, it is certainly possible to argue that there was tacit acceptance of behaviour bordering the line of legality, if not actually crossing it. One of the most controversial documents in the archive – a memorandum from the Attorney-General to the Governor of Kenya in 1957 – tried to draw a distinction between various uses of force: legal and illegal, compelling and punitive, overwhelming and beating. This secret internal debate was exposed to public view – and public dismay – by the inquest into the deaths of 11 Mau Mau detainees at the Hola detention camp in 1959.

Even as he settled the Mutua litigation, the British Foreign Secretary, William Hague, in an unprecedented step, published an official apology and also adopted a highly tendentious argument from Elkins' book. She had claimed that "officially...some eighteen hundred African civilians (ie, Kikuyu who rejected Mau Mau) died at the hands of Mau Mau; in contrast, the British reported that more than eleven thousand Mau Mau were killed in action". That formulation – which, she claimed, showed where the "moral balance" in the conflict lay – was directly reflected in Hague's public statement, even though it is demonstrably false.

2. The "unaccounted for" Kikuyu deaths

Why this claim is so misleading will be explained below. But it is not the only, or even the most important, false claim made in her book by Elkins. She asserted that hundreds of thousands of Kikuyu were "unaccounted for" during the Mau Mau uprising, citing census data suggesting that there were nearly 300,000 fewer Kikuyu than would have been expected if growth data for the Kikuyu had matched that for other tribes between the 1948 population survey and that in 1962. On p 366 of her book, she claims the census data shows that "between 130,000 and 300,000 Kikuyu were unaccounted for". She quotes a Kenyan advocate, Fitz de Souza, who might have given evidence in the second court case, but for ill health, as believing "there were several hundred thousand killed" (ibid). Elkins used a figure of 400,000 in a BBC documentary (see below). For this she blamed, not Mau Mau, but British policies, directly or indirectly, causing actual deaths ("mass murder" of detainees, p 351) or a reduction in female fertility as a result of "malnourishment, disease, miscarriage, the absence of regular partners and the psychological stress resulting from war trauma" (p 366); according to her, "tens of thousands" died as a result of "torture, exhaustion, disease and starvation" (p 234). However, apart from the census data, she offered no direct evidence for any of these claims. And even this data must have been unearthed by her quite late in her research, as there is no mention of it in papers she had published not long before her book came out.

Clearly, the absence of thousands of Kikuyu males for varying periods of time during the Emergency (whether fighting in the forests or held in prison or detention) could potentially reduce fertility in the short term. However, beyond that, Elkins' diagnosis is purely speculative. Dr John Blacker, until his recent death the leading expert on Kenyan census-taking (he supervised or was a consultant on all the relevant census exercises in Kenya before and after independence), dismissed Elkins' arguments on both counts: fertility and mortality. That he was encouraged by both Anderson and Lonsdale in writing his authoritative paper "The Demography of Mau Mau: Fertility and Mortality in Kenya in the 1950s", published by the Journal of African Affairs in April 2007, was significant.

Lonsdale, despite having maintained close contact with Elkins during the writing of her thesis, was privately dismissive of her reliance on anecdotal evidence and described some of her figures as "frankly incredible". However, that did not dissuade him from citing the census data, in a letter to author David Lovatt Smith (a veteran of the Emergency, and writer of various books on it), saying they showed "that at least 100,000 Kikuyu were 'missing' (in my view probably because of female malnutrition and thus infertility from amenorrhea)".

Blacker indeed identified a dip in Kikuyu fertility during the Emergency, but concluded that this was most likely simply the result of a delay in raising families rather than an absolute loss. Any differences in fertility compared to other tribal groups "were primarily due, not to the 'malnourishment, disease, miscarriage, the absence of regular male partners, and the psychological stress resulting from war trauma' ascribed by Elkins, but to higher age at marriage", itself partly attributable to Kikuyu girls staying at school for longer than those from other tribes.

Blacker anyway found a far lower figure for "missing" Kikuyu than Elkins provided: though she still holds to her estimate, despite conclusive evidence that she had fudged the figures in her book. The 300,000 "unaccounted for" claimed by her was a figure based on her comparison of population growth as between the three Kikuyu-speaking tribes (Kikuyu, Embu and Meru, or KEM) and three others (Kamba, Luhya and Luo, or KLL), between the 1948 census and the 1962 census, covering the period of the Emergency. In her book, Elkins published the breakdown between the three KLL tribes, but failed to do so for the KEM. When I checked the actual individual outcomes, this failure was exposed (parts of my critique were published in both the *New York Review of Books* and the *London Review of Books* in 2005, and can be found online).

The fact is that the aggregation of two sets of three tribes was a structure Elkins imposed on the census data, not anything on which the census itself reported. Indeed, she could only provide the aggregate figures by adding together individual tribal totals. Clearly, she knew perfectly well what the individual figures were for the Kikuyu, Embu and Meru, but chose not to publish them: so I did.

The great majority of the apparently "missing" KEM, as calculated by Elkins, turned out to be Embu or Meru (EM), not Kikuyu (K). No one has ever suggested that the British targeted these Kikuyu-speaking tribes, rather than the Kikuyu themselves. Between the two census dates, the Meru population had reportedly increased by only 35% and the Embu had seemingly declined by 15%, with the Kikuyu numbers increasing by 56%. Even if the entirely artificial aggregation of the KLL tribes was used as a yardstick, I calculated that the ostensible shortfall amongst just the Kikuyu was no more than about 50,000 over the period 1948-62. The sleight of hand in averaging the Kamba, Luhya and Luo rates of population growth (which were very different – 52%, 66% and 64% respectively) edged into something approaching deceit by then averaging the KEM growth without revealing the startling differences between the three tribes.

Blacker's analysis was much deeper than mine. He showed how Elkins had simply misunderstood the different bases for the two censuses in 1948 and 1962, both in terms of methodology and tribal classification. Much of the apparent decline of the Embu and slow growth of the Meru was a result of the Mbere and Tharaka being separately enumerated in 1962, whereas they had been included with the Embu and Meru in 1948 (he accordingly re-labelled the KEM as KEMMT, to include the Mbere and Tharaka in both surveys). Taking into account other re-allocations of tribal groups, and drawing on a sophisticated analysis of data gathered for the 1962 census and that of 1969, Blacker offered some tentative conclusions.

He proposed a range of "excess" deaths, over and above the normal mortality rate, of between 30,000 and 60,000 – "perhaps a round figure of 50,000 is as good a guess as any". Even this exercise could not precisely distinguish between the years of the Emergency (about half the period) and the years before and after.

It was the "age-sex pyramids" which most obviously disproved Elkins' claim. These are the demographer's building blocks, layering each 5-year age group upwards, one on top of the other, with the largest, the 0-5s, at the base and the 75+ at the top. "Even a momentary reflection, "says Blacker, "suggests that Elkins' figures are implausible...[the figure of 300,000] implies that perhaps half of the adult male [Kikuyu] population would have been wiped out. Yet the censuses of 1962, 1969 and subsequent years show no evidence of this. The age-sex pyramids for the Kikuyu districts do not even show indentations."

Even more notable was the breakdown of what Blacker termed "excess" deaths in his analysis: "rather more than half, say 26,000, will have been children under 10 years of age"; "of the remaining 24,000 adult excess deaths, perhaps some 17,000 were of males and 7,000 of females". Somewhat strangely, at this point in his paper, having concluded that "there is no evidence to support the claims made by Elkins (which) are based on a misunderstanding of the data", Blacker relies on Elkins to explain the preponderance of young children amongst the estimated "excess" deaths. According to Elkins, "there was hardly a woman of childbearing age during the Emergency who did not lose a son or daughter, or elderly relative, to the combined effects of famine and disease" (she has, it is worth noting, provided no support other than anecdotes for this vast claim).

There is no evidence in the demographic surveys for supposing an increase in deaths amongst the elderly. Indeed, through the 1950s, before, during and after the Emergency, the underlying annual death rate amongst the Kikuyu was a steady 28,000, and there was no measurable change in life expectancy. Nor is it obvious why children under the age of 10 would have been so massively more vulnerable to famine and disease (assuming they were prevalent) than older children, though Lonsdale has suggested there is some evidence in other periods of food scarcity for older children to be favoured over young ones in sharing out what was available.

Blacker's calculations from what he calls "fitted model life tables" show that, during the 1950s, KEMMT had an expectation at birth to live to the age of 53, against 44 for KLL; and KEMMT under-5 mortality rates, even allowing for the disproportionate presence of under-10s in the "excess" deaths, were 190 per thousand live births, against 290 for KLL. Amongst KEMMT, 15-year-olds had a 73% chance of surviving to 60; against 66% for KLL.

Sadly, Blacker died before Ken Lees had written his memoir. For Ken, there was a very obvious reason why so many young children died: they could not run fast enough to escape the Mau Mau gangs that were killing their parents. The confessions he listened to day after day confirmed that parents and the small children with them were murdered together. (Below I note an observation from the official history of Mau Mau that boys aged 10-14 were subjected to mass oathing, which would again help explain the Blacker differential.)

If we subtract the known deaths in battle and from hanging from the 17,000 males Blacker calculated as part of his "best guess" total of 50,000 excess deaths, we are left with between 4,000 and 6,000 (depending on which figures for Mau Mau casualties are used and how many of those who died through hanging – a normal feature of the Kenyan penal system – would be classified as "excess"), to add to the 7,000 females. If we go back to the upper end of Blacker's 30,000-60,000 "range", we could perhaps add another 10,000 adult males to his total. That fits with Ken's estimate of at least 15,000, and up to 30,000, adult Kikuyu killed by Mau Mau: and 26,000 "excess" deaths of those under the age of 10 would be an entirely plausible number if it included those who died with their parents. The total number of Kikuyu victims of Mau Mau could have been somewhere between 30,000 and 50,000.

Interestingly, both Anderson and Lonsdale chose to publish their interpretations of Blacker before his paper actually appeared. Lonsdale, in a paper entitled "Britain's Mau Mau", directly cited his findings, but – in my view – subtly misinterpreted them. Because of the temporarily lower fertility during the Emergency, for which he now accepted Blacker's judgment as being attributable to later marriage, Lonsdale wrote that Blacker "cannot say how many of these [26,000] Kikuyu children died and how many were yet to be born". Actually, Blacker is quite clear. Delayed marriage temporarily delayed first births, but any shortfall during the Emergency must have been rectified by the time of the 1962 census. The 26,000 were "excess deaths", not missing births.

Moreover, Blacker undertook a number of sophisticated reverse calculations (which he acknowledged as somewhat artificial) using the 1969 census data and certain unpublished reports on detailed surveys, revising the overall average annual growth rate for the whole of Kenya between 1948 and 1962 to 2.7%, compared with just 2.65% for the KEMMT group. This would have lowered his overall estimate of "excess deaths" to below his tentative estimate of 50,000, but he preferred to stick with that figure.

More importantly, he focused even more closely on the 26,000 "excess" under-10s, and noted that the sharpest increase in child mortality (actual deaths as opposed to delayed births) was in the period 1949-54, at 22%, compared with 17% for the period 1954-59. As villagisation did not begin until 1954, it would have been impossible for at least 15,000 of the 26,000 deaths to have been caused by malnutrition and disease, as hypothecated by Elkins, and uncritically accepted by Blacker. Ken Lees' explanation – these were children too small to run fast enough when Mau Mau gangs murdered their parents – seems far more plausible; and would also make much more sense of the 15,000 adult males and females not killed or hanged by the British.

Indeed, if the children had died as Elkins theorised, why would their graves not be readily identifiable, and their deaths go unrecorded? There is no sign in the 1969 census of any increase in child mortality having occurred during the Emergency. In 1969, mothers aged from 15-49, split into five-year age groupings, were asked how many children they had living and how many had died. In every grouping, including those aged over 30 (who would have been giving birth during the Emergency) the proportion of children reported as having died showed no blips, and was far lower for KEMMT than any of the KLL tribes. What Blacker had identified was missing numbers, but not a higher reported instance of child deaths: and that is consistent with Lees' version of events, where parents and young children were killed together, leaving no graves and no reports. If mothers survived Mau Mau attacks and punishments, so too would their children have survived

Anderson published an article in the New Statesman in July 2006, clearly having read Blacker's paper, in which he dismissed Elkins' figure of 300,000 "missing" as "demonstrably wrong", asserting that "demographic analysis indicates that, between late 1952 and 1956, the war accounted for between 20,000 and 30,000 African dead...the vast majority civilians". There is actually nothing in Blacker to support such a claim: that range of mortality and years is nowhere in the published paper. Moreover, Anderson takes for granted that these deaths were inflicted by "British forces", seemingly unable to consider the possibility that the majority of the "excess deaths" identified by Blacker might have been the result of Mau Mau actions. After all, does he really think British forces would have killed 26,000 Kikuyu children under the age of 10? As for the idea of up to 30,000 African civilian dead between 1952 and 1956, we need to look closely at what the available records and literature tell us.

3. The "moral balance"

It is time to deal with Elkins' other misleading figure, of 1,800 African civilian fatalities (actually, 1,819 in the source she cites), which, in an eerie pre-echo of Elkins' belated discovery of the census data she used in her book, is drawn from a late addition (it does not appear in the original draft) attached to Appendix H of the official inquiry into "The Origins and Growth of Mau Mau: an Historical Survey". This report was commissioned by the Nairobi government from a senior colonial official in Kenya, Frank Corfield, and published in May 1960 as a Sessional Paper in Kenya (No.5 1959/60) and a Command Paper in the UK (No.1030). Corfield had spent most of his overseas career in the Sudan, and had also served as a District Commissioner in Acre and Galilee during the Arab Revolt in Palestine in 1938. After retiring, he went to live in Kenya, and was promptly hired by the Nairobi authorities to take on various tasks, starting in the Cabinet Office. Before he could take up his post as Government Commissioner on the Mau Mau history, he had to finish his work as secretary of the colony's game policy review. The table of casualties in his Mau Mau report takes up less than a third of the final page.

Anyone who has read the report cannot fail to realize that the 1,800 figure refers only to the *known* deaths of "African civilians" (ie Kikuyu) at the hands of Mau Mau; such known deaths nearly all happening *after* the declaration of the Emergency in October 1952. The notion that the British government would deploy battalions of soldiers, regiments of locally recruited soldiers and Home Guards, squadrons of aircraft, hundreds of British policemen and even naval assets to crush a rebellion that had almost no victims *before* the Emergency was declared seems unlikely.

Tracking the Corfield files in the National Archive, it is easy to see how the figures were gradually changed month by month, arriving at the numbers he provides "up to end 1956". "Terrorists killed 11,503", "Security Forces killed 167" (of whom 101 were African), and "Loyal Civilians 1,877" (of whom 1,819 were African). A later version (April 30 1959, National Archive file CO141/6300) of the fortnightly reports which underpinned his table offers different figures, showing fewer Mau Mau killed (10,540) but slightly greater numbers of Mau Mau captured wounded, captured unwounded or arrested (by police, rather than by troops: just over 27,000). In the Corfield papers, which include his unpublished summary of his Report for ministerial use, he explicitly uses the 10,540 figure, as the most up-to-date and authoritative. There is no good reason for preferring the 1956 estimate to the 1959 one.

The "killed or wounded" numbers for security forces in the later document were virtually unchanged for Europeans and Asians; but for Africans the reported number of wounded was much lower (465 versus 1,469), whereas there was a fourfold increase in those reported killed: 525. I have not tracked down how and why these large changes (a thousand fewer wounded, four hundred more killed) came about. The number of both total civilian deaths and of African civilian deaths was 13 higher, bringing the African total to 1,832. The strong presumption is that virtually all the African "loyal civilians" were Kikuyu, as Mau Mau almost solely targeted fellow Kikuyus in attacking Africans.

According to Corfield's privately circulated briefing paper, 667 members of the Home Guard (nominally civilians, usually unpaid, but essentially, an armed and organised Kikuyu defence force) were killed by Mau Mau. As this figure is in itself higher than the final reported figure for Africans in the security forces reported killed (525, even in the 1959 version, 101 in the 1956 version), there is reason to believe that Home Guard deaths may not all, or even substantially, have been incorporated into the security forces total. The Home Guard was by default a civilian force, as it had no basis in law, so such a re-classification may have been advisable after it had been wound up at the end of 1954.

There is a clear implication of a change in categorization at some point between 1955 and 1959, in that in February 1955, Viscount Swinton told the House of Lords that the known number of civilian Africans deaths was 1,300: as it happens, a figure he immediately qualified, saying "I am sure that is a considerable understatement". But it is wholly improbable that 500 more civilian Africans were killed between 1955 and 1956, given that the shooting war against Mau Mau had effectively ended by early 1955; so it is quite possible that Home Guard fatalities were included in the number of *known* civilian African deaths.

The timeline that constitutes the bulk of Appendix H refers to "fifty-nine loyal Africans, including Chief Waruhiu, murdered" between May and October 1952; evidently, the great mass of the 1,819 deaths (or 1,832 in the amended 1959 version) tabulated by Corfield occurred *after* the Emergency was declared in October 1952. Indeed, on the very first page of the report, Corfield states that although his main task was to survey the origins of Mau Mau – by definition pre-dating the Emergency – he "was also asked to report on terrorist strengths, methods and organization during the Emergency...and extent of casualties inflicted by and on Mau Mau" – which is the context for the table added to Appendix H. Notably, he was not asked to report on the number of such casualties *before* the Emergency; and this may well have been a deliberate omission from his brief.

That it is relegated to the very last page of the report perhaps indicates his own view as to the relevance of the Appendix H table to his main task of analysing events before October 1952. As he knew, much of the contemporary evidence argued that the vast majority of Mau Mau murders of Kikuyus occurred *before* the Emergency was declared. Indeed, even as he asked the Ministry of Defence for the latest figures, he added "one last query: I presume that 'Casualties to Loyal Civilians' covers Africans known to have been murdered (eg in the Lari massacre) but does not include the many Africans whose murder came to light during the later stages of the Emergency following the extensive confessions. Is there a reliable estimate of the number of bodies discovered? I remember that at one stage the total for Kiambu district alone was over 800". Bodies discovered, however, would only have been a small proportion of those killed in the more remote areas, where the dead were disposed of in rivers and wells, left for carrion, or, as Tony France (who served in many roles during his 21 years in the Kenya Police) puts it, "buried under slum plots in Nairobi or dumped down 'long drop' latrines".

It was, for perhaps obvious reasons, easier to count the African civilian dead *after* the start of the Emergency, as far more of the Mau Mau fighters were then engaged in direct combat with British and loyalist forces than previously, when the bulk of killing took place either in Nairobi (where Mau Mau held considerable sway) or the remote *shambas* such that they were obscured from possible police investigation, or even reporting by relatives of victims (for fear of retaliation). The post–Emergency killings were normally in full view of the heavily re-inforced colonial authorities. Even if the number of dead at Lari is disputed (with Anderson's figure of 74 being the lowest, but other estimates ranging up to 100 or even 150), most of the victims were readily identifiable by name, however mutilated or burned their bodies might be. The official report on this massacre, in March 1953, said that large and well-organised Mau Mau gangs more than 100 strong left at least 71 dead (one report claimed the figure was 150), with 51 missing, and many women and children burned alive (CO 5659/97). One of the reasons why the chief who was the main target for this attack, Luka, failed to mount an organised defence of the homesteads at Lari (he himself was reportedly cut into small pieces) was that some of his armed guards were drawn away to help deal with a near-simultaneous attack on the nearby Naivasha Police Station, led by Dedan Kimathi, where the fatalities were much fewer (just three policemen) but the loss of rifles, automatic weapons and ammunition, together with the release of 137 Mau Mau suspects, represented a serious defeat. Reprisals for these attacks were ruthless and extensive, and probably cost even more lives than were lost at Lari (which was situated in the Uplands district, 25 miles from Nairobi).

Other encounters were documented by some of the 200 veterans of the Emergency who responded to David Lovatt Smith's invitation to contribute to his book "Kenya, the Kikuyu and Mau Mau". Most notable of these was probably W H Thompson, a District Officer at the heart of the battle in Fort Hall (and whom we will encounter again in the section below, on Hola, by which time he had risen to the position of District Commissioner; his final posting was as Governor of Montserrat). Thompson's unpublished memoirs, collated in 1978, when he was 49 years old, are repeatedly cited by Lovatt Smith, along with personal communications from him, of which a striking example was as follows:

"I still believe, and from the testimony of my own ears and eyes, I know that Kenyatta built up a murderous, and murdering, organisation that killed thousands of his own tribesmen. I remember only too well the day he exhorted the Fort Hall Kikuyu to 'Go out and water the Tree of Freedom with blood'. And I was there the very next morning when the machete-hacked bodies of seven persons known to be his opponents were brought into my District Headquarters".

Thompson was one of many DOs and DCs (Wally Coutts was another – and Ken Lees agrees with them) who named Jomo Kenyatta as the prime mover of Mau Mau. For Lees, Kenyatta's studies in Moscow would have educated him in Leninist revolutionary principles (including the use of terror, slogans and tightly controlled leadership): key ingredients, as Lees saw them, of Mau Mau as an organisation. For the purposes of this analysis, the accuracy of that judgment is immaterial (and is disputed, in whole or in part, by most current historians). The question is rather the detail of civilian Kikuyu deaths after the Emergency was declared, and how an estimate can be established for the number killed before then, irrespective of which individuals within Mau Mau were giving the orders.

One of the reasons why such an estimate is hard to provide is that the Kikuyu Tribal Reserve, which was bounded by Nyeri in the north, Kiambu in the south and Fort Hall in the east, was under the control of the civilian administration, supported by Chiefs, Headmen and Tribal Police, with the Kenya police service (reporting to the Commissioner of Police) having only limited authority. Given the huge scale of Mau Mau oathing, few tribal leaders could publicly stand up and oppose Mau Mau. Indeed, says one of Lovatt Smith's contributors, they were directly targeted, either in being forced to take oaths, or killed: "The Headmen in nearly all cases were oathed, because if they failed to do so, they knew they would die... murders increased daily. Things became really grim in the months of August and September 1952. Ten days before the declaration of the Emergency...a Church Elder, who has since been murdered by the Mau Mau, [took me] to a Mau Mau oathing ceremony. I had one Tribal Police escort...and the only weapon we had between us was a walking stick. We sat on the side of the hill and watched about 900 people oathing. There was nothing we could do. The people laughed and spat at us."

Mau Mau and the administering of Mau Mau oaths had been outlawed, but the prohibition was widely ignored. According to Lovatt Smith, "Senior Chief Nderi of Nyeri, accompanied by two Tribal Policemen, came across a crowd of several hundred at an oathing ceremony organised by Dedan Kimathi. When he ordered them to disperse, they rounded on him and hacked him and his two policemen to death." He continues: "Chiefs and Headmen, and particularly the Tribal Police force, were all targets and many

were murdered in the months before the declaration of the Emergency...
for at least two years before the Emergency...the Mau Mau were highly
successful in their relentless slaughter of those that did not toe the line."
In Fort Hall "was a redoubtable force of Tribal Police who only numbered
thirty at the beginning of the Emergency. Twenty-eight was the number
of fatal casualties they were to suffer in the ensuing months. The Mau Mau
made a dead set at them and if they could not get them, they got their wives
and families and butchered them for their husband's loyalty".

Lovatt Smith acknowledges that "the number of those who refused
[taking] oaths and were cut down for their pains will never be known. But
in Fort Hall alone, there are plenty of records to show that considerable
numbers lost their lives in the most horrific manner." He does not cite
any of those records, but quotes Thompson again: "Anyone refusing was
quickly threatened and subjected to savage physical violence. If they [still]
refused they were killed in the presence of others attending the ceremony,
thereby ensuring that the threats were not seen as empty words. Many very
bravely did refuse, but we could never find out, nor will it ever be known
how many thousands of 'missing' Kikuyu were executed in this way. The
chiefs were forever reporting the discovery of chopped up bodies, burnt
out huts, missing persons, slaughtered animals and other depravities...time
and again we came upon or were taken to see slashed or violated bodies."

According to Lovatt Smith, it was the then Fort Hall DC, Frank Loyd,
who was persuaded by his DOs, Tommy Thompson and Tony Soutar, to
support Senior Chief Njiri's appeal for arms and assistance in creating the
self-defence force that became the Home Guard. This force then bore the
brunt of the fighting with Mau Mau in the Reserve during the Emergency
itself. The first allocation of fifty rifles from the British Army was received
in April 1953.

This period also saw the start of a card index system to record
intelligence and confessions, initiated by a Kikuyu assistant DO, Jerome
Kihore: later, murdered by Mau Mau. The value of the system was noted
by DO Thompson, in an observation later echoed by Sir Vincent Glenday
(see below), who was deputed in 1955 to investigate abuses by Home
Guards, and, of course, much later by Ken Lees. "The strength of the card
index system," said Thompson, "lay in the recorded inaccuracies as much as
the truths. Time and again, when false confessions had been made and set
down, they stood out like the proverbial 'sore thumbs'." As we now know

from Ken Lees, the 4" x 2" cards were fairly primitive as compared with his later use of foolscap sheets in ever-fattening files as a means of identifying the most active Mau Mau members, but the technique of cross-referencing seems to have had some success even in this early form.

Inevitably, the Home Guard posts, and their arms supplies, became primary targets for Mau Mau gangs. Peter Lloyd, another DO, in Nyeri district told Lovatt Smith: "Eventually, a group of terrorists led by Waruhiu Itote, the self-styled 'General China', mounted a determined attack on my Senior Chief's guard post. Mercifully, the Chief together with his police bodyguards managed to escape, but seeing the mutilated corpses of several other individuals I had known, respected and admired, was traumatic."

Tommy Thompson told a similar story. After the village of Ndaikini had resisted an attempt by a Mau Mau gang to enforce oath-taking, "a week later, the gang came at night and slaughtered some thirty women and children, either hacking them to death or burning them alive in their huts... My own headquarters was also attacked by a very large and well-armed gang...we found out later that the main purpose was to capture our local armoury in the village hall. They ransacked and burnt part of the school and two houses together with the tiny three-roomed stone building into which I had only recently moved. But most sadly of all, the six rondavel huts built for the Tribal Police had been the focus of appalling savagery. Three of the wives and four children were slashed to death, the children lay beheaded."

Tony France, who joined the Kenya Police in 1953, was quickly immersed in this struggle. "I was one of the first KP officers to arrive at the scene of the massacre of the 'loyalist' occupants of the ill-fated Uthiru Kikuyu Home Guard post, whose only survivor, Headman Ruben, ran across country at night to sound the alarm at my Kabete police station. The scene at Uthiru was almost indescribable: methodically hacked corpses in ragged clothes, scorched human flesh and smouldering remains of huts. Nothing had been spared from the savaging, deliberate damage, from kids' soft toys to smashed china, and mangled household utensils. In the surprise attack, most of the victims had been shot from a Bren-gun stolen from a Kenya Police armoury. The rage expended by the MM gang was totally disproportionate in what might be roughly interpreted as a struggle for power by atrocious means. I still retain B and W photos of that destroyed village and some of the bodies. Obviously the gang members had become thoroughly brutalized and desensitized to human suffering." France, in a private communication, accepted that "Mau Mau murdered several thousand of their own", whilst rejecting "the very unlikely figure of 36,000 African deaths during the MM Emergency" that he was once quoted. An Australian journalist (like Ken Lees, France eventually emigrated to Australia) cited a figure of 18,000 African dead, but, says France, that "has never, to my knowledge, been properly verified".

According to Jock Rutherford's "A History of the Kikuyu Guard", in April 1953 a post at Ruathia in the Fort Hall district "was attacked and overrun by a gang of fifty Mau Mau, armed with at least one automatic... although the Tribal Police and Kikuyu Guard fought well, their ammunition was limited and they were soon overcome. The Tribal Policemen were found later. Some had had their hands tied and had then been shot and cut to pieces. Four Kikuyu Guard were also killed."

Lovatt Smith tells us that "whenever a Kikuyu Guard Post was overrun and its defenders killed, it was re-built and made operational within a single day [so as] never to concede a single gain to the Mau Mau" (this policy was described to him by former DO Bob Otter). He also cites the unpublished memoir of Stan Bleazard, a Kikuyu Regiment soldier assigned to training Kikuyu Guards, whom he refers to as "brave stalwarts...many of whom lost their lives [in] appalling instances of everyday murder and violence against those Kikuyu who did not support Mau Mau".

Another Mau Mau tactic was ambush: Chief James Kiru of Location 14, Fort Hall, and Assistant District Officer Jerome Kihore (the architect of the confession system) were shot to death in August 1953 as they drove their Land Rover, when halted by a tree so as to create a road block: "the gang made their escape," writes Lovatt Smith, "though not before mutilating the bodies". (For those who might doubt the tenor and credibility of these accounts, as all from one perspective, there are Mau Mau memoirs, too. Gucu Gikoyo describes a gang of one hundred ambushing a DO's Land Rover: "When the District Officer's bodyguards saw how tough things were bound to get, they took to flight leaving their master [Richard Wood-White] behind. We got hold of the thug who had insulted our people and hacked him to pieces before setting his Land Rover on fire. We removed three sub-machine gun magazines fully loaded from his jacket pocket before we finished him off.")

With the recruitment of thousands of new volunteers, the Home Guard gradually gained the upper hand in Fort Hall in late 1953, but not before, as

Lovatt Smith puts it, "many posts were overrun and their occupants killed... [while] several District Officers and Kikuyu Guard DOs were ambushed and killed in the most bloody and savage attacks."

According to John Pinney, Fort Hall District Commissioner at the time of Ken Lees' assignment there, during the first 13 months of the Emergency those killed by Mau Mau included "three District Officers, one Chief, nine Headmen, twenty-eight Tribal Policemen and two-hundred and thirty four Kikuyu Guard". Despite these losses, during the two years when the Kikuyu Guard was operating, it "accounted for 63% of all Mau Mau killed or captured" (says Lovatt Smith, without citing a reference). After it was disbanded at the end of 1954, a new force of Tribal Police was established.

What can we conclude from this mixture of anecdotal and official evidence? First, that it is relatively easy to see how a total of some 1,800 Kikuyu civilian deaths can be calculated from the reports of massacres, smaller incidents and cumulative statistics (as in John Pinney's analysis), especially if we include the Tribal Police and Kikuyu Home Guard casualties. Clearly, apart from a few score reported killings in the weeks before the Emergency, virtually all the "known" deaths date from after October 20 1952.

So what happened before October 1952? On page 2 of his report, Corfield refers to "the holocaust of the Mau Mau rebellion", an expression that could scarcely be applied to the weekly average of eight civilian African deaths for the post-Emergency period that he reported. It was a choice of words highlighted by one of the participants in the debate on his report held in the Kenyan legislature in 1960.

If we read further into the report, we find the following passage on page 136: "On 15th May 1952, the bodies of two Kikuyu were found in the Kirichwa River near Nairobi. Both men had been shot and their bodies mutilated. One of them had given information to the tribal authorities concerning Mau Mau activities in the Nyeri area some weeks previously. Six persons were charged with these murders and committed for trial. The person who discovered the bodies and reported to the police was later murdered. This was the first reported instance of a Mau Mau execution. But it is known from confessions made in the later stages of the Emergency that the organised campaign of assassination which started about this time increased in intensity. The number of Kikuyu who were murdered will never be known, but in Kiambu district alone over 500 bodies were eventually found" (this copies almost exactly the wording in the letter cited above, apart from changing 800 to 500).

Given that the confessions Corfield referred to regularly claimed that bodies had been thrown into rivers, abandoned to wild animals or otherwise left in remote locations, that as many as 500 bodies in one district were eventually recovered suggests a large multiple of that number for the actual total of victims: thousands, even tens of thousands.

On page 166, Corfield takes up the story. The Mau Mau attempt to achieve dominance of the Kikuyu tribe, and then lead a nationalist bid to drive out the British, was, he says, organised around a campaign to persuade members of the tribe to take an oath of loyalty. This campaign had first been noticed in 1948 and had gathered strength through 1950 and 1951. It was continuing apace when in May 1952 police encountered a second oath, the so-called "killing oath", which – so the British authorities claimed – entailed the penalty of death for anyone taking it who failed to carry out Mau Mau orders, be they for murder, theft, refusal to help drive Europeans out of the country, or to worship Jomo Kenyatta.

"A reign of terror," said Corfield, "shortly to be backed by assassination, had already got a hold in the Kikuyu reserves and in other Kikuyu-dominated areas, and if any refused to take the oath they were quickly threatened and subjected to physical violence. If they still refused, they were killed in the presence of others attending the ceremony, thereby ensuring that the others fully realized that the threats were not empty words. Many did however refuse, but it will never be known how many thousands of 'missing' Kikuyu have been murdered in this way."

That last sentence is an echo of a line in the 1954 book, "Defeating Mau Mau", by one of the witnesses that most impressed Corfield – the palaeontologist and expert on Kikuyu culture, Louis Leakey. Leakey claimed that the Mau Mau leadership could not afford to let anyone who refused to swear the second oath report having done so to colonial officials. "Therefore those who refused had to die, and no one will ever know how many of the thousands of 'missing' Kikuyu have died in this way."

On page 284, Corfield directly cites Father Trevor Huddleston's description of Mau Mau as "wholly evil" and "the worst enemy of African progress in Kenya", in having about it "all the horrors of the powers of darkness". Then he adds his own assessment of the impact of what he described as a "civil war" amongst the Kikuyu: "Such was the power of

Mau Mau that a large number of those who resisted were assassinated. Some 1,800 are known to have died, but the true number will never be known."

Corfield privately described the Lari massacre – the worst of the Mau Mau atrocities – where, he says, some 100 inhabitants of a loyalist village were hacked and burned to death (Elkins says 97, a figure cited in the House of Commons debate four days after the killings, but Anderson says 74) – as itself a "holocaust". But he was almost certainly aware that the "confessions" to which he referred had described the murder of many thousands, possibly tens of thousands, of Kikuyu adults, along with many thousands of children too small to run away when the Mau Mau gangs struck. In a letter to The Times in early 1961, he referred to the "many thousands of Africans, some of whom might well have been the present leaders in Kenya, [who] were cruelly liquidated" (many key political opponents of Mau Mau were assassinated: not just tribal chiefs, but young leaders from other tribes such as Tom Mbotela). In his papers, held by the Bodleian Library in Oxford, he kept a copy of a letter to the Manchester Guardian, from a Mr A L Holt, published in March 1961, claiming that Mau Mau "brought about the deaths of more than 15,000 Africans"; and a clipping from Time magazine, asserting that 12,423 [sic] Africans were victims of Mau Mau (the edition of Time Africa published a week after Lari reported 300 deaths there).

The Governor of Kenya, Sir Evelyn Baring, wrote in secret to the Colonial Secretary, Alan Lennox-Boyd, in September 1955, of the challenge of Mau Mau rehabilitation, when there were still 47,000 Mau Mau in detention and 15,000 in prison. A key task was to keep "fanatical irreconcilables" well away from those areas where Mau Mau murders took place during "the appalling reign of terror which prevailed at the end of 1952". He added darkly: "from the number of corpses produced during the last few months we now know that the number of these murders far exceeded anything imagined in 1952". As at this point the confessions evidence was not available, Baring must have been referring to the physical evidence that Corfield had inquired about – the 500, or 800, bodies in Kiambu, for instance, the corpses with ropes around their necks disinterred in Nairobi (as described by S H Fazan below) and the remains abandoned at the Nairobi mortuary (see Anderson below).

A full year before Corfield reported, a Conservative Member of Parliament, Bernard Braine, who had been part of one of the regular all-party parliamentary delegations that visited Kenya during the Emergency (he inspected Mariira and other detention camps in the Fort Hall area on February 17th 1958, accompanied by a Labour MP, Austen Albu, and had previously visited on January 14th 1957, accompanied by three MPs and a member of the House of Lords), spoke in the House of Commons on February 24th 1959. He reported that amongst those detained "are some who did not hesitate to butcher thousands of their fellow tribesmen...in the most savage and bestial fashion that one could think of...if we had let these men loose we should never have been forgiven by tens of thousands of loyal Kikuyu who withstood the tortures and the hellish persecution and terrorism of Mau Mau".

Another Conservative MP who visited Kenya, Frederic Bennett, told the House of Commons as early as June 6th 1956 that "many thousands" of civilian Kikuyu "had been butchered by the Mau Mau".

The strong likelihood is that the underlying source for both Corfield's reference to information from confessions and Braine's citing of "thousands" being butchered was the interrogation process at the Fort Hall camps, which was supervised from 1956 to 1959 by Ken Lees, the young Inspector of Police, recruited from the UK on a 3-year contract, originally posted to the traffic department in Nairobi and then swiftly assigned to Special Branch in Fort Hall: his account of his experiences forms the first half of this book. Lees did not speak directly to Braine about the number of killings (though he was at Mariira for Braine's visit), or to Corfield, but the results of his interrogations were closely monitored by the Assistant District Commissioner at Fort Hall, Bill Pollok-Morris, as Lees explains in this book; and it is highly likely that the District Commissioner, John Pinney, communicated his findings to the Nairobi hierarchy.

Other Kenya police officers were involved in the taking of confessions. Lovatt Smith tells us he still retains copies of the 70 confessions made to him when he was serving in Special Branch. Likewise, Tony France, during his assignments to Manyani, where Jomo Kenyatta's son Peter Mugai was one of his team, said he interrogated "scores if not hundreds" of detainees. "Manyani camp's corrugated iron Special Branch office held many hundreds of index cards that recorded interviews with detainees...By cross-references from SB's voluminous index files we were able to use that foreknowledge to question detainees, who thereafter freely admitted any role in the MM. Indeed...when discovered in their evasions, they most usually cheerfully confessed, often in great detail." Such "cheerful confession" was also very much Ken Lees' own experience. But the sheer volume of confessions made at Fort Hall gives greater weight to his estimates as to the proportion of murderers amongst those interrogated.

Elkins refers to the 1,819 enumerated in Appendix H as if it were the official total of all the Kikuyu killed by Mau Mau. Anderson, in "Histories of the Hanged", has a different formulation. "According to Corfield's Historical Survey of the rebellion, only 32 European civilians were killed in Kenya as a result of Mau Mau attacks, with another 26 being wounded. More European civilians would die in traffic accidents in Kenya between 1952 and 1960 than were killed by Mau Mau. These figures should be contrasted with the 1,819 African civilians assassinated by Mau Mau, and another 916 civilians wounded over the same period."

Anderson then directly cites the relevant page in the Corfield Report for these figures, and continues: "these figures do not include the many *hundreds* (my italics) of Africans who 'disappeared', and whose bodies were never found." Anderson offers no reason for substituting "hundreds" for Corfield's actual reference to "thousands", nor does he tell his readers he has made such a substitution; and he makes no mention of any "holocaust". It is unlikely that this was an unconscious piece of drafting. John Lonsdale tells me that Anderson is one of the few historians who actually went through all the annual reports from the DCs in Kikuyuland for the years before the Emergency, and could find evidence for hundreds, but not thousands, of Mau Mau murders of fellow Kikuyu.

Indeed, Lonsdale posed the direct question to me: why is there so little evidence in the colonial records for the scale of killing alleged by Ken Lees? It is entirely unsurprising to me that reports from District Commissioners and Provincial Commissioners should fail to mention hundreds or even thousands of murders: how were these men even to find out about the killings in the remotest parts of the large territory they were administering? At best, they were stretched to breaking point, with barely 200 officers, assistants and regular police, supported by tribal police, overseeing a population of 750,000. Even if there were survivors from Mau Mau attacks in the areas furthest from the reach of law and order, what incentive did they have to report the crimes? And even if they told the DOs and DCs, what could these officers do about them? They were dealing with a central administration that consistently believed agrarian reform would wean the Kikuyu from their nationalist aspirations.

There were plenty of reports of various kinds that flowed into Nairobi, as both Corfield and Lovatt Smith attest. But with Special Branch entirely absent from the Reserves, organising such reports into meaningful intelligence assessments rarely happened. A committee charged with oversight of intelligence gathering met just once, in November 1951. In the Commons debate on the Lari (Uplands) massacre, a Tory backbencher put on record that "we all know that at the beginning of the trouble in Kenya there was a breakdown in the intelligence services advising the government as to what was taking place inside the country". DC reports repeatedly alerted the Government to the spread of oathing and other subversive activities – and directly warned of "a rising against the Europeans" – but it was the prospect of rebellion rather than wholesale killing of Kikuyu by Mau Mau that registered as a strategic threat requiring action.

The earliest alarm call – unfortunately from a controversial and not always reliable source – came from the notorious Colonel Meinertzhagen, in April 1949, claiming that a Nyeri chief who knew him well "fears an outbreak of violence against Europeans involving murders on a large scale under the direction of a secret society now in existence called Maw Maw, whose influence in the tribe is rapidly growing and whose oaths, taken in utmost secrecy, are binding on all those compelled to take them". The chief had not told his local DO because he thought "he would not be believed". Although Corfield unearthed a copy of this letter, there was no trace of it in the Governor's files, and Governor Mitchell denied ever receiving it or reading it.

This was par for the course. Even when the Provincial Commissioner for Central Province, citing annual reports from his own District Commissioners in Fort Hall and Nyeri, flagged "the worsening tone of public meetings", the Chief Native Commissioner, E H Windley, deleted the more alarming passages before passing it on to the Governor, who then commented that "it is a very good report of an excellent and encouraging year's work". As it happens, Corfield complained to Windley privately that the Government House filing system was "chaotic"; and Windley complained to Corfield that Mitchell not once asked for a private meeting in 1951 or 1952 to discuss the crisis in the Reserve.

Not until April 1952 did a newly appointed Director of Intelligence and Security pull together a report that Corfield praised as "first class" in "marshalling concisely and accurately all facts then known about Mau Mau". It overturned complacent estimates that oathing had spread to barely

10% of Kikuyu, and warned that "the Mau Mau menace will continue to increase"; for the first time, Corfield noted, came the recognition that "the whole campaign of subversion, intimidation and oathing was centrally organised". Yet even this memorandum made no mention of widespread killings, which, if they had indeed already started, were beyond the reach and ken of the provincial administration. Moreover, the DIS report took three and half agonizing months to reach the Governor, and longer still to be distributed to key provincial officers: even then, it was not distributed to District Commissioners because their offices were thought to be insecure. They would have to visit their PC to read it.

The delay in distributing this document – which was only approved even for limited circulation on September 25th, less than a month before the declaration of the State of Emergency – was down to John Whyatt, the Member for Law and Order and Attorney-General. Corfield presumes the cause: the message that "the menace of Mau Mau 'would continue to increase until the organizers can be adequately dealt with' was not in accord with Government policy", even as reports to the contrary were flowing in to Nairobi from the provincial administration, the police and European residents. As the DC Nyeri, Tony Swann, reported in August, many chiefs had warned him that "their days were numbered", while the DC Rumuruti begged that "the emergency should be admitted or it will be too late".

But Whyatt felt Swann was "over-painting" the situation and was persuaded that a de-oathing campaign was making headway (what Corfield described in a letter to Windley as "clutching at any straw in the wind"). He wrote to the Colonial Office in September 1952: "I think we shall succeed in rolling back the Mau Mau movement before too long". Corfield's note on this claim – Chapter V, p 153, note 32 – reads: "This appreciation of the position in fact bore little relation to the current trend of events. In Fort Hall alone eight known murders were reported with no prospect of arrest" – and in the two following weeks, another 14 murders were reported, including two women and three children. The previous month, August, just in Fort Hall, Corfield says "there were nine reported murders (NB there were in fact many more) and the small force of police were out night after night, but not a single arrest was made...they became completely overwhelmed".

Whyatt was opposed to making any arrests without 100% certainty of convictions, was reluctant to legislate for more "fire brigade" powers, and "categorically denied that there is a state of emergency" as late as August 19th 1952. Yet his Commissioner of Police had just informed him that Mau Mau had at least a quarter of a million followers, that Kiambu was 60-70% oathed, that "a general revolt" was brewing, and that there was not enough prison space to accommodate the "tens of thousands" who would be convicted if even the present laws against Mau Mau and oathing were to be enforced.

As Corfield wrote to Richard Turnbull, "it is a little frightening to see the storm clouds gathering with so little realization by the 'high ups' of the impending typhoon". Even as Whyatt was reassuring the Colonial Office that "things have got very much quieter during the last few weeks, both in Nairobi and the Reserves", a Fort Hall DO was noting that "during the months of July and August hardly a day went by without the report of a corpse or a missing person, and always these were those who had informed or given evidence against the early Mau Mau oathings...an old man at Ruathia was chopped into two halves because he had given evidence against Mau Mau in the Court at Fort Hall...the whole family of a Chief's retainer had been murdered because the retainer had given evidence in the same Court, and down in the river below Gituge we found the corpse of an African Court Server who had likewise been strangled for informing against Mau Mau. That was the pattern and it has largely been forgotten."

In fact, the flood of incidents effectively swamped the paper-thin local officialdom: as Corfield puts it, "the all too few administrative officers and police, who were well aware of the seriousness of the situation in their own districts, were working at high pressure against almost impossible odds". Tony France puts it succinctly: "much of the ordinary police procedures in normal times were flooded by a string of almost continuous MM incidents – the system commonly fell apart at the seams". Frank Loyd told Corfield that "he, with his handful of police, were so desperately busy chasing here and chasing there, attempting to maintain the semblance of law and order, that he had no time, so to speak, to rise above himself and assess the overall position". Even reporting what was known seemed pointless: "a very general feeling of frustration had descended on the Provinces – what was the use of calling for more and more drastic action from Nairobi when previous reactions had all been so disappointing?" Tony Swann (who later became Minister of Defence) submitted "many excellent reports" as DC Nyeri, so Corfield told Windley, but "failed completely to make any impression on Mitchell".

It is easy to lose sight of a key issue in all this: that before Mau Mau could directly challenge the authority of the Chiefs, the provincial administration and the police, they first had to secure their base of support within the Kikuyu tribe. Mass oathing could only begin after a large part of the population of the Reserve had been induced or persuaded to swear loyalty, if necessary after a sustained campaign of intimidation and murder. Most of that preliminary process would have been conducted out of sight of the authorities. So, when Mau Mau was proscribed in August 1950, the oathing campaign must have already accomplished a large part of its initial objective.

Once the Mau Mau oaths became illegal, the next stage was to challenge enforcement of the law, thereby undermining Kikuyu confidence in colonial authority, and demonstrating that those collaborating with it would be ruthlessly dealt with, in ways designed to generate fear and silence. What overwhelmed the DOs, DCs, Chiefs, Tribal Police and Kenya Police in 1952 was the brazen display of defiance, in which, as Corfield was told, "gangs would arrive from Nairobi by night and, with the precision of a military movement, would surround small groups of huts, and a forcible oathing of occupants would take place. There was no chance of escape." The known unknown here is simply the scale of threats and murder used during the early phase of oathing to bolster the voluntary recruitment process: that such killings would total no more than some hundreds seems highly unlikely, however little documentation might be found in annual reports by District and Provincial Commissioners.

Sir Evelyn Baring finally arrived in Kenya on September 29th 1952, and was sworn in as Governor the next day. A week later, Mau Mau carried out what Corfield calls a Chicago-style assassination of Chief Waruhiu, in broad daylight, on the open road just outside Nairobi. Baring – who had been conducting a lightning tour of the colony – immediately asked the Secretary of State for permission to declare a State of Emergency, which was granted a week after the shooting. A week later, the State of Emergency was proclaimed, the new powers it provided were used to start detaining Mau Mau suspects, and military forces were flown in to support the civil power.

Modern historians have concentrated on the alleged abuses of those new powers, with the recent lawsuits reflecting that focus. Perhaps as a result, the shameful abandonment of over a million people to whatever fate Mau Mau inflicted on them has attracted much less attention: ironically, the very people who have spent years in the High Court pursuing compensation claims against the UK represent a movement that apparently slaughtered fellow Kikuyu by the thousands, even tens of thousands. Families of those victims will never see a penny of compensation: to add insult to injury, the very fact of their deaths is routinely denied.

Remarkably, Anderson's book ends with an eloquent coda on the subject of recovered skeletons from the conflict period. All the remains of the hanged were interred in unmarked graves at Kamiti prison. But Nairobi's chief pathologist, Dr Morris Rogoff (who played such an important role in the Hola inquest) also retained the unclaimed remains of 475 disinterred victims of violence. They include, says Anderson, "the victims of Mau Mau courts in Nairobi, dug up during Operation Anvil, and the many loyalists who were murdered in Mau Mau assaults. They come from all over Kikuyuland". That skeletons were actually discovered was unusual. That families of victims failed to collect them for burial, even after the peak of the Emergency was over, was also unusual. These 475 must have been only a fraction of the actual number of victims. Yet Anderson does not, at this point, revise his earlier reference to "hundreds" rather than Corfield's "thousands" of Mau Mau victims.

A similar discrepancy can be found in the writings of Sidney Fazan (entitled "Colonial Kenya Observed", published in 2015 and edited by John Lonsdale). Fazan was a key colonial official in pre-war Kenya, who emerged from retirement to serve on the Advisory Committee on Appeals, with Sir Owen Corrie (that nearly half the 2,319 appellants succeeded in having their detention orders cancelled suggests that there were at least some meaningful checks and balances within the detention regime – and there were many examples of people being compensated for wrongful detention). Fazan notes the severity with which secret Mau Mau courts dealt with offenders, and that "when the sites of these courts were discovered and the neighbourhood searched, large numbers of corpses were found with ropes around their necks. The Mau Mau method of keeping order...was by reign of terror".

Yet even though such formal executions played only a minor part in Mau Mau enforcement, the "large numbers" of such corpses did not prevent Fazan from concluding that probably only 2,000 – and at most 3,000 – civilians were killed by Mau Mau. Lonsdale notes that this figure is "calmer than lurid estimates of up to 30,000 at the time – a figure quoted in military circles". As a serving officer in the King's Africa Regiment during the Emergency, Lonsdale no doubt heard the "lurid" figure from his own colleagues. But he may not be aware that Corfield's private papers reveal that the senior colonial ministers whom he criticised so strongly for ignoring the weight of reports from their own officials and law enforcement agencies concerning Mau Mau atrocities before October 1952 used that very word, "lurid", to dismiss such reports (Corfield letter to Richard Turnbull, 1958). Fazan, compiling his account at the same time as Corfield wrote his report, lacked access to the papers, witnesses and confessions that persuaded Corfield to use the word "holocaust".

What is simply impossible is for the figure of 1,800 used by Elkins, Hague and others to be correct. In October, 1956, it was noted that there were 1,364 self-confessed murderers known to the authorities, of whom only 50 were in custody. According to National Archive file CO 6308, Attorney-General Eric Griffith-Jones recognised that, although it was desirable to try to prosecute in cases of "important" murders (where the victim or the murderer were so deemed), or where there was sufficient evidence to mount a case, "absence of a corpus delicti greatly complicates an investigation". Moreover, it was not possible to follow up every case, "by reason of the number of alleged Mau Mau murders".

Through 1957, the issue was debated between the Attorney-General, the Minister for African Affairs, the Minister for Community Development, the Special Commissioner (who also took on the African Affairs and Community Development roles during this period), the Minister of Defence and the Commissioner of Police, sometimes meeting in Griffith-Jones' office to thrash out the difficulties. Griffith-Jones, as much a bureaucrat as a lawyer, tried to separate these men into different categories. 156 of the self-confessed murderers were classified as "unacceptables *[that is, not acceptable as returnees to their home districts]* not in custody": but as the Permanent Secretary at the Ministry of Defence, A C Small, said in July 1957, "some of these men have been living in their home districts for up to two years, so it is difficult to argue that they are unacceptable". They appeared to be no threat to public order, but nonetheless should they be "left at large"? Nor was the figure of 1,364 even close to the full total: in the Hanslope Park documents, we also find examples such as a Police Superintendent writing to Terence Gavaghan, the District Officer in Charge of Rehabilitation at the Mwea detention camps in March 1958, asking what he should do with 11 self-confessed murderers he was holding, awaiting release. In April, another

27 were identified at Gathigiriri camp. 123 were being held at Hola, with many more confessions emerging.

These self-confessed murderers, very few of whom had been tried, let alone convicted for that crime, and mostly not even detained, were more than enough to have been responsible for just 1,819 (or 1,832) victims. As the process of confession and rehabilitation finally built momentum in 1957 and 1958, Ken Lees discovered during detailed interrogation that, in the Fort Hall district works camps alone, thousands of Mau Mau detainees admitted having murdered fellow Kikuyu.

Long before then, 346 Mau Mau had already been hanged, after being tried for, and convicted of, murder (this was less than a third of the total hanged for committing offences under the Emergency laws, such as unauthorised possession of firearms). Anderson's exhaustive study of the trials of the 1,090 hanged concluded that some of those executed were probably innocent (the legal structures, especially for mass trials such as for the alleged perpetrators of the Lari massacre, were demonstrably deficient); but that does not significantly diminish the number of known murderers. So we already have over 1,700 self-confessed or convicted murderers, without including a single guerrilla fighter, and only a handful from the mass of detainees.

By definition, none of those executed was amongst the fighters who were killed by British troops and auxiliaries in combat (whether we use the figure of 11,503 or 10,540), within the larger total of over 20,000 armed Mau Mau who managed to retreat to the mountains and forests after the Emergency was declared and the tide of battle turned against them. The likelihood that not a single one of these had committed even one murder is minimal. Equally unlikely, even if Ken Lees were not alive to tell us otherwise, is that almost none of the scores of thousands of Mau Mau and suspected Mau Mau who had been detained for short or long periods – anything from a month to eight years – was a murderer (see below for analysis of the detainees numbers).

As the man responsible for authorising the release, by his estimate, of 69,000 detainees through the works and detention camps at Fort Hall (known these days as Murang'a) between 1956 and 1959, Lees reckoned that 20% of those interrogated by him and his team as a preliminary to their release had confessed to murder; often, to multiple murders. The great majority of Mariira detainees were involved in multiple murders.

One Mau Mau killer held at Hola is reported to have boasted of murdering 35 victims. Yet caution needs to be exercised in assessing these estimates. It was standard Mau Mau practice to force several individuals to participate in killings, with many hands on the machete, or gun or rope. Ken Lees regarded 10,000 of the roughly 14,000 "killers" held at Fort Hall as minor players, concentrating on the 4,000 with "fat files", which constituted the leadership of Mau Mau as he encountered them. Would there be more murderers than victims? Or the other way round? We simply have no mechanism for making that calculation, so need to count murderers and murdered separately.

Overwhelmingly, Mau Mau targeted fellow Kikuyu: few Europeans, Asians or members of other tribes were killed. There were many contemporary accounts claiming that 20,000 to 30,000 Kikuyu were killed by Mau Mau. Sir Philip Mitchell, Governor of Kenya until May 1952, was bitterly criticised in private letters written by Corfield during his research: he was "self-satisfied", had "lost touch", "refused to listen to any advice on the necessity to take stronger action against Mau Mau"", allowed "the ship of state" to be "wrecked", "failed to see that the balloon was about to go up", and represented "the ultimate failure in judgment" that allowed the slaughter in Kikuyuland (his "wilful blindness" was compounded by having a second in command, law officer John Whyatt, who was the "ultimate clutcher at straws", who lived in a "cocoon of complacency", displaying "blinding self-conceit" and "complacent self-deception"; supported – if that is the right word – by "a particularly weak Chief Native Commissioner"). None of this did Corfield feel he could publish in his report, but Mitchell was, to his credit, quick to recognize his own failings.

In his memoirs (published in 1954, long before Corfield reported a "holocaust"), he acknowledged that Mau Mau "murders of Kikuyu, Embu and Meru tribes people with unspeakable cruelty and depravity, now run into thousands". He had also written to the Manchester Guardian on May 18th 1954, saying that Mau Mau, according to the official running total up to that point, had murdered "close on a thousand Africans, almost entirely Kikuyu, according to official figures. The number of Africans must, in fact, run into thousands by this time, if account is taken of secret, unreported killings in the forests and bamboo thickets, and the little hamlets in the depths of the country."

Writing much later, in an unpublished memoir, a Police Inspector working in the South Nyeri Kikuyu Reserve in 1953 described "the terrible slaughter and mutilation of men, women and children including babies", with "thousands of victims". "Each morning for months on end I set out to deal with these murders. I lost count of how many, but if I said 100 I would not be exaggerating. This was repeated in many other police areas. The number of murders dropped dramatically when people moved into fortified villages." Terence Gavaghan, the man who became so controversial for his period in charge of rehabilitation at the Mwea group of detention camps (see below), estimated that the villagisation policy, which was adopted in 1954, saved 20,000 Kikuyu lives (implying that this was the number of lives lost before the policy was introduced).

Why, then, should the British government endorse the Elkins formulation, when it is so self-evidently and self-servingly false? The Corfield Report itself is the best evidence we have on that question. Corfield felt that he had to tread with great care in presenting his findings so as to avoid an obvious conclusion, which is that the outgoing Governor of Kenya in 1952, Sir Philip Mitchell, had blatantly and negligently ignored or played down the mounting cries of anguish from Kikuyuland.

The Mau Mau leadership had adapted the Kikuyu practice of using oaths, such as those used to seal contracts, to compel the overwhelming majority of adults to swear bloodthirsty pledges of loyalty – a process enforced where deemed necessary by slaughtering those who refused to comply, along with their families. As many participants as possible were dragged into the killings, so as to reduce the likelihood of anyone being reported to the authorities. In one ghastly case, the dismembered body of a resister was dug up nearly two weeks after his execution, for the purpose of terrorising his family and neighbours into hacking further at the corpse and pressing decomposing flesh against their lips. Anderson, telling this disturbing story, claims it was "utterly exceptional": but, then, he did not interrogate thousands of murderers, or listen to their harrowing confessions, as Ken Lees did.

The prevailing myth of colonial benevolence – European supervision of subject races for their own benefit, embodied in the Devonshire Declaration of 1923 – would scarcely have survived full publication of the evidence of pre-Emergency negligence, and the drawing of the necessary lessons. Corfield soft-pedalled his report, and spared Mitchell the criticism he deserved. If the Colonial Secretary at the time of publication in 1960, Iain Macleod, had had his way, the whole of the report would have been buried.

Corfield came under strong pressure to modify his language and conclusions. He was forced to delete virtually every reference to sitting Members of Parliament, especially those who gave moral support to Mau Mau: ostensibly on the egregious grounds that his report was not "privileged" in the UK, even though it was in Kenya. Most references to Peter Mbui (or Mbuyi) Koinange, a key figure, whose family was heavily involved in Mau Mau, and who was by then engaged in talks about future independence, were also expunged. A list of over 100 deletions has been preserved in Corfield's private papers. Corfield also blamed Macleod for blocking wide distribution of the report in the United States, where an enthusiastic publisher had noted the blockbuster sales (20,000 copies) in the UK and Kenya, only to be subjected to lengthy delaying tactics, eventually losing interest.

Later, Corfield privately complained that his many months of work on the report had not earned him a mention in the Honours List. To add injury to insult, Macleod implied to the House of Commons that Corfield had laboured over the text for five years, whereas he had actually taken just 16 months – Macleod apologised to him in writing, but only for this slight, not for his generally obstructive behaviour, or failure to offer formal thanks.

This absence of commendation Corfield attributed to his findings being so unwelcome in Whitehall: "not so much as even a letter from Macleod: understandable, perhaps, as he did his best to squash it...it exposed the shaky foundations on which he thought he could build a multi-racial government in Kenya." (Letter to Richard Turnbull, 4/2/64, Corfield archive, Bodleian Library). It was not just the scandalous negligence of the pre-Emergency period that was sensitive. Corfield's direct criticism of Jomo Kenyatta for repeatedly failing to denounce Mau Mau in 1952 – before he was arrested as soon as the Emergency was promulgated, put on trial, convicted, and sent to a remote prison in northern Kenya for eight years – was a further embarrassment for a government which had decided to release Kenyatta and back him as a possible future leader of an independent Kenya.

Kenyatta, who had been educated in London and Moscow in the 1930s and 1940s, was the most charismatic of Kikuyu public figures in the pre-Emergency period, and maintained a careful, almost mocking, ambiguity when asked about Mau Mau. He certainly knew the Mau Mau organisers, and clearly influenced their political demands for "land and freedom". Whether his ambiguity was a ploy to avoid arrest by the British, or assassination by Mau Mau, is unclear (Elkins dismisses him as an Uncle Tom who betrayed Mau Mau; Lonsdale labels him "the man in the middle"): but Corfield in his report unhesitatingly concluded that Kenyatta was actually the "founder" of the "society of assassins", was responsible for "conjuring up demons", and had created a "Frankenstein monster".

So publication of the report was very inconveniently timed with regard to the new Conservative policy of granting Kenya independence under majority African rule. Giving too much "air" to the scale of Mau Mau killings would have seriously embarrassed the British government in the midst of a delicate manoeuvre, and have undermined a key figure – Kenyatta – in Britain's plans for Kenya's future. Even though at that stage Kenyatta had not even been released from his imprisonment (after conviction in a trial of dubious legality), the expectation that he would play a leading role in an independent Kenya was high, not least because Tom Mboya (a negotiator who much impressed the British) deferred to him.

Macleod's own brother was a farmer in Kenya, who took a dim view of the hard-line white settlers demanding that any independence constitution entrenched their privileged position. When Kenyatta demonstrated a change of heart – or of plan – on his release, many settlers chose to put the past behind them, at his urging: after becoming President of Kenya in 1963, he did indeed denounce and proscribe Mau Mau. Within two years, Corfield was also persuaded, and wrote to one of Kenyatta's ministers, praising Kenyatta's meeting with a group of European farmers at Nakuru, where he said there had been mistakes on both sides, as a "turning point". He even claimed to "have always been sympathetic to the aims and aspirations of African Nationalism" (letter, 4/10/65).

But in 1960 Corfield had felt that the speedy granting of independence and of black majority rule was not just a gamble, but unfair to the white settlers. He accepted an invitation to join the Monday Club, which had emerged as a pressure group within the Conservative Party, lobbying against Prime Minister Macmillan's perceived tilt to the left, and the decolonisation policy foreshadowed by his famous "Winds of Change" speech, given in Cape Town in February 1960.

He later deplored the Monday Club's extremism, and said he "detested" another right-wing pressure group, the League of Empire Loyalists; but in showing his hand in this way – and failing to understand the way the "winds" were blowing – he exposed his report to criticism as the product of a backward-looking mindset. On balance, it would seem that his trenchant critique of Mau Mau was as much coloured by his disgust and dismay at what he was told about the Mau Mau oaths, and the carnage inflicted by those who swore them – and by one meeting with hostile detainees – as by any element of racism in his personality.

Anderson dismisses Corfield's report as "second-rate", without explanation. Certainly, it is – as Corfield admits himself – at times tedious to read, as he laboriously works his way through the available material; and shorn of its more damning elements, as "not in the public interest" to reveal, it lacks punch. But his confidential summary, to be found in his private papers, was not just scathing, but precise in its apportionment of blame: Governor Mitchell was so wrapped up in his schemes for land and political reform that he hoped progress on that front would outpace the rise of subversion as a pathway to change. This was the "supreme" lesson of Corfield's deliberations: but that a British colonial administration should allow thousands of its subjects to fall victim to a failure of law and order, through a mixture of negligence and wishful thinking, was a conclusion neither he nor his masters wished to proclaim out loud. Even today, it would seem, the scale of the failure is obscured by an opportunistic alliance between the British government and revisionist historians.

4. The second legal case

In the second group legal case against the British government, torture was not admitted by the defendants, and the only allegations that were allowed to go forward were for "batteries": assaults of one kind or another. This had an important impact on the conduct of the case, with Mr Justice Stewart having to decide whether uncorroborated claims, presented for the first time fifty years or more after the alleged offences, should benefit from the court's discretion under section 33 of the Limitation Act of 1980. He had already rejected use of section 32, where fraud or concealment on the part of the defendant is alleged: that had been a live issue in 2013 with the "Mutua" litigation, in the light of the Hanslope Park revelation, but was much less clearly arguable in a mass of claims for assault. The judge also rejected an attempt to classify "fear" as a basis for compensation.

Section 33 discretion can be exercised where there is good reason for delay. However, in the first Test Case to reach the stage of final submissions,

TC34, the judge could find no good reason why the complaint had not been raised a decade, two decades or even more decades earlier. The State of Emergency had ended in 1960, Kenya had become independent at the end of 1963, and although Mau Mau as an organisation had been proscribed by successive Kenyan governments till 2003, even a claim lodged then might have given the defendants more opportunity to find witnesses or documents to refute the allegations made. The prejudice to the defence was simply too great to allow the court to exercise section 33 discretion. This judgment was handed down in August 2018.

Tandem Law immediately sought leave to appeal: this was rejected by two Appeal Court judges, who saw no prospect of Mr Justice Stewart's approach to the issues, or principles applied, being overturned. They went further: "his judgment is a masterly synthesis of the complex web of facts, and absence of facts" (in fact, he made a few errors, such as mis-dating the resignation of Sir Arthur Young as Police Commissioner, and the Glenday report on screening camps).

The final blow to the litigants came in late November 2018, when Mr Justice Stewart refused to exercise his section 33 discretion in the case of TC20, 90-year-old Mrs Waithaka. She, her husband and all her family had been Mau Mau supporters (and still were), and she claimed that she had been forced to move to a protected village, where she was often beaten, and had also been beaten in a Kikuyu Guard police station when being questioned about her Mau Mau oath. But the only assailants she was able to name were long since dead, or untraceable; there were no surviving witnesses or documents; and even the village she claimed to have been removed from, Githanga, had itself disappeared without trace.

The judge was even more dismissive of this claim than that of TC34. The defendants had spent "an enormous amount of time and money trying to trace any witness", and had effectively "drawn a blank" – "there cannot now be a fair trial". Of 57 colonial officials listed as serving in 1956, just one was still alive, but was unable to throw any light on Mrs Waithaka's allegations. Borrowing some nautical comparisons, he described this attempt to float a claim for damages after 65 years as like "putting to sea in a sieve" that was "doomed to sink immediately".

With those words, he torpedoed all 40,000 claims, and Tandem Law was instructed by the Court to abandon the litigation, with the likely loss of millions of pounds in contingency fee expenditure. In defiant mode, Tandem Law issued a public statement containing no less than four questionable claims. It said that "it was accepted" that the two test claimants were "telling the truth": in fact, all that had been accepted was that, even if they were telling the truth, there was no way of proving or disproving it, which is why the claims failed. The statement said that none of the claimants was accused of exaggeration, but it is not possible to reconcile that statement with the judge's reaction to Test Claimant 34's evidence that he had been shown a collection of severed heads, stored in desk drawers, in the offices of Nairobi CID. Perhaps fortunately for the claimant, his statement that he was still a detainee in 1963 went unremarked: by early 1961, there were only 25 people still detained – by 1963, he must have been unique.

The Tandem Law statement also said that the judge "came to his decision despite evidence that there was a deliberate strategy to avoid investigation of abuses at the time"; and "despite decisions not to prosecute abuses at the time". Yet scores of policemen, soldiers, chiefs, headmen, Home Guards, prison warders and other officials were prosecuted for a wide variety of offences, ranging from assault to murder; and there were lengthy investigations into alleged abuses, such as the inquiry by Sir Vincent Glenday in 1955 (visiting 68 locations where those arrested were held or screened), the Heaton Report on prisons and detention camps in 1956, the Fairn Inquiry into Hola and subsequently into the whole detention system, and (in the same year, 1959) the months-long investigation by the Director of Public Prosecutions, A P Jack, into the complaints made by Victor Shuter (see below: all Shuter's allegations were eventually rejected as uncorroborated).

One of the issues left unresolved by the failed claim was the status of protected villages. A key element of the anti-Mau Mau strategy was to cut the guerrilla fighters off from their supporters and food suppliers. This was done by requiring nearly all Kikuyu to move to villages with protective moats or fences, patrolled by guards, sometimes armed. As it happened, such a tactic was a standard Kikuyu response to Masai attacks in the pre-British days; and had also been very important in helping quell the Communist uprising in Malaya.

A seasoned Kenyan civil servant, Thomas Askwith, who had been despatched to Malaya in 1953 to see what could be learned from that campaign, became the architect of two crucial policies: rehabilitation of

Mau Mau detainees, and villagisation, both as a means of protection and of re-vitalising communal life (he talked of"model villages"); a connection that goes unremarked by Elkins, who much admired Askwith, but fiercely criticised villagisation (she does manage to praise his attempts to mitigate hardship in the villages). Dr J C Carothers, whose analysis of the so-called pathology of Mau Mau was a highly influential document in the early 1950s, was a strong supporter of Askwith's villagisation strategy.

Many commentators – including visiting British MPs – warmly approved of villagisation; not least because it was deemed to encourage much more productive use of available land than traditional Kikuyu methods (Kenyatta was one of many Kikuyu leaders who appeared to support land reform and consolidation of small plots of land, but – according to DCs like Wally Coutts – in practice frustrated such initiatives). Terence Gavaghan, as we have already noted, reckoned that villagisation saved 20,000 Kikuyu lives, by making much rarer the murderous attacks by Mau Mau gangs on unprotected villages that had characterised the pre-Emergency period – the massacre at Lari (a collection of homesteads rather than an actual village) was a notable post-Emergency exception.

Against that, Mau Mau supporters and sympathisers, notably Professor Elkins, have described the protected villages as a form of concentration camp, where beatings for disobedience were frequent and forced labour prevalent; even that starvation was a deliberate policy. One of the Tandem Law clients claimed £5,000 for each of the five years he was compelled to stay in a protected village (by the standards of the 1950s, a very large sum of money). Yet there is no doubt that the policy was lawful at the time, was highly effective in helping suppress the rebellion, and inevitably became a target of Mau Mau protest because of that success. The only witnesses found by the Crown in the second legal case who had any knowledge of villagisation denied seeing any abuse, or hearing of any. And Mr Justice Stewart declined to accept as "corroboration" of claims of abuse that there were thousands of Tandem Law clients making such claims: in his view, plaintiffs bringing similar complaints could scarcely constitute mutual corroboration.

That 40,000 Mau Mau veterans had survived until now, and had been located by the Tandem Law solicitors, was itself remarkable. At the end of the Emergency, according to the 1962 census, there were about 400,000 adult Kikuyu, male and female between the ages of 20 and 35 (anyone older would not have survived till now, and anyone younger would not have been an adult at the time). At least 30%, and maybe more than 40%, would not have been Mau Mau, so when the litigation commenced, only about 160,000 of the age category would be possible litigants. Blacker's estimation of life expectancy in 1962 suggests that at least a quarter of these would not have survived to the age of 60. As none of the claimants could be younger than 75, a conservative estimate is that another quarter would not have survived to even that age. It would be surprising if even 80,000 former Mau Mau were still alive.

Given that maximum potential number of claimants, finding and deposing 40,000 of them was an impressive feat, especially considering that a large proportion were illiterate and therefore harder to reach. It was the strategy of using Mau Mau veteran associations to find claimants that helped build a formidable looking lawsuit: but that many of the claimants, especially female, had to rely on the uncorroborated allegations of abuse in the protected villages, in the end served to undermine the litigation. Only abuse in detention camps and screening locations was likely to survive the court's requirement for a fair trial, and with the claimants alleging torture in those locations already compensated, the narrower claims of battery failed to reach the level of seriousness that could trigger waiving the statute of limitations. Of course, that does not mean the assaults never happened.

5. The start of abuse of detainees

Abuse of those arrested as Mau Mau suspects started early on in the Emergency. Unsurprisingly, the core of the problem was in the Home Guard posts that sprang up as the first line of defence for Kikuyu loyalists, and the screening process for interrogating those arrested. Personal knowledge of who had sided with Mau Mau, let alone been active in Mau Mau attacks on loyalists, was the immediate impetus for seizing people, not least for the purposes of revenge. Torture – whether as a means of retaliation for Mau Mau atrocities, or to extract information about other Mau Mau supporters – became commonplace, and extra-judicial killings were sometimes inflicted to cover up these illegal processes. There were also many examples of local chiefs and headmen exploiting the conflict to extract money from those arrested. Record-keeping of who was in custody, or for how long, was patchy, though there was a legal limit of 17 days to the period that anyone seized could be held before being formally detained, charged with an offence, or released.

For the local colonial officials – District Officers, District Commissioners and Provincial Commissioners – these abuses and crimes presented a difficult choice. There was no question but that Kikuyuland in 1952, 1953 and 1954 was riven by a brutal war, in which British forces, civil and military, were fully engaged. Retaining the support of loyal Kikuyu was seen as essential. As a consequence, at the local level, district officials not only turned a blind eye to abuses, but even became complicit in them. Routinely, the local police station (part of a parallel but different line of authority) was often the last to hear about an arrest, even where the Home Guard post was close by (in some instances, the police station telephone was used to inform district officials of something that had happened, whilst the police themselves were left in the dark). European settlers, whether in the uniform of the Kenya Regiment or the Kenya Police Reserve, were also responsible for many grisly episodes of torture and murder.

These abuses could not survive the scrutiny of what was a largely independent judiciary, nor the advent of senior British police officers, recruited to bolster the colony's over-stretched force. Just as General Erskine, the army commander who led the military campaign against Mau Mau, was repelled by the settlers, their ruthless behaviour and their racist attitudes, telling his wife that he could not stand their guts, so the Metropolitan Police Commissioner, Sir Arthur Young, switching from London to Nairobi, was equally dismayed by the lawlessness he encountered. He served less than a year before resigning in protest at the end of 1954, frustrated by the administration's toleration of the way local officials colluded in allowing loyalists and settlers to evade justice, and by Governor Baring's failure to respond to three letters of complaint Young sent to him.

Perhaps surprisingly – for those commentators and historians who imagined the Hanslope Park documents would prove to be incriminating, or be some form of subtle management of documents by junior officials to discredit those more senior – the newly released archive shone a bright light on the whole Arthur Young episode. The information about misdeeds in the Home Guard and screening process primarily came from one of Young's most senior officers, another UK policeman, Assistant Commissioner (CID) Duncan MacPherson. Young had instructed MacPherson to compile reports documenting the improper procedures (no doubt to justify his planned resignation letter to Baring).

Until the Hanslope Park disclosure, the most important fact we knew about this officer was a long letter he had sent to the firebrand Labour MP, Barbara Castle, parts of which she read out to the House of Commons in the heated debate of June 16th 1959 over the Hola massacre, saying that he had been "got rid of" after being told to stop investigating murders in detention camps, where he had seen "horrifying" conditions and had investigated an "appalling number of deaths". He told her he had departed from Kenya "a disgusted man". It was an explosive letter, designed to maximize the embarrassment the government was enduring as the Hola inquest findings were being debated. Why did he write to her in particular? Elkins describes a secret meeting between MacPherson and Mrs Castle in Kenya nearly four years earlier, on November 1st 1955, during which he reportedly told her of the abuses he had found.

If that meeting indeed happened, it was immediately followed by Macpherson's departure from Kenya that month, on vacation leave, to New Zealand (with no mention of "disgust"). Anderson claims he was driven out by his colleagues, after having been ostracized and hounded; but there is no evidence for this in the archive; rather, the contrary. Puzzlingly, neither Elkins nor Anderson seems to have been aware of the 1959 letter to Barbara Castle and the major row it caused. But in the archive we find, not only the original reports MacPherson sent Young at the end of 1954, but the detailed rebuttal of many of MacPherson's 1959 claims by Young's successor, Commissioner Robert Catling.

MacPherson had indeed investigated a score of incidents in which chiefs and headmen had extorted, tortured or killed Mau Mau suspects, and then been partly shielded by local colonial officials: but these were all in Home Guard posts and screening camps, not detention camps. However, although he somewhat self-righteously listed all the obstruction and obfuscation he had encountered, MacPherson's reports also made clear that in nearly all the cases he cited, the culprits were arrested: 36 in all, for 23 crimes. In one case, as he himself conceded, the perpetrator had evaded justice as a result of a temporary amnesty that had been granted to Mau Mau and loyalists alike.

That did not stop him taking umbrage when a District Commissioner called Pedraza invited one of his officers to spend more time catching Mau Mau terrorists ("an unnecessary and uncalled for remark"). He was also irritated when Provincial Commissioner Carruthers "Monkey" Johnston told Governor Baring that a Senior Superintendent of Police was too junior an officer to take a statement from him regarding the prospective arrest of a chief (which only a PC could authorize, according to government policy).

Catling could find no evidence that MacPherson had ever set foot inside a detention camp (there was no reason why the head of CID should do so – nearly all his reports relate to Home Guard posts, with "one or two" relating to screening camps, according to Catling), let alone seen an "appalling number of deaths". He referred in his letter to Mrs Castle to another officer's visit to a detention camp, after an "affair" where, he claimed "two men died and several suffered severe injuries". It transpired that one man had died at Theta Road camp from violence, but the other fatality was from natural causes; as for the "severe injuries", all that Catling found on the record was that 15 men had been briefly hospitalized for fatigue (hard labour and heavy "exercise" were unquestionably a feature of camp discipline – see below).

More disturbingly, it emerged that MacPherson had not resigned "in disgust". Having taken vacation leave, nearly a year after Young's departure, and soon after receiving a promotion, he moved over to sick leave in March 1956, reporting high blood pressure and headaches. Then – ignoring the strong advice from Catling and other colleagues that he should continue to extend his sick leave – he resigned on grounds of ill-health at the end of October 1956, nearly two years after Young's departure and nearly a year after the reported meeting with Mrs Castle: yet still no mention was made of "disgust".

Indeed, he subsequently tried repeatedly to return to Kenya, but his old position had been filled (just as he had been warned), and no suitable other vacancy presented itself. Instead, he went on to serve in other British colonies. What Catling added in his report was that for years afterwards MacPherson had written repeatedly to him, to Attorney-General Eric Griffith-Jones and to the Colonial Office, asking to be allowed to return: scarcely the behaviour of someone who had left in disgust.

By then, Catling says, he "had lost confidence in MacPherson". "Certainly, during the whole of my time with him not once did he say, or even intimate, that he felt that he could not do what he considered to be his duty because of interference or because of lack of support of police or legal officers. My own view of him is that although he had undoubted ability and energy as a police officer he was obsessed (at any rate throughout his time in Kenya) with the idea that almost the entire Government service was corrupt and that only he could expose the evil".

Eventually, Catling wrote to MacPherson: "there is nothing for you here", forbearing to tell him that, if he had indeed returned, he would most likely have had to face a charge of gross dereliction of duty with regard to a former Superintendent of Police, Milner, whom he had inexplicably sidelined for many weeks. The investigating officer dealing with a complaint from Milner (who had indeed resigned in disgust) concluded that "this is a most unfortunate case of serious mismanagement, mishandled from the start by Mr MacPherson, which has resulted in the loss of a sound police officer to the Colony".

It is possible, of course, that MacPherson had realised that a meeting with Mrs Castle might lead to disciplinary or even criminal proceedings, and that the sick leave, resignation and attempts to return were designed to flush out any risk of exposure and proceedings. The file makes clear that Catling knew nothing of the meeting (assuming it happened) and was genuinely puzzled that MacPherson had behaved so oddly. What is beyond dispute is that Young quickly realised he had made a mistake in taking the Kenya post, just as quickly decided to resign (on the perfectly genuine grounds that politics was over-riding policing) and used MacPherson to assemble a basis for his resignation letters. Equally beyond dispute is that, three years later, MacPherson grossly misrepresented his reasons for leaving Kenya.

Although Baring had tried to shrug off Young's resignation, it was impossible to ignore the scale of the misdeeds that MacPherson had reported: whatever his "obsessions", no one disputed the facts that he unearthed, nor the core issue of the tension between the police and the civil administration. In 1955, Baring's deputy, Crawford, oversaw an investigation by a veteran of colonial Africa, Sir Vincent Glenday, who visited most of the screening camps, detention camps and guard posts before compiling a brief report. Crawford opposed its publication, on the grounds that it was (in his view) ill-written, but was persuaded to release a copy to the House of Commons, at Barbara Castle's request, in July 1955. Neither Elkins nor Anderson refers to it: perhaps they have not read it – at nine pages, scarcely an arduous task.

Glenday found poor record-keeping with regard to custody details, recommended lengthening the period during which a suspect could be held for questioning, asked for regular medical inspections of Guard posts and screening camps, and urged that Home Guard posts should no longer be allowed to hold prisoners: a key point. He recommended that uncorroborated confessions obtained during screening not be used for prosecutions (something the Attorney General claimed had already been implemented). He commended the Fort Hall system of maintaining an index card for every detainee, to accompany the individual from camp to camp. Special Branch put forward a bid for 32 staff and 60,000 index cards for individual detainees: a forerunner to Ken Lees' more elaborate cross-indexing of individual records to create incident files.

In an interesting pre-echo of Lees' experience, Glenday noted that the card-index systems at Meru, Subukia and Nanyuki provided a "web of information" which "enmeshes a person", so that "there is today no longer any need for pressure or threats...all that is required is infinite patience". This somewhat Panglossian conclusion was surely premature; but Glenday's recommendations encountered no resistance, and the screening abuses were largely eliminated. Thereafter, new and different points of tension within the administration were to arise as the pivot of policy moved from the screening process to detention and rehabilitation.

6. How many detainees were there?

The scale of the detention programme is a source of much debate amongst historians, mostly because of confusion over the way in which detainee numbers were documented. Elkins asserts that the most frequently used "official" figure of about 80,000 detainees is far too low, offering her own estimate that at least double, if not quadruple, or 320,000, was closer to the truth (this out of an adult population of little more than 1 million Kikuyu). In his book "Histories of the Hanged", David Anderson offers a figure of 150,000, without explanation, other than that the "snapshot" official monthly totals included in his text (themselves suggesting a total well below 100,000) misleadingly elide the flow of detainees in and out of camps. Subsequently, after studying the Hanslope Park papers, Anderson wrote to me to say he had revised that figure down to 125,000.

Some of the confusion arises out of the range of categories used. Detainees were initially arrested under GDOs (Governor's Detention Orders), but as the scale of detention increased, DDOs (Delegated Detention Orders) were used more frequently. Moreover, convicted prisoners, including those convicted under Emergency regulations, were often held alongside detainees; and to avoid detention orders, some Mau Mau cadres chose to plead guilty to minor offences, so as to serve short prison sentences before returning to their previous activities – which in turn persuaded the authorities to impose DDOs on many prisoners as they completed sentences (a process called "form C-ed" as Elkins terms it). Thus in late 1958, nearly all remaining Mau Mau convicts – 3,400 – were transferred to GDOs, as part of the "pipeline" process. At Hola, there was yet another category: the 189 farmers at the open camp, some with their families, who were under "restricted orders". Anderson tells me he was just estimating the total of those actually subjected to detention orders, be they DDOs or GDOs, whereas Elkins must have been counting anyone ever arrested.

One document in the files (CO 141/6300), dating from early 1955, refers to 278,560 arrests up to that point, of which 167,027 were released immediately after questioning or soon afterwards. It also says that 111,032 were tried, 18,461 acquitted and 18,210 convicted of Mau Mau-related charges. By implication, 74,361 were convicted of some other unspecified charge, which seems a remarkably large number, especially in the context of Mau Mau sweeps; nor is it fully reflected in a similar number of convicted prisoners, implying non-custodial sentences.

As for Operation Anvil – the mass round-up in Nairobi in April 1954 to break Mau Mau's stranglehold on the capital – this document offers a figure of 33,500 arrests, with 10,500 being quickly released and a further 5,348 let go after screening, implicitly leaving 17,652 being either detained or tried. This is the fourth different "official" figure for Anvil, if we include the estimate of 30,000 in the 1959 Fairn Report on the Hola deaths, and two other official estimates of 25,000 and 27,000. The roundness of these numbers suggests they should be treated with caution.

It would seem that Viscount Swinton, the Secretary of State for Commonwealth Relations, must have been using the same database when, in February 1955, he told the House of Lords that 266,000 had been "detained" (which presumably means "arrested") in the first 30 months of the Emergency, of which 53,000 had been released "at once", and 103,900 a few days or weeks afterwards, after screening. This leaves a remaining total of about 110,000, which is very similar to the figure in CO141/6300, but he went into no detail as to how many of those were tried (whether convicted or acquitted) and how many either detained or convicted of Mau Mau offences.

The "Treatment of Offenders" annual report of 1956, published in Nairobi at a price of 2 shillings (10p in modern money) is a typical example, like the annual prison reports, of documents packed with statistics: for instance, that the cost of the prisons department had risen from £1m a year to £4m during the Emergency, whilst the cost per inmate had risen from £26 per head per annum to £52. Neither Elkins nor Anderson refers to these; and the findings and detailed background in the Fairn Report, containing highly relevant material, are also largely ignored by them, despite their providing estimates of detainee numbers that at least deserved to be analysed.

In fact, nor do Elkins and Anderson cite the abundant detail available in the reports of parliamentary delegations to Kenya, or of debates in the House of Commons and House of Lords libraries, such as that addressed by Viscount Swinton. These offer useful insights into how information flowed from Kenya to London – in the Swinton debate, several versions of the number of detainees currently held were offered: Lord Lloyd, Under-Secretary of State for the Colonies, reported that there were (as of February 1955) 46,200 in detention, of which 15,000 were in works camps and 31,200 in holding camps and reception centres at Manyani, Mackinnon Road and Langata. (It was in this speech that he revealed that 26 men had been convicted of killing or maltreating Mau Mau suspects, with 6 Home Guards convicted of shooting two suspects.) Lord Lucan (a Tory critic of government policy) challenged this estimate, claiming that the true figure was 58,000 in detention, while Earl Jowitt (for the Labour Party) claimed it was 60,000.

As it happens, all of these figures would represent "snapshot" totals: the ebb and flow of releases and detentions – the average length of time for any period of detention was just four months – meant that the overall number of people detained for any period of time in any year clearly had the potential to justify a much higher figure than the largest intra-year snapshot. Yet there is no way now of ascertaining whether individuals were detained once, more than once, or even multiple times. So a case can certainly be made for the Anderson estimate of 125,000 actually detained at one point or another under GDOs or DDOs; though if a large number of people were detained more than once, the total number of individuals ever detained might be little more than 100,000. As for Elkins' highest estimate of 320,000, not only is Anderson surely right to say this was a figure for all those ever arrested, even if quickly released, or never subject to a detention order; but even then, her assumption must have been that few individuals were detained more than once.

Even at the end of the Emergency, Kenyan civil servants could not agree on the figures. The District Commissioner for Fort Hall, John Pinney (who had access to the daily figures reported by Ken Lees to Bill Pollok-Morris, his Assistant District Commissioner) sent in a paper claiming that 90,000 had passed through the Fort Hall group of works camps and been released to the supervision of village chiefs; only for Monkey Johnston to ask Baring to amend the figure to just 13,000, claiming that most of the larger figure would have been "repatriates" on their way home. As it happens, Pinney's tally includes about 20,000 such "repatriates" (Kikuyu living outside the Reserve being returned there as an Emergency security measure), leaving a net figure of 70,000 detainees. Baring compromised at 14,000. Lees himself, in calculating a total of 69,000, seemingly supports the Pinney numbers, but provides his own estimate of annual figures at variance with those in the official Fort Hall numbers: lower for early years, higher for later ones.

Meanwhile, a briefing note for the Provincial Commissioner giving evidence to the Hola inquest provided the astonishingly precise information (with an equally precise monthly breakdown, below) that "77,517 Mau Mau detainees had been released". An independent estimate comes from the International Red Cross, which visited the detention camps regularly, and reported in 1959 that 85,000 detainees had passed through the detention camps. The figures Fairn supplied, also in 1959, tell a story consistent with most of the official documents and estimates. He says that 78,000 detainees passed through the system and that, at the peak, in 1955, there were 53,000 Mau Mau detainees and 16,000 Mau Mau convicts; together with, of course, many thousands of non-Mau Mau convicts and detainees: according to the Heaton Report, the prison establishment had swelled by 1956 to a total of 86,634 across 176 establishments – at that time, 15,800 were held at Manyani and 7,000 at Mackinnon Road. The size of these establishments was heavily criticised by Heaton as making prison management, let alone rehabilitation, extremely difficult. When John 'Taxi' Lewis was ending his term as Prisons Commissioner in 1959, Baring (trying to justify leniency

over the Hola affair and praising Lewis' lengthy service in an overstretched
system) cited a lower peak of 81,920, in December 1954.

Lennox-Boyd's predecessor, Oliver Lyttelton, told the Commons in
1953 – before Operation Anvil, the mass sweep of Nairobi in April 1954 –
that in the first four months of the Emergency 61,907 had been arrested,
3,053 had been quickly released, and the remaining 58,854 screened, leading
to the release of 39,002 and trials for 17,613 (nothing was said about the
remaining 2,239). How many of those tried were imprisoned, how many
detained and how many acquitted was not stated: but, again, we can assume
that a single database was being consulted.

A further complication was that detention had pre-dated the Emergency
as part of the colony's legal system, in the shape of clause 80 of the Laws
of Kenya. So we find in the published data for the prisons department in
1956 that there were 39,454 Emergency detainees, but also 5,171 "ordinary"
detainees, just as there were 10,222 Mau Mau prisoners, but also 8,129
"ordinary" prisoners. In addition, there were 969 remand prisoners. Added
together, the daily average of persons in custody through the year was
53,945 – a significant reduction on the figure for 1955, which was 74,678,
including 11,236 "ordinary" detainees, itself a big reduction on the pre-
Emergency total of over 23,000 "ordinary" detainees, and an average of
17,300 for the years 1948-51.

Clearly, the system was under such pressure that "ordinary" detention
was used less and less often. In any event, only 10% of detainees were
held for five months or longer, while over 40% were released within a
month. The scale of turnover can be judged by the total number of those
committed to detention camps between 1953 and 1957 (183,600) and
the snapshot end-of-year number of detainees (eg 44,947 in 1955, 31,532
in 1956 and 13,894 in 1957): clearly, thousands of detainees were being
counted multiple times as they passed in and out of detention and along
the "pipeline".

Tentatively, we can try to reconcile the different (and confusing) numbers
and definitions by separating the "headcount" totals (how many in custody
on any day or in any year) from the "personal" totals. All convicts would
have name and fingerprint details recorded. If each detainee was identified
by name and number, as Karimi Gathirike (see below) was, with the number
33540, and as suggested by the Special Branch request for 60,000 index
cards to allocate to individual detainees, then however many times he or

she was imprisoned, detained, transferred, released, re-arrested or sent up and down the pipeline, just one name and number would be involved, despite the accumulation of headcounts suggesting a much higher total. How widespread the practice was of detainees wearing bracelets imprinted with their number is not known.

Conversely, we can assume that individuals released as rehabilitated were rarely re-arrested and detained again. So when the Security Council was advised in March 1959 that 45,663 detainees had been released as rehabilitated as of April 30 1957, with monthly releases thereafter of 2,440, 1,511, 1,798, 1,991, 1,867, 1,768 and 1,699 (so 14,899 for May–December 1957), followed in 1958 by 1,424, 966, 802, 952, 1,297, 769, 1,997, 1,356, 1,035, 1,273, 717 and 761 (so 13,359 for January–December 1958), and then 1,548 and 786 (so 2,334 for January–February 1959), the total of individual releases of 77,517 up to March 1959 almost certainly refers to separate individuals. That is why so many officials – Fairn, Baring, Macleod, Pinney – talk in terms of 77,000–80,000 detainees.

De-duplication is a standard discipline in data management systems: for instance, company billing systems regularly have to remove redundant data for customers who have more than one account, or have changed their telephone number, their email address or their postal address, or re-joined as customers after a period of non-subscribing. Publicly-quoted cable or satellite TV companies, for instance, must regularly declare their actual number of customers, as well as the number of different services for which those customers subscribe. Auditors will carefully check to ensure that de-duplication has been conducted, and investors can then see accurate figures for quarterly shifts in customer numbers (previous total, less cancellations, plus new customers) as well as for uptake of services (basic channel package, premium channels, broadband, mobile phones, landlines etc). Typically, these figures will move roughly in parallel, but the market will scrutinize them carefully to see if there is any discrepancy. The mystery of detainee numbers may not be as mysterious as it first appears.

The prison estate was also vast: 112 detention camps in 1955 (71 for "ordinary" detainees and 41 for Emergency detainees), as well as two "ordinary" prisons and six just for Mau Mau prisoners. The number of Emergency camps had already been reduced from 68 in 1954, and was further reduced to 27 in 1957. Unsurprisingly, during the expansion of the prison system, the speedy recruitment of a large number of prison officers was required, which in turn led to much higher levels of poor discipline. By 1956, there were 545 European officers in the prison service, supported by 14,394 African staff (compared with 1,406 in 1952), of whom 948 were dismissed during the year for misconduct, and 42 dismissed after being convicted of criminal offences. In 1955, 821 African staff had been dismissed for misconduct, and 56 for committing crimes, with the total number of those subjected to disciplinary punishment being 6,648. In 1954, there had been 5,906 disciplinary offences: it seems nearly half of those hired were in one way or another found wanting.

All kinds of data were recorded in the annual prison reports, including numbers of prisoners and detainees subjected to corporal punishment, and deaths in custody. In 1955, an unusually high number of 343 deaths was recorded within the prisons department, the great majority of victims being convicted prisoners: 56 from dysentery, 22 from typhoid, 9 by drowning, 5 suicides, 10 from accidents and 106 "various". (As it happens, the current annual death rate in UK prisons, with a similar number of prisoners, is also over 300, though suicide features much more prominently.) During 1955, there were 30,247 committals to detention camps (the daily average number of detainees was 4,247, illustrating the relative brevity of periods of detention). The following year, there were over 40,000 committals (as convicted prisoners completing their sentences were held under detention orders), but as the pace of release increased, the year–end total of detainees declined from 44,947 to 31,532. Although the UK government regularly stated that few, if any, detainees died as a result of ill-treatment, the official figure for detainee deaths, even in 1958, when the camps were being rapidly closed, was 78, compared with 45 in 1954 and 49 in 1955 (though it would be speculative to regard these as even primarily the result of ill-treatment).

Was the government lying? The evidence from the Hanslope Park papers suggests not. Deaths from ill-treatment were regularly noted, by name, as there was always a possibility that prosecutions and convictions might follow, given the independence of the CID and the courts. Covering up murder would have been a high risk option for camp commandants; and, as we shall see (below), prison officers were briefed to watch out for excesses by rehabilitation staff.

Anderson understandably condemns the number of deaths from diseases such as pellagra and typhoid, and especially the dysentery outbreak at Manyani, which caused over 100 deaths. (It would be interesting to hear his view on the current Kenyan government, which presides over a health system that sees 45,000 children die of salmonella *every year* – the equivalent figure in the UK is effectively zero.) The Heaton Report in 1956 also condemned the level of overcrowding that had contributed to the outbreak. Neither mentioned a potential contributory factor noted by one police officer visiting Manyani: that Mau Mau re-oathing, allegedly involving the use of human faeces, had been rife there. That the epidemic had been contained by importing a new and expensive American drug, streptomycin, only marginally mitigates the systemic failures that allowed the massive over-crowding which made the spread of disease so easy.

7. Rehabilitation

By 1959, the Fort Hall camps were closed, all the detainees having been released, other than a few hundred who were either unwilling to confess to their Mau Mau past, or were unacceptable in their home district because of it; these were mostly transferred to the remote location of Hola, where a closed detention camp held about two hundred hard core Mau Mau, and a neighbouring open camp held twice as many. Still others worked the four acres of land that had been allocated to them, whilst awaiting the arrival of their families: a kind of internal exile for those "unacceptable" in their home villages, by virtue of the crimes they had committed there. At one time, a capacity of 6,000 for such Hola "exiles" had been envisaged, but the final number of land plots was 500, and of men who had qualified for such a plot, and been assigned a new status of "restrictee", just 189 had been joined by their families.

It was the beating to death of eleven Hola closed camp detainees by their African guards in March 1959 – and the immense uproar the atrocity generated in the UK Parliament – that ended the careers of Kenya Governor Sir Evelyn Baring and his London boss, Colonial Secretary Alan Lennox-Boyd (nominally, Baring retired on grounds of ill-health, but lived for another 14 years; Lennox-Boyd stayed in office till the general election in September). The new minister, Iain Macleod, having failed to suppress the Corfield Report (with its underlying message of dismal failure and complacency on the part of Baring's predecessor, Sir Philip Mitchell) instead forced through – with backing from Prime Minister Harold Macmillan – a swift passage to independence for Kenya, and the release of Jomo Kenyatta, after eight years of being held in near isolation in the far north of Kenya (a punishment imposed after his conviction as the ostensible leader of Mau Mau, in a controversial trial – shortly before the release, a key witness at his trial, Rawson Macharia, the only person to have claimed in court to have witnessed Kenyatta administering a Mau Mau oath, had confessed to perjury). It was Kenyatta who became the nation's first President in 1963.

Even in February 1959, such an outcome must have seemed a remote prospect. The fighting war against the Mau Mau guerrillas, who had mostly holed up in the Aberdare forest, was effectively over by the end of 1954, but was followed by a prolonged and draining battle over the tens of thousands of those who remained in prison or detention, and whose plight became a potent weapon for Mau Mau in its propaganda war against the colonial government. Indeed, Mau Mau leaders gained control of many camps and prisons, or parts of them, using that control to impose discipline and undertake further oathing. Paradoxically, detention may have inadvertently strengthened that leadership, just as internment in Northern Ireland acted as a recruiting sergeant for the IRA.

In 1954, the civil servant who became the main architect of rehabilitation of Mau Mau detainees, Thomas Askwith, reported from one prison, Sakwa (also known as Sinyanya, in Nyanza), where, he claimed, the leadership even printed a book of 62 rules (his report says 64, but the attachments only itemize 62), listing punishments to be inflicted for breaches of discipline. Some of the rules were coolly practical, such as those outlawing escape attempts ("this brings hardships on those remaining"). Askwith noted that this might explain why so few detainees had taken advantage of the thick Sakwa bush to run away – though elsewhere in the vast complex of camps there were determined and successful escape attempts (there was even an attack by Mau Mau on Lukenia prison camp that allowed many prisoners to make a bid for freedom).

Askwith also recorded that the camp had an overall Mau Mau leader, a deputy and a secretary, along with an informer; and each compound had a commander and sometimes a deputy commander: "their idea is to perpetuate Mau Mau after their prison life, and at the same time maintain a rigid control of their fellow inmates". The "sentences" for breaking the rules ("six months", "one year", "outlawing") were usually converted into punishments, including some later adopted by the colonial authorities, such as the knee-march ("walking on one's knees the length of the dormitory – being equivalent to a year's imprisonment or part thereof") and the bucket fatigue (parading with a bucket of mud or stones on one's head). Terence Gavaghan, years later when in charge of rehabilitation at the Mwea camps, acknowledged using such techniques, but only – so he insisted privately – in retaliation against those Mau Mau leaders who had used them to discipline non-compliant cadres.

Not that such a justification necessarily made these punishments legal. As late as December 1958, Attorney-General Eric Griffith-Jones was warning Carruthers "Monkey" Johnston "that there is no power in the Emergency (Detained Person) Regulations 1954 to impose 'heavy labour' as a punishment" – this included running with 50 pounds of earth in buckets and earth-filled shirts – "nothing should be done which might lead to scandal". Little did Griffith-Jones realize that a "scandal" on an unimagined scale was about to break (though he personally survived it, and, indeed, ended his days in colonial Kenya as Acting Governor, complete with knighthood).

The problem for Johnston was that heavy labour and caning were effective with the least co-operative detainees in a way that no other technique could match. For a long time, it suited Mau Mau to keep the detention system going, to embarrass the Nairobi administration: which it certainly did, as ministers struggled with the sheer scale of detention, and with the lack of an agreed policy for "de-fanging" known terrorists. The original strategy – rehabilitation – was developed by Askwith, who incorporated it into his community development brief within the Ministry of African Affairs (thereby receiving a pay rise of £200 pa). He had been posted to Malaya in 1953 to study the policies used to suppress and then to eliminate the communist insurgency there.

But there was a crucial difference between Malaya and Kenya: most of the Malayan guerrillas were Chinese, who were relatively easy to identify within the population. Once the insurgency had been sufficiently contained, it was a realistic prospect to send the most intransigent captives into exile, thereby making it easier to "re-educate" the more co-operative. As there were never more than 30,000 detained in Malaya, half of whom were eventually exiled, the task of rehabilitation was limited.

In Kenya, that did not apply: Askwith was firmly told that actual exile was impractical, and internal exile on any scale similar to the Malaya experience unfeasible. Askwith's initial instinct was that the task was akin to "isolating lepers", after which he could concentrate on rehabilitation of the least contaminated. This he saw as involving hard work (land reclamation, bush clearing, dam digging and quarrying), training (especially in farming techniques), re-education (including reading his book, "The Story of Kenya's Progress") and restoration of moral values ("the approach must be Christian"). The moral imperative was to return terrorists to being law-abiding citizens. Those detainees confessing their oaths and accepting rehabilitation could be transferred up a "pipeline" to works camps in their home areas, where detailed confessions could be recorded and family visits arranged, followed by release to open camps, and then home villages, under careful supervision by Chiefs and Headmen. At any stage, rejects could be sent back down the pipeline, awaiting a change of attitude.

At other times, it seemed to Askwith that "the interrogation and classification process" was "of much more importance than anything else at this moment" (January 1954); a few months later, he was "very averse to recommending the use of detainees for proselytizing" (whereby those who had renounced their oaths urged others to follow suit); later still, a proper process "must be considered" before anyone ostensibly rehabilitated should be released, and "the Special Branch view must prevail". As the detainee issue metastasized, it is hard not to sympathize with Askwith, an idealist in a colony characterized by opportunist settlers, rampant racial inequality, silo-minded civil servants mostly out of their depth, and a brutal civil war that had been allowed to burst into flames by an indolent and blinkered administration.

Undeterred by initial opposition, Askwith continued to call for removal of the most difficult detainees to a place where they could not influence the mass of their followers. The Tana River Irrigation Scheme on the coast was the chosen location for the Hola camp, where selected exiled Mau Mau would be forcibly resettled, and allocated a few acres of land to cultivate. There they might in due course be joined by family members, but Askwith assumed that years after the Emergency ended, the exile settlements would still be expanding. Places for up to 6,000 such exiles were planned, but in the end fewer than 500 were allocated (and, as noted above, just 189 taken up). However, Hola also housed an open camp for those awaiting transfer to the plots of land, together with a closed camp for the most intransigent detainees. The notoriety of events in the closed camp on March 3rd 1959 has wholly eclipsed the story of the irrigation scheme (it also largely eclipsed events in the nearby British dependency of Nyasaland, where a State of

Emergency was declared that same day in the midst of a crisis that cost more than 50 Africans their lives, shot dead by security forces).

Askwith also advocated confiscation of land from convicted and irreconcilable Mau Mau members: something the Attorney-General had to tell him would have been illegal as a penalty for Mau Mau offences. One of his preoccupations was his view that tens of thousands of Kikuyu needed to be re-settled anyway, or found jobs, because of land shortages in Central Province. Exile and confiscation were ways of releasing precious land. Askwith had volunteered the opinion that there would be "vast hordes of irreconcilables"; but that, contrarily, it should in theory be no more difficult to wean susceptible Kikuyu from Mau Mau as Chinese Malay communists from Marx.

All these ideas were buzzing around in his head, along with a propensity to see himself as the hero of the story. He had to be reprimanded for preparing a lengthy press release naming himself in the first paragraph ("premature and inappropriate" was the official rebuke). His title was actually Secretary for Community Development, later expanded to Permanent Secretary, but his limitations were steadily exposed, even as his bids for scope and budget were enlarged. His unconcealed ambitions and gargantuan proposal papers alienated many colleagues over the years.

As the provider of the foreword to his memoir puts it, he was not afraid "to infuriate Provincial Commissioners" and he would "blitz" his colleagues with "circulars, memos, articles and points of information". His occasional attempts to take capable officers on secondment from other ministries, without prior consultation, let alone consent, and intervene in delicate handling of Mau Mau suspects all over the colony, reduced more than one District Commissioner and Provincial Commissioner to outraged protest: the Kiambu and Lamu DCs were joined by the PCs at Nyeri, Coast and Rift Valley in registering angry complaints, to the effect that Askwith's premature actions had caused "a great deal of embarrassment" which had been "very humiliating".

Askwith's establishment included nearly 70 rehabilitation officers and hundreds of assistants. The most prominent of the rehabilitation specialists were Major James Breckenridge and his wife Caroline, who pioneered an intensive "tutorial system" for potential renouncers of Mau Mau oaths. This required weeks of work on individual detainees, culminating in public confessions, recorded and played over loudspeakers to village gatherings.

These "baraza" sessions reportedly caused as much resentment as persuasion, as did the continuous emphasis on Christianity: the controversial evangelical movement, MRA (Moral Re-Armament), originating in Oxford, played an influential role in this approach.

Walter Magor, at the Ministry of Defence, told Askwith he was "a cynic" about rehabilitation in general and MRA in particular. Even Askwith conceded that barely one in eight detainees at Athi River "may be regarded as having responded to treatment". Magor ensured Askwith's removal from the Athi River inspection committee after Askwith had tried to take control of it. He also blocked Askwith's attempt to insert himself in a proposed Christian Council of Kenya Advisory Committee on Rehabilitation. Fortunately for Askwith, Magor's successor, John "Jake" Cusack, was more supportive.

Caroline Breckenridge, as late as May 1958 (according to Colonial Office file 141/6608), was nonetheless still urging the importance of religion "filling the gap" for men giving up the Mau Mau oaths to which they had clung for so long: "hence the great necessity of leading men into Christian fellowship wherever it was possible". Confession must be followed by "cleansing", partly as a religious process, partly in recognition of the fact that oath-takers had rendered themselves ritually unclean according to tribal custom. However, even the Catholic priest who played a central role in rehabilitation "felt there were dangers of over-zealousness on the part of Christian workers who regarded themselves as 'saved' and required the same profession from any detainee". This did not stop him insisting that every camp with more than 600 detainees should have a Catholic church as well as a Protestant one.

Askwith, claiming that "progress was encouraging", despite the limited numbers passing up the pipeline, contented himself with the formulation that "if hard work, a fair chance for every man to make a fresh start and, most important of all, a simple form of confession will not produce the change which is our object, there is nothing else that will". He was undeterred by the Chief Native Commissioner's rejection of his "exile and model villages" strategy, seeing his biggest obstacle as "a conflict of outlook" between his own staff – "commissioned officers" – and prison staff – "NCOs". He complained that his rehabilitation team – the equivalent of commandants – were better equipped than prison officers – equivalent to quartermasters – to run the detention system, and if that task were allocated to them, it "would remove many of the causes of friction resulting from divided control"; but they were "unlikely to agree to take charge of camps, even if requested to do so, unless the emphasis was placed on rehabilitation".

Yet at the same time, in 1956, he was admitting to – of all people – Frank Corfield, then working in Government House in Nairobi, that the MRA methods at Athi River "have met with little success", being too "evangelical"; that "it is unlikely that the present methods of rehabilitation, which have proved effective with the rank and file of Mau Mau, will succeed with the leaders"; and that insofar as there had been successes with the rank and file, it had been military failure which "persuaded them to turn against Mau Mau".

For some Mau Mau adherents, experiencing or witnessing defeat, and surviving surrender without being struck dead, was enough to break the power of the oath. For others, it was seeing their comrades co-operating with the detention regime, and making their way home, that was persuasive. For some, engaging in work – whether voluntarily or under threat or experience of violence – was the first breach of the power of the oath. Even acknowledging the taking of an oath could be the start of a process of renunciation. And then there were those for whom the state of ritual uncleanness, or the burdens of conscience after committing horrific crimes, proved no longer bearable. For the teams of self-trained rehabilitators, there was no single pathway to success.

The Mau Mau intelligentsia, mostly held at Takwa (and whose prospective transfer to Hola would play an integral part in the 1959 tragedy), were a particularly difficult challenge. Only "paragons of knowledge, intellect and virtue could hope to succeed with them", and "no such officer exists in the Ministry of Community Development at present". A colleague of Askwith's, Tatton-Brown, concurred: "at present, it is not possible to rehabilitate these people, for lack of staff with the necessary intellectual abilities".

Another problem was the sheer expense of this kind of intensive effort: at one point, Askwith put forward a budget for over £300,000 for one of his projects, roughly 5% of the entire annual Emergency expenditure. By contrast, when Sir Vincent Glenday spent three months compiling his report on 68 screening and detention centres, the entire cost, including fees, accommodation and per diems came to just £615 (all itemised in the archive documents).

The Breckenridges operated primarily from the camp at Athi River. Soon after the Hola disaster, and perhaps influenced by that calamity, Monkey Johnston, who served as Special Commissioner for Rehabilitation admitted to Baring that Athi River had failed. The numbers being released as fully rehabilitated were disappointingly low. Askwith had declined even to attempt to deal with convicted prisoners. Special Branch reckoned that 80% of the prisoners at Manyani would never become "acceptable". Askwith put the figure much lower, at 33%, but even that would leave thousands upon thousands of hard core Mau Mau with nowhere to go except internal exile. It was small wonder that official projections as late as 1958 showed detention still in force as late as 1970, with any possible date for independence being pushed back to 1975.

Yet another report on prisons and detention, in 1956, from G R Heaton, a prisons commissioner, recommended that responsibility for rehabilitation be shifted from Community Development to the Prisons Department. Heaton's logic was that, insofar as Askwith had made any headway, it was with the "low-hanging fruit" of detainees classified as Xs and Ys (that is, least dangerous), with the Zs and the convicts remaining to be dealt with (though how, he did not specify). Askwith protested long and hard, appealing to his minister to intervene, and even managing to delay the switch by invoking the technicality of when the budget year started. Heaton had noted "a great deal of friction" between prison staff and rehabilitators. On the touchy issue of the use of force, he settled for the unhelpful nostrum that "discipline should be strictly maintained...if discipline is threatened, the minimum amount of force to maintain it must be used and no more".

Elkins – working from a partial view of the archives, before the Hanslope Park declaration, and from personal testimony from Askwith – concluded that the Breckenridges were strongly opposed to using force in their rehabilitation process. The new files reveal the superficiality of that judgment. In November 1957, James Breckenridge was attributing the slowdown in obtaining confessions to the "very stringent prohibition of any form of physical persuasion". Such a complaint perhaps explains another telling document in the archive, dated February 19 1959, where the Prisons Commissioner, John "Taxi" Lewis, issued a formal warning to the prison staff at Athi River, in dealing with Breckenridge's rehabilitation officers, to watch out in case the latter resorted to "extreme measures".

"Detainees transferred from Manyani are unlikely to respond to rehabilitation in any form. While you should support and assist any reasonable tactics it is your duty to ensure that no ['unnecessary' has been redacted in the original document, presumably by Lewis himself before it was issued] beating or other brutality takes place." He spelled out his instructions further, this time not deleting the qualifying adjective: prison warders "should prevent any unnecessary violence" by rehabilitation, officers.

Remarkably, this instruction was issued almost contemporaneously with Lewis's note to the Minister of Defence, Jake Cusack, with regard to the planned attempt to induce the latest intake of ultra-hostile detainees at Hola camp to work for the first time: an attempt, he warned, that might result in injury, or even death. This would be a central document in the inquiry into the Hola killings (see below).

The failure by Askwith to unblock the detainee pipeline, which in turn was preventing any potential move towards political progress and perhaps even independence, eventually led Monkey Johnston to embark on a "left field" appointment in March 1957. He turned to a 35-year-old civilian official, who had served as a District Commissioner and District Officer in various parts of Kenya since 1944, but had had minimal contact with Mau Mau.

Terence Gavaghan, an Irishman born in India, was in hospital – having ruptured his Achilles tendon while playing squash – when Johnston dropped by to invite him to take responsibility for rehabilitation at the Mwea group of camps, in the Embu district, through which it was hoped the bulk of the then daunting total of 20,000 remaining detainees, mostly hard core and mostly at Manyani, would progress up the pipeline. As Lennox-Boyd admitted to the House of Commons, in 1959, at the time of Gavaghan's appointment "these figures seemed impossible to achieve".

Gavaghan worked alongside a Senior Superintendent of Police, John Cowan, who had been assigned to the Mwea the previous year. They were put in joint charge of the five detention camps that made up the complex, and immediately realised that re-gaining control of the main camp, at Thiba, from its Mau Mau leaders, and then maintaining their authority, would require in the first instance the use of enough force to break up the 1,000 detainees into manageable groups of 250. This was no easy task: similar attempts at Manyani and Athi River resulted in failure and riots.

They brought in a squad of tough, young, loyalist Kikuyu, and once these had been trained in the use of short batons without causing any lasting physical damage, Gavaghan and Cowan announced to the assembled inmates their intention of splitting up the accommodation. The detainees responded by clustering in a tight mass (what Gavaghan termed a "Mau Mau pyramid"), noisily protesting. In the absence of co-operation, Gavaghan and Cowan simply moved in with their squad, and physically ejected man after man until they could safely call in a building team to undertake the planned division of the camp into four separate units. The whole operation took two hours, and resulted in a few minor injuries: "evenly distributed" – according to Gavaghan – between detainees and warders. He was now ready to receive prisoners and detainees from Manyani.

What then happened has become a flashpoint in the argument between defenders of the colonial regime and the revisionist historians who currently hold the field in Kenyan studies. Gavaghan invited a group of ministers and officials to observe, on June 6th 1957, an intake of 80 'Z' detainees being transferred, first by train and then by lorry, from Manyani to Kandongu, one of the five Mwea camps (he describes the event in his memoir, "Of Lions and Dungbeetles", and his account matches closely with that secretly given to Nairobi by one of the observer group, the Attorney-General, Eric Griffith-Jones).

The theory of "dilution" (rather than individual rehabilitation) was that small groups of non-co-operators should be exposed to large groups of co-operating detainees who had admitted oath-taking and repudiated Mau Mau. Askwith had expressly rejected the use of co-operators in this fashion, but Gavaghan and Cowan embraced it. In front of an exuberant crowd of detainees who had already accepted the new regime, and were looking forward to eventually moving up the pipeline on the way to release, newcomers – as soon as they stepped down from the lorries in groups of 20 – were required to have their heads shaved and to change into clean camp clothing (hygiene and discipline were the declared motives for this demand). Any refusing were quickly seized, thrown to the ground, and held down whilst the shaving and changing were forcibly achieved. Resistance to a legally issued order was punished with a caning of up to twelve strokes administered under the supervision of Cowan, as specified under Regulation 17a of the Emergency laws issued in 1954.

Griffith-Jones, who had himself been a held as a prisoner of war by the Japanese, wrote a detailed "secret and confidential" account of the process, accompanied by a request for a change in regulations to bring detainees under the same provisions as convicted prisoners, in terms of explicit authority to use force to impose discipline. It was sent on to the Colonial Secretary, Alan Lennox-Boyd, by the Governor, Sir Evelyn Baring, who provided a covering note urging acceptance of the change. Gavaghan was left entirely in ignorance. Griffith-Jones distinguished between illegal and legal uses of force: essentially, the difference between using force to punish and using it to compel compliance with legal orders. This has been widely interpreted – most notably, by Caroline Elkins, but also other historians, and other officials at the time – as a plan to legalize state violence (see the section below on the question of Elkins and Gavaghan).

Reading the Griffith-Jones document, along with Baring's covering note, it is clear that there is some nervousness about what might otherwise seem like a minor regulatory adjustment; nervousness over-ridden by the enticing prospect (as offered by Gavaghan, according to both Griffith-Jones and Baring) that this new process could finally unblock the detainee pipeline. Nairobi's ambivalence about the whole process led to Griffith-Jones meeting Gavaghan two weeks later to suggest using reduced force so as to "prevent serious injury".

But even before Lennox-Boyd could give a decision, a familiar face had turned up at the Mwea, on July 11th, uninvited, to watch an intake: that of Tom Askwith. Askwith and Gavaghan knew each other. Askwith had been the senior District Officer in Kitui district when Gavaghan served his first stint as a cadet District Officer in Kitui in 1944. That prior acquaintance proved no barrier to Askwith's shocked reaction to what he witnessed. He immediately protested bitterly to his own minister, with a copy sent to virtually all members of the colony's cabinet. He listed thirteen objections.

Askwith's first argument was that Gavaghan knew nothing about rehabilitation (and little about Mau Mau, having had almost no contact with them in his previous postings): he was a mere District Officer, whose methods were "the negation of everything that rehabilitation has stood for so far" – he seems to be "not required to conform to accepted ministerial policy". Why should Gavaghan be answerable to the Provincial Commissioner, Johnston, rather than the Minister for African Affairs, Edward Windley? More importantly, Askwith was genuinely horrified by what he saw during the induction day: for such punishments as canings and beatings to become routine was not just likely to be counter-productive but also risked "death or serious injury". Detainees, he said "were completely cowed...[into] terrified submission".

"Were the CID to investigate the numerous cases of assault which are occurring daily, a large number of prison officers and Mr Gavaghan himself would be likely to find themselves charged in court", he asserted in the lengthy memorandum he sent the next day. In this judgment, as it happens, Askwith was by no means mistaken. In the immediate aftermath of the Hola calamity, Sam Githu, a much-decorated prison warder, was jailed for assaulting a detainee. Gavaghan was one of those who protested, saying Githu's actions were no different from those of scores of fellow prison officers; he helped organise fund-raisers to support Githu's family.

The minutes of the Fort Hall Intelligence Committee, chaired by Bill Pollok-Morris, reveal the depth of bitterness amongst administration officials and loyalists at Githu's punishment: their "faith in Government had suffered a severe blow – why had his previous outstanding loyalty and hard work apparently been totally disregarded by Government? – opposition elements are overjoyed, regarding his imprisonment as just reward for his fight against Mau Mau".

Shortly after writing his scathing document, Askwith tried to claim credit for some traditional rehabilitation, in the successful transfer of 217 Manyani "Zs" to Mariira, in the Fort Hall camp system, of whom 100 had confessed fully. As we will see below, Mariira, which was taking far fewer from Manyani than the Mwea did, was very much part of Ken Lees' sphere of responsibility, and his techniques were quite different from those of Askwith, let alone Gavaghan. Moreover, the decision to send detainees and convicts directly to divisional works camps like Mariira was one taken explicitly by the War Cabinet as an experiment. But now the tide turned against Askwith.

Griffith-Jones protested at "personal attacks on individuals: [they] are unfair and will not be permitted". One of the recipients of the Askwith complaint, Frank Loyd, also a Provincial Commissioner, rebuked Windley about it – "I take the greatest exception" – and deplored Askwith's "penchant for unnecessary interference". Noticing the absence of a copy to Gavaghan, Loyd sent him one anyway, and – like any experienced bureaucrat – Gavaghan responded swiftly, copying his riposte to all the original addressees, rejecting the charge of using illegitimate force.

"Terrified submission is a fantastic phrase to use especially as Mr Askwith the self-same evening saw *all* of Thiba camp pour unassisted out of their huts to sports full of fun." Of course, he said, "this task is distasteful to any normal man", but "the detainee is not ordered to confess though this nearly always follows upon compliance with other orders". Confession was simply the admission that oaths had been taken (Gavaghan elsewhere referred to this acknowledgement as taking a few steps forward when asked to confirm oath-taking). He claimed that, typically, even the "Zs" started to co-operate within 1-3 days. Gavaghan ended with an observation that can be replicated in any number of accounts by Europeans dealing with Mau Mau relinquishing their oaths (from Frank Kitson, conducting his anti-guerilla campaign, to Caroline Breckenridge and to Ken Lees): "the intention here is to turn a half-hypnotized brute into a normally thinking and behaving human – it is this astounding 'volte-face' of the most brutalized men which gives most of us pleasure".

Neither of the protagonists made any reference to this explosive exchange in their respective memoirs, Gavaghan simply noting that "Tom Askwith had expressed mistaken umbrage when the responsibility for Rehabilitation had been withdrawn from him and had impugned an assumed new policy of force to secure confessions by someone more amenable!" But Gavaghan did acknowledge – in referring to Hola – that Askwith, "a man of dogged and insistently liberal values...had taken care to warn that the use of force in obtaining confessions...could lead to disaster".

Only "Taxi" Lewis, the Prisons Commissioner, sided with Askwith (even though his man, Cowan, was jointly responsible with Gavaghan for what was being done at Mwea). Gavaghan says of Lewis that his "mild temperament...rendered him unsuited to the rough and tumble of mass detention", unlike the more senior Cusack, whose "sympathy was not likely to be engaged by the disciplining of recalcitrant detainees". As Lewis answered to Cusack, his support for Askwith cut little ice. Askwith suffered the humiliation of being summoned to the Governor's office for a personal reprimand, after "a long private session". Cowan and Gavaghan were meanwhile invited to Government House for a meeting on August 8th with Baring and his key ministers. The die was cast.

In due course, some months later, Askwith was actually dismissed as a civil servant (a rare event), and if he still had fears about Gavaghan's methods risking fatal consequences, there were no fatalities he could actually report, even though by then Gavaghan was more than half way through his Mwea assignment. Gavaghan insists in his memoir that no one died or was even seriously injured during his 15 months in charge – rather, that 18,000 of the last 20,000 detainees had been successfully transferred up the pipeline, ready for the next stage in the release process, after having acknowledged to him that they had taken Mau Mau oaths (which indicated to him that they might no longer feel bound by them).

Gavaghan was duly recognized in the 1958 honours list: his MBE, or Membership of the Order of the British Empire, is the most junior "gong" in that category, behind Officer of the Order, or OBE, and, even more senior, Commander of the Order, or CBE. Elkins mistakenly substituted OBE for MBE as his honour in her book, an error which the most cursory check could have avoided. But then she also insisted that it was the Mwea detainees who had bestowed on Gavaghan the nickname Karuga Ndua, translating it as "Big Troublemaker", even though in his memoir, published five years ahead of her book, he three times tells the story of its true origin, long before his time at the Mwea, when he was a junior officer in Limuru township, tasked with breaking up illicit brewing in private dwellings. "Crawling through muddy entrances, I could detect the sickly smell of illegal rotgut Nubian Gin stored in large Kubayas (root vats). I tipped them all over." The literal translation of Karuga Ndua was "he who jumps over the cooking pot rather than going round it": indicating rashness and defiance of custom. Elkins is guilty not so much of a lazy error as of a deliberate mistake, designed to denigrate Gavaghan and validate the claims of her interviewees: she simply scores an own goal.

After leaving the Mwea, Gavaghan returned to Kiambu as District Commissioner (under Frank Loyd, the Provincial Commissioner), but eventually fell victim to politics, having offended Monkey Johnston with his views on the failure of the pre-Baring regime in dealing with the nascent Mau Mau threat, and on the future need for full voting rights for all adults, including released Mau Mau. He was assigned to the Ministry of Local Government in Nairobi, where his tasks included Africanising the civil service (in a typically snide aside, Elkins describes this as "transitioning loyalists into the administration", ignoring Gavaghan's published claim to have treated loyalists and ex-Mau Mau identically). His fortunes then recovered somewhat, and his last postings were as acting Permanent Secretary Governor's Office (PSGO) and then, when Frank Loyd assumed the substantive role, Under Secretary (USGO), working in Government House alongside Griffith-Jones, who had been promoted to Deputy and then Acting Governor of the colony. Gavaghan told me that neither the visit to the Kandongu intake in June 1957, nor the lengthy memorandum to the Governor, was ever mentioned by Griffith-Jones at any point.

Ironically, Lennox-Boyd never approved the proposed change in regulations, probably because he realized it was not actually necessary, and that Nairobi was trying to cover its back. In the end, once Gavaghan had, by August, reduced to 8% the proportion of those being transferred from Manyani who were subjected to physical punishment for failing to obey orders, the colonial administration was much too impressed by his success rate to continue chivvying him about his methods. By September, there had been three intakes with no physical punishment. Even so, at the very top, there was the lurking worry that events from the early days of screening might yet come back to haunt them. Griffith-Jones noted in 1958 that "we have had impressive testimony from responsible people on all sides that violence, not just corporal punishment, was often used in the past by 'screening teams' to compel confessions".

Gavaghan himself wrote to Cowan in late 1957 confirming the limits to "the use of force", which ranged from a "compelling slap" to "punitive caning": "we need to secure obedience and order, suppress fanatics' intimidation, and 'break the sound barrier' between concealment and confession which seals off so many indoctrinated minds". He also sent a letter to all Mwea staff in November saying "we must clearly stop short of brutality, be satisfied with a fair minimum" and balance "present impact against possible lasting resentment": "we must prefer delay or rejection to over-indulgence in punishment". By October, it was reported that "force is now used only in exceptional cases".

But doubts remained. Taxi Lewis had asked Griffith-Jones for an indemnity for the use of excessive force, and had been sharply rebuffed ("this is an improper request" – "excessive" force should never be used, and reasonable use of force is legally permissible anyway). So Lewis imposed a ruling that only after three refused requests could a detainee be formally caned in the orderly room. Nonetheless, Jake Cusack noted a report in December from Lewis's deputy, Gregory-Smith, that one intake had been subject to "very severe measures and too much force". Two weeks later, according to a note from Frank Loyd to Johnston, a Special Branch inspector alleged ill-treatment at Mwea by rehabilitation officers using "excessive force", though he modified his allegation when it became clear that a reported broken leg and arm were actually bruising and a cracked rib. The report confirmed that 80% of each intake admitted to taking an oath on the first day after arrival, and the remainder within two or three days; so enabling "the main object of the rehabilitation programme – to transfer the detainee within four months of his arrival to his district of origin."

Gregory-Smith thought Gavaghan in December 1957 was "done in, at the end of his tether", and recommended replacement. Johnston sent a response to Cusack, saying he was keeping Gavaghan on ("he did not appear to me to be looking 'under the weather'"), but at the same time told the new commandant at Athi River that he could adopt all Mwea methods except "use of the cane to enforce discipline on new intakes". Yet the pressing need to empty Manyani was re-emphasised by an outbreak of violence there in August. Gavaghan was asked to visit two days later and report. His terse note provided a chilling summary: "compound 16, no 2 camp, had rioted and killed a Kamba warder on Saturday 17th, after a set-to with some 70 Askari and 20 officers who were compelled to withdraw in face of superior numbers and weapons (nailed maces, rocks, etc)". A second warder later died from his injuries, and six of the rioters were eventually hanged for murder. This may have been the fracas reported by Tony France: "I was on the scene shortly after one African warder was bludgeoned to death, another seriously injured, with timbers the inmates had wrested from the A-frame structure".

Perhaps it was this incident that persuaded Askwith to write to Johnston three days later, telling him to "let the Mwea concentrate on clearing Manyani as quickly as possible". In a message the previous day, he had modified his claims for Mariira: rehabilitation there, and at Aguthi and Gatundu, "has not been a great success since virtually no dilution was possible". It was the presence of crowds of co-operators that seemed to make a difference. "I suggest that the tougher type of detainee should continue to go to the Mwea Camps or Athi River...it appears that dilution offers the best hope of rehabilitating Zs at the present time". It was now "essential" that the Ys "be made use of to the maximum extent with the rehabilitation of the Zs". (The true story of Mariira was rather different: see below.)

This about-turn by Askwith is not referenced in his memoir, "From Mau Mau to Harambee", and challenges the accuracy of the claim in the introduction to that volume, by a Cambridge historian, that "he opposed the use of force against Mau Mau prisoners who refused to work". At one stage he did, to the point of trying to drive Gavaghan out of his job and into prison; but the realities of the task of returning the Zs to normal life within their communities were such that, however reluctantly, he endorsed the Mwea dilution system – implicitly with its harsh discipline – as the only option.

As if to underline the uncertainties of the world these civil servants were trying to navigate, out of the archive steps detainee number 33540, Karimi Gathirike. He was 32 years old, and had been arrested in October 1953. His story, or "petition", describes his "safari ubogo", or short journey, which started in Nairobi prison, encompassing Mackinnon Road, Nairobi Special Camp, Lamu, Mwana, Kamiti, Manyani and Mara River before he reached Mwea.

He tells of the Mau Mau committees and prayers that he encountered everywhere (though Manyani had prayers but no committee – he was there for the compound 16 riot on which Gavaghan reported). In November 1957, he had been sent to Mwea, where he says he was beaten by Gavaghan and the warders: there were no Mau Mau structures there (allegedly, Kandongu was mostly occupied by Kiama Kia Muingi, which, like Kiama Kia Ngoro, was assumed by the authorities to be a re-invention of Mau Mau), and he confessed one oath, but even so was sent back to Manyani rather than up the pipeline. Then he was transferred to Athi River, as one of five "hard core fanatics" that the officer in charge of Athi River was keeping apart from each other.

Breckenridge and 15 screeners were reported to be "working on them", and three were said to be now talking (resisters were sometimes called "non-talkers"). Gathirike's confession is variously dated as February 23 and February 28 1959, so probably took some days to compile: this was, as it happens, the week before the Hola massacre. The confession document was signed off by a "special team" of five elders: it is preserved in full in the archive.

"The subject has willingly confessed taken one mau mau oath. He has given a very good start. He paid 17 shillings for the mau mau collections and paid 60 shillings instead of ram promised when oathed. He attended two mau mau ceremonies and within those ceremonies, he escorted three persons to be oathed there. He also guarded one of those mau mau ceremonies. He has never joined any political bodies but he attended Kenya

Africa Union meeting held in Nakuru in 1947. He has given a good general information. His Camp and Prison activities are good. He has promised to co-operate with the Government. Ready to tell the hard cores to do away with the mau mau. He smiled before the elders and answered questions very nicely. And as nobody could see inside anybody (soul) the team has recommended him for a transfer to his District for they were satisfied with his confession, knowing it is only God who can see in his heart."

Gathirike felt he had been treated fairly by Major Breckenridge, who must have savoured this victory for his targeted approach all the more after the failure of Gavaghan's methods in this instance. The case is an example of how the archive captures the mixed fortunes of the rehabilitation campaign at the cutting edge, with advocates of different methods caught between the pressures of mass detention, the need to embrace the tribal identity of a detainee (which Ken Lees regarded as crucial) and the understandable human response to the needs of individuals. Breckenridge made an equally determined effort to "turn" James Koinange, a scion of a leading Mau Mau family who had been unsuccessfully prosecuted for organising the assassination of Senior Chief Waruhiu in 1952, but in that instance Breckenridge had to admit defeat. In the rough ready-reckoner of results, it was Gavaghan who achieved most on the part of the administration.

Much later, Baring's successor, Sir Patrick Renison, who had far less "investment" in Gavaghan's methods, felt free to voice his disapproval of them (much easier to do once the pipeline had been unblocked). As for Cowan, even after Mwea closed, he was using its techniques: in December 1958 at Karaka, 172 out of an intake of 177 (including 95 "unmanageables" from Aguthi) quickly confessed to having taken at least one Mau Mau oath. The five non-co-operators were harangued by 150 co-operators, but even after head-shaving and changing of clothes, refused to be screened. Eventually, 92 of the 95 were induced to co-operate, 12 after heavy labour, 10 after caning. Cowan also reported confessions induced by caning at Karaba (in September 1958); also, that in two days at Kandongu, "heavy labour" had generated 180 confessions.

How that differed from the heavy labour frowned upon by Griffith-Jones is not clear. In September 1958, Gavaghan's successor at the Mwea, Galton-Fenzi, reported to the Ministry of African Affairs that one detainee, Kamau Chege, having been returned from Gathiga because of "poor quality confessions", had collapsed and died after "a very short period of heavy labour" – "at no time was any physical violence used", and the post mortem confirmed death from "natural causes".

When Cowan's turn came to feature in the Honours List, it was excruciatingly badly timed: recommended (for his support of Gavaghan at Mwea) before the Hola scandal, listed for his award after the "Cowan plan" (a course of action at Hola recommended by Cowan but poorly implemented) became notorious, and then vilified in the press after the Hola inquest, he was suitably grateful that Lennox-Boyd did not fold under pressure, not least from the Cabinet Secretary, who advised rescinding the recommendation. Cowan sent Lennox-Boyd a handwritten note in May 1959, followed by a typewritten one in June. Elkins, characteristically, fails to understand the sequence of events, imagining that Lennox-Boyd had deliberately chosen to honour Cowan in defiance of the Hola uproar. The actual citation gave primary credit to Gavaghan, but said his "remarkable achievement could not have been obtained without the administrative ability and example provided by Mr Cowan."

In the newly-released archive, in one of the 1959 files, there is an unsigned hand-written note defending the Mwea system, regretting only that the first sweeps in the detention process had been too broad and indiscriminate, thereafter distorting the attempts at rehabilitation. Too many people were left for too long in holding camps, without any rehabilitation or work, whilst the Askwith teams concentrated on "easy targets", using public confessions broadcast over Tannoy. This methodology proved counter-productive, as the larger group of harder targets were wary of such a risky exposure. In the absence of adequate segregation, the hard core Mau Mau leaders were able to impose their own disciplinary code, along with a "barbed wire mentality".

A clue to the authorship of the note came in the next section. The key, said the author, was to ensure that orders were being obeyed before screening could begin. The "government should assert authority" – "when dealing with hard core must first administer psychological shock by transferring non-co-operating detainees from holding camps to filter camps; changing of clothes and shaving of heads while addressed by co-operative detainees; then being asked whether they were prepared to obey lawful orders – if not, a formal inquiry by an Assistant Commissioner of Police would immediately follow, resulting in caning and solitary confinement; and being made to work by use of compelling force".

This so obviously reflects what Gavaghan and Cowan did at Mwea that I sent a copy of part of the note to Gavaghan's widow, who in turn sent it to Cowan's daughter: and his daughter confirmed the handwriting was her father's. As Griffith-Jones and Baring never discussed their proposal to London with Gavaghan, it is highly likely they also excluded Cowan from the correspondence; so the use of the phrase "psychological shock" in the note suggests that this concept was not some gloss put by Griffith-Jones and Baring on the process, but a deliberate part of the methods chosen by Gavaghan and Cowan.

8. Elkins and Gavaghan

When Elkins wrote her account of the dispute between Askwith and Gavaghan, she chose to demonize Gavaghan as the worst of the worst: but even among her 137 interviewees (Mau Mau veterans and their families) whose testimony underpinned her research findings, she found not one who witnessed him ever committing a wrongful act. Lacking a copy of Askwith's condemnatory memorandum, she instead concocted a version, using quotes from other interviewees, and even from Gavaghan himself (who had, with a touch of ill-judged bravado, described the forcible changing of clothing as "a kind of rape" in a television programme). She did not disclose this sleight of hand.

The television programme – made by the BBC in 2002 – provided further evidence of her seeming bad faith. It was, as she confirmed in her book, a "project" effectively based on her research ("the BBC...brought my research to the screen"). At one point the BBC approached David Anderson to be an advisor on the programme, but he declined, no doubt realizing that its course had already been set by Elkins. The programme's accredited researcher was her own thesis researcher, Terry Wairimu (though using a different name).

The reporter was a freelance, John McGhie, who happened to be John Lonsdale's son-in-law. The invitation to Gavaghan to appear in the programme had come from Lonsdale, in whose specialist sessions on modern African history Gavaghan had from time to time participated. It was not entirely clear how the invitation came about until eventually Gavaghan's wife tracked down an email from Lonsdale: "would Terence be prepared to talk over, 'without prejudice or commitment', a possible

TV episode, put together by my son-in-law, who reports for Channel 4, comparing, say the impact of Hola and Guantanamo? My son-in-law needs the commission."

Six months later, McGhie, having replaced Channel 4 as an outlet for the Elkins thesis with a BBC documentary series called "Correspondent", finally called Gavaghan. He made no mention of the programme's content or title ("Kenya: White Terror"), nor that the programme was complete apart from this last interview: both glaring breaches of the BBC's editorial code, which require production teams to keep interviewees fully informed at all times about the context of their proposed contribution.

Lonsdale readily concedes that memory is fallible, which is one of the reasons he is so dismissive of Elkins' reliance on anecdotal evidence (he also, in a letter to Gavaghan, described her estimate of Mau Mau deaths, as well as some of the content of the BBC programme, as "incredible"). He loyally supported his son-in-law at the eventual regulatory hearing of Gavaghan's complaint, but also regretted – so he told a former colleague of Gavaghan's – dropping Terry "in the shit", as collateral damage in the battle over reparations. To be fair to Lonsdale, Gavaghan had always been keen, in person and in those academic seminars at Cambridge, to defend his regime at the Mwea, openly and robustly. What Lonsdale may not have anticipated was the way the Griffith-Jones document might be used by a hostile interviewer.

In fact, when the BBC unit turned up at Gavaghan's home – and stayed for five hours – the interview meandered somewhat pointlessly until McGhie eventually turned to the Griffith-Jones document, which Elkins had given to him, and which he flourished at Gavaghan. At one point, after he had been asked the same question a third time ("did you ever stuff a detainee's mouth with mud, or order anyone else to do so?"), Gavaghan paused lengthily – furious with himself for having walked into what he now identified as an ambush – before again replying "no". The broadcast programme left in the 23-second pause, but excised the "no". I have spent 40 years in senior editorial roles in UK broadcasting, but have never come across so blatant an example of prejudice. The multiple breaches of the BBC's own code of conduct, and of the similar code issued by the UK's new broadcasting regulator, Ofcom, eventually led to the BBC being required to broadcast a 2-minute statement acknowledging the degree of unfairness with which Gavaghan had been treated.

The BBC defended its interrogation of Gavaghan by claiming he knew perfectly well what he was being questioned about, as he had seen the document himself – Elkins had told them so. Indeed, she assured the BBC – and through the BBC, the Ofcom adjudicators – that she had personally handed the document to Gavaghan in his home: she "presented this file to Terence in part to see what sort of reaction it would elicit (which he read through at the time of our meeting)".

Gavaghan flatly denied this ever happened. He had indeed had several meetings with Elkins during her research at the National Archive at Kew, and she had indeed shown him extracts from a number of documents she had copied, to assist him with completing his own memoir: every meeting was carefully noted in his diaries, including all the Kew reference numbers. There are notes in his file, in her handwriting, that she gave him in June 1998, citing Colonial Office files 822/836, 822/888, 822/1230, 822/1237, 822/1334 and 822/2093: but there is no mention of 822/1251, which is the file containing the Griffith-Jones memorandum, the covering Baring letter and correspondence with London: 23 pages in all.

Later, Elkins provided Gavaghan with an extract from the Baring letter, including the file reference, and she felt her claim of prior provision was clinched by the fact that the extract and the reference were included in his memoir, noting her as the source. But the text has been subtly altered in Gavaghan's book. What follows is what Baring wrote, with the section Elkins chose to pass on italicised:

"An administrative officer named Gavaghan, who has taken charge of all the Mwea camps, has introduced a number of changes and the result... has been good...He has generally improved co-operation and organisation all round...Last month we were back to a net release figure of 2,000 and... it should be possible to increase it soon on one condition...We find that, with the type of men from Manyani with whom we are now dealing, there are a certain number who arrive determined to resist and cause others to resist. We also find that the resistance of these men breaks down quickly in the great majority of cases under a form of psychological shock.

"*Gavaghan has been perfectly open with us.* He has said he can stop secret beatings such as that which occurred in the case of Jasiel Njau. He has said he can cope with a regular flow of Manyani 'Zs' and turn them out later to the district camps. We believe that he will be able to go on doing this a very long way down the list of the worst detainees. But he can only do this if *the hard cases are dealt with on arrival in a rough way. We have instituted careful safeguards, a medical examination before and after the arrival of the intake, the presence of the officer in charge all the time, the force being used by European staff only.*

"We have felt that either we must forbid Gavaghan and his staff to proceed in this way, in which case the dilution technique will be ineffective and we will find that we cannot deal with many of the worst detainees, or, alternatively, we must give him and his staff cover provided they do as they say they are doing. That is the reason why the Attorney General has prepared a new draft regulation...

"We can probably go further with the more fanatical Mau Mau in the way of release than we had ever hoped eighteen months ago. But to do so there must with some be a phase of violent shock. I privately discussed this question with Dr Junod of the International Red Cross...He has no doubt in his own mind that if the violent shock was the price to be paid for pushing detainees out to the detention camps near their districts, away from the big camps, and then onward to release, we should pay it."

There is no possibility that Gavaghan himself would have edited the Baring letter down to the brief section cited in his memoir. That could only have been done by Elkins. Nor would he have removed the "if" before "the hard cases". He would immediately have picked up on the reference to Dr Junod, who had told him directly something very similar when he inspected the Mwea camps. He would have scoffed at the notion of medical examinations before and after intake. And if he had seen the reference to the Griffith-Jones memorandum in the letter, he would unquestionably have wanted to peruse it. There he would have found the paragraphs where Griffith-Jones describes the forcible change of clothing as "a deliberate, calculated and robust assault" and his claim that Gavaghan told him that on previous intakes, a resistor was "put on the ground, a foot placed on his throat, and mud stuffed in his mouth; and...in the last resort knocked unconscious".

When he eventually read this, Gavaghan angrily wrote comments in capital letters in the margin. Of the first claim, he wrote "not accurate – quite out of order – they were compelled to change or held down to do it". Of the second claim, he underlined the phrase "past intakes", and asked "which? where? when?" (the one witnessed by Griffith-Jones was the first organised by Gavaghan). On "a foot placed on his throat and mud stuffed in his mouth", he wrote "no"; on "knocked unconscious" he wrote "never".

It is perhaps worth noting that anyone who has watched the British television documentary series "Prison", filmed in Durham Prison in the north of England, will have seen repeated instances of disruptive inmates being forced to the ground and then handcuffed behind their backs by squads of warders wearing body armour and helmets, and armed with shields, batons and tasers. Fists were legally used to subdue those resisting who might otherwise represent a danger to a warder.

Of course, Griffith-Jones may have been right in his account, and Gavaghan may have been protesting against that version in retrospect, 45 years later. It took him some hours to complete his annotations (including the fact that he had never heard of Jasiel Njau or secret beatings). But what is beyond dispute is that he could not possibly have been shown the Griffith-Jones memorandum when Elkins claimed, or at any point by her. It is also extremely unlikely that she could have shown the full Baring letter to Gavaghan: he would have undoubtedly included it in his own text, along with some of the many comments he eventually made, including the reference to Jasiel Njau. The more detailed her account of what she claimed, the stronger the suspicion that Elkins was consciously deceptive. She seems deliberately to have misled Gavaghan, and also the BBC and Ofcom. The evidence that this was not an incidence of faulty memory is close to conclusive.

As it happens, Lonsdale was also fully aware of the Griffith-Jones memorandum for at least four years before the programme was transmitted, but concedes that he never mentioned it to Gavaghan, despite their regular interactions, which included his writing a foreword for Gavaghan's memoir, published in 1999, in which he remarked on "the physical violence used to break the detainees' will", but also commended Gavaghan for succeeding in the task of rehabilitation "with so little force", largely thanks to his decision to use Kikuyu staff in achieving his objectives. The great majority of staff at Mwea were Kikuyu, which made co-operation that much easier. By contrast, just 8% at Hola were Kikuyu.

No one was recorded as having died from maltreatment during Gavaghan's Mwea period: indeed, in 1959, the government actually claimed that throughout the period since 1952, there had been no such deaths before Hola, which is clearly untrue, as even in 1958, junior minister Julian Amery reported to the House of Commons that there had been two prison deaths in 1956 and 1957, and that although only one officer had been convicted for one of these deaths, 56 officers in 1956 and 73 in 1957 had been convicted of lesser offences. One of these was Commandant L W Lemon, of Mara River camp, charged with actual bodily harm and convicted of common assault. The slipperiness here is Amery's reference to "prison" deaths; after all, Lord Lloyd had told the House of Lords in 1955 that between October 1952 and May 1954 twenty-six persons had been convicted of killing or maltreating Mau Mau suspects.

In fact, the archives list name after name of those who died. In 1953, two Europeans were fined for battery after the death of Elijah Njeru. In 1954, Kabugi Njuma was beaten to death at Agathi. In January 1957, Machiri Githuma died at Gathigiriri; Jasiel Njau was convicted of manslaughter, and given a sentence of 12 months imprisonment, with other "co-operating detainees" being convicted of actual bodily harm. In July that year, seven detainees were charged with manslaughter after Kariuki Muriithi died from cold water shock at Athi River (allegedly acting "under orders" from Major Breckenridge): six were found guilty and sentenced to one month of imprisonment. In the same year, two African interrogators, accused of murder, were convicted of manslaughter and jailed for three years. In September 1958, the death of Kabebe Macharia led to the conviction of two screeners for manslaughter. In the same month, another prisoner died on reception at Aguthi: the following month, the beating of 87 detainees on reception at Aguthi led to a CID investigation into unauthorized caning.

An ominous note in the files reports that there were at one time as many as three deaths per day at Embakasi, whose prisoners were deployed in building Nairobi's main airport (work was compulsory in nearly all camps and prisons, and sometimes paid). It is highly unlikely that such a death rate could have persisted at Embakasi without official intervention, as the camp was closely monitored: even so, a colleague of Tony France, Tony Murphy, told him that the conditions there "sickened him". The 3,800 inmates were all convicts, and all but 86 were KEM.

According to a report to the War Council from the ministries of defence and community development in 1956 (CO 6274/39), there were seven compounds at Embakasi, one of which was for Mau Mau leaders only, who wore "clothing of distinctive colouring". There was also a Special Rehabilitation Camp (SRC) "some distance away". Every evening, the 17 rehabilitation staff would hold a 1-hour baraza in one of the compounds, filtering leaders to the leader compound and the likeliest co-operators to the SRC, 40 at a time. There, no work was required, and the emphasis was on classes, games, family and elder visits and contact with co-operators: "usually sufficient to bring about the desired change in the course of three to four days". Different clothing was then issued, extra privileges granted, and a transfer to Kajiado (also known as Mile 37) followed. The plan was for 250 such transfers per month.

If anything like a death rate of three per day was prevailing when this report was written, it is very hard to imagine that the ministers would have deliberately concealed it. In fact, by the time the airport was ready for use, and the Embakasi convicts were dispersed, 15 months later, there were still 2,318 inmates, who were despatched to Nyeri (990), Fort Hall (630) and Kiambu (698). If even half the planned rate of release of 250 a month had been achieved, at least 1,500 of the original 3,800 would have been sent up the pipeline. That would leave almost no room for any substantial level of deaths. Based on interviews, Elkins describes Embakasi as a particularly brutal prison: but offers no estimate of deaths that occurred, whether through overwork or ill-treatment.

Nonetheless, if we add the known reported deaths in the screening camps and Home Guard posts during the early years of the Emergency (such as when Headman Wamai Muriu was convicted of murder and illegal detention in December 1954 by Mr Justice Cram), we can be sure there were scores of such victims, probably hundreds. Conversely, the fact that the archives tabulate so many individuals perhaps suggests that Hola was highly unusual, and that claims of thousands of detainee murders (as made by Professor Elkins) lack supporting evidence. As so often with the archives, the knowledge that they are incomplete, because so many documents were destroyed before independence, leaves open the possibility of incriminating behaviour being covered up.

9. The Hanslope Park archive

My detailed review of the section of the Hanslope Park archive dealing with document destruction reveals a rather different scenario. The operation, far from being a last-minute "burn everything" panic, as with the US officials abandoning Saigon to the Vietcong, was a carefully rehearsed process conducted under rules that applied to a series of de-colonisations.

As one official put it: "no sensible person would expect the transition to independence to be unaccompanied by the destruction or removal of some paper".

Over a lengthy period, a system called "Watch" replaced the old reporting and filing habits of the colonial decades (in Uganda, the new system was codenamed "DG"). Copies of new documents, with their carefully noted levels of secrecy, were strictly controlled, keeping access tightly limited so as to minimize the task of editing what was to be handed over to the incoming government. Meanwhile, all the accumulated documents were assessed to see which needed to be kept – so as to ensure an orderly handover with a clear history of decision-making – and which could either be destroyed (as no longer having any relevance, or being too sensitive to be handed over), or could be sent back to the UK (as part of the record of the colony's administration).

A subtle additional consideration was to ensure that there was a sufficiently coherent and known set of documents that accurately told the history of the colony, so that an incoming government minded to re-invent that history would be deprived of that option ("just in case a future nationalist government wished to erase all record of the colonial past and re-write history to accord with their point of view," wrote Chief Commissioner Robin Wainwright to Margery Perham, of Nuffield College, Oxford). This comment, it would seem, undermines the view that the UK itself was determined to "erase all record of the colonial past". Indeed, to protect that record, Wainwright encouraged Provincial Commissioners to co-operate with Dick Cashmore (a long-serving Africa hand) and Ms Perham in preserving archives "of historical value", which the two of them were proposing to microfilm for the benefit of Oxford and Cambridge universities. Those archives stretched back to 1895. Much of that material had no useful purpose for the incoming government, but was of great interest to historians, geographers, ethnographers, sociologists and – not least – archivists.

A key "sensitivity" was the tens of thousands of intelligence files, which could have become a source of considerable conflict as incoming politicians worked out who had been Special Branch informers and which Mau Mau operatives had killed which victims. As Ken Lees has pointed out, his own files served no useful further purpose once all the Fort Hall detainees had been released: they had not been compiled with a view to mounting prosecutions, only to ensure truthful confession. It would have been a travesty then to hand such explosive material to a set of African ministers starting afresh and trying to put the past behind them, as Kenyatta was urging.

A further sensitivity was to avoid leaving behind anything that might "embarrass" the UK government. This could range from reports on foreign countries, relationships with allies, or even something as basic as racist comments in documents, be they made by British officials or friendly ones, such as those from the US ("criticism by other races of Africans in any context should be destroyed"). Ironically, US citizens were restricted from viewing a range of classified documents: in the archive, we find a communication to Treasury being destroyed unopened because it was marked "Guard" (that is, not to be seen by US citizens), and its addressees happened both to be American.

As the restrictions became tighter, we find two of the most senior officials – the Chief Commissioner and the Permanent Secretary at the Ministry of Defence – restricting communications between them to two lockable metal boxes, to which only they, Wainwright's secretary and "Mrs Weeks in MoD Secret Registry" had the combination. Like some Gabriel Garcia Marquez novel, the system progressively retracted into itself, until just 13 authorised persons remained: all District Commissioners, all permanent secretaries bar three, even the Prisons Commissioner and the resident naval officer were excluded. One civil servant, Alastair Matheson, was prosecuted on six charges of failing to take reasonable care of documents (he was acquitted). The Ministry of Defence warned that Kenyan students were being taught techniques of subversion in communist countries: "we will eventually be faced with the presence of semi-trained intruders and saboteurs".

Pulling in the opposite direction were longer-term considerations. The Colonial Office wanted for its own archive everything of importance, so it is reasonable to assume that little if anything was deliberately destroyed simply to avoid potential embarrassment domestically: hence we find a lengthy exchange between the Colonial Office and Nairobi as Lennox-Boyd tried desperately to keep track of what had happened in Hola, including very bad-tempered responses to demands to know what "compelling force" meant ("read the exchange of messages of June 1957!", Nairobi signalled in disbelieving fury, referring him to the Griffith-Jones report from the Mwea, Baring's covering letter and Lennox-Boyd's reply).

The Lennox-Boyd message was accompanied by an inquiry from the UK Attorney-General, Reginald Manningham-Buller, asking that the Police Commissioner, the Minister of Defence and the Minister of African Affairs denounce the Cowan plan (see above and below) as illegal (in other words, endorsing the verdict of the magistrate who investigated the Hola deaths, William Goudie). Historians should be thankful that telephone calls were extremely rare – not least for security reasons – and that a full paper trail was typically retained. The ministers concerned were outraged by the telegram from Manningham-Buller (CO 141/6289 D156), and were unrestrained in deploring it: "Minister of Defence, Minister of African Affairs and Prison Commissioner all agreed that no illegal force was contemplated or would ever have been approved or tolerated".

Deputy Governor Crawford wrote to Lennox-Boyd insisting that "throughout the whole process of rehabilitation the use of illegal force has never at any time been contemplated by anyone. The contrary has been expressly ordered....[the] rather odd message from Manningham-Buller has very much upset us all here". When Lennox-Boyd, in the post-Hola panic, instructed putting an end to compulsory work, Crawford bluntly reminded him (June 12th 1959): "without compulsory work some 6,000 of the most recalcitrant detainees would never have been released to freedom...this is considered an integral first step in rehabilitation".

On small matters, too, avoiding embarrassment seemed not an issue. Someone with a sense of humour retained a lengthy sequence of inter-departmental memoranda over a period of some years, dealing with the travel and living costs of an official ostensibly from the Post Office in London who flew to Kenya, Tanganyika and Uganda in March 1951 to advise on postal services. There was meant to be an equal bearing of the cost between the three dependencies, but for some reason nobody would take on the Kenyan share until, belatedly, the Commissioner of Police grudgingly agreed to do so in August 1953. The junior clerks who had been chasing the missing amount were not cleared to understand what was really going on. It transpired that the Post Office gentleman was actually from the Security Service ("Colonel Allen's deputy"), advising on how to intercept and censor letters. It is not evident from the file whether the full censorship proposal was adopted, but the 1953 projection was for 200 staff and an annual cost of £716,000 in Kenya alone.

That the Watch system needed itself to be secret from most people raised its own problems – there was already a sophisticated hierarchy of secrecy: "confidential", "secret", "top secret", "guard", "UK eyes only", "secret and personal", "confidential and personal", "confidential and restricted" and so on – not least the possibility that some of the new African civil servants would work out that a "shadow" set of files was being created, even though clues as to its existence were carefully hidden. So be it, said a senior official: "it will not be possible to conceal from an alert Parliamentary Secretary the existence of these covert files".

This section of the archive is the last we see of Terence Gavaghan, who by 1962, as retirements, repatriations and relocations filleted the ranks in Nairobi, had become USGO (Under Secretary Governor's Office). Like all his senior colleagues, he is helping decide which files to keep for the incoming administration and the historical record ("should the new cabinet have access to the minutes of its predecessor?", "I have put to one side the papers relating to the early influence of MRA in rehabilitation camps") and which to destroy or return to the UK. His own departure was imminent – to a career in humanitarian projects, on behalf of the United Nations, governments, NGOs and commercial companies – but he would return every year to Kenya, where two of his children lived, until his 80s, regularly greeted by those he encountered in the streets of Nairobi as "Karuga Ndua", be they former detainees or former loyalists. He died in 2011 at the age of 88.

Governors also came and went. Baring was succeeded briefly by Sir Patrick Renison, who promptly blotted his copybook by denouncing the prospective release of Kenyatta, "the leader to darkness and death" (he had obviously read his Corfield and spoken to Wally Coutts). Summoned to London, he was brusquely dismissed by Duncan Sandys, the Commonwealth Secretary, leaving the son of the Labour Party's most reviled leader, Ramsay Macdonald, the questionable honour of presiding over the transfer of power in 1963. When Renison returned to Nairobi after his humiliation, Frank Loyd recorded that "the entire Council of Ministers turned out to greet him at the airport," in protest at the "inhuman performance put up by Sandys".

Like the pre-existing National Archive files on colonial Kenya, the Hanslope Park files reflect the life and problems of the colony as viewed from Kenya itself, seen through the prism of Government House. On file, we find plenty of special pleading, as with ministerial commentary on the Hola inquest findings (see below); the tensions over rehabilitation, detention, the "Mwea techniques" and relations with London are there for us to view; but no smoking gun revealing a secret plan to exterminate the Kikuyu is to be found.

10. Mariira and Shuter

As Ken Lees explains in an earlier chapter, Mariira was the only Fort Hall camp where it would have been imprudent to wander about chatting to people. In March 1959, John Pinney, the Fort Hall District Commissioner, wrote to the Minister of African Affairs, saying: "At the end of 1956, it became apparent that the only place where real progress could be made with the rehabilitation of hard core detainees was in a camp in the district of origin which was the subject of some home influence and where it could be demonstrated on the ground that Mau Mau was a thing of the past.

"Accordingly, in January 1957 it was decided that detainees in this category should be filtered into the pipeline through a Special Camp to be established in each of the Districts concerned. Mariira Camp...was selected in this District, and with a very good quarry within its precincts it was ideal for the purpose, but unfortunately with a capacity of only 400 it was not really big enough and one of the Mwea Camps in Embu District had also to be used as a subsidiary.

"The results achieved at this camp were quite remarkable. Detainees on admission from Manyani and other Camps were sullen and unco-operative, but within a very few weeks their attitude was completely changed and after two to four months their state of mind was such that they could be transferred to a Divisional Works Camp on their way to freedom.

"By the end of 1958, the Camp had completed its work and was closed but not before 2,117 hard core detainees had passed through it to Divisional Camps. During the two years of its operation no more than 20 had failed to respond to the process of rehabilitation practised in the District and had to be returned whence they came."

Including 20,000 convicts and repatriates in his overview, Pinney concluded: "I consider that the re-absorption into the District and the rehabilitation of some 88,000 persons to play a useful part in the life of the country reflects the very greatest credit on those District Officers, Chiefs and Headmen, Special Branch Officers, Prison Officers, Rehabilitation

Officers, Screening Staff and all Government Servants concerned with the operation."

As reported by Pinney, life in the Divisional Work Camp "consisted of hard work, the occupation of the mind throughout all the working hours, evening discussions on the new life in the Reserve, visits from relatives and regular screening whenever a subject asked for it and was willing to make a confession of his misdeeds, until such time as the Administration (including the Chief), the Special Branch and the Head Screener were satisfied that his state of mind was such that he could be safely released." Even then, after a few days in an open camp, and suspension of the detention order, there was still a requirement for regular monitoring.

By contrast with what Ken Lees tells us, this was a somewhat top down overview, but nonetheless correlates reasonably well. There is no mention of "dilution" or co-operatives haranguing recalcitrants. Did Askwith even visit Mariira? Lees disagrees with Pinney's figures, reckoning that more than 3,000 passed through Mariira (though his estimate for all Fort Hall degtainees released accords almost exactly with Pinney's, at 69,000). And he also disputes Elkins' claim of an alleged murder at Mariira, which she based on a letter (see p 337 of her book) from a group of detainees. His lengthy response not only rebuts the claim, but also provides enough detail to give pause to those who doubt whether he really did what he claims to have done in Kenya.

"I witnessed from start to finish the alleged 'murder' Elkins claims occurred at the Mariira Camp in 1958. Similarly, Eliul Mutoni [presumably a variation of Eluid or Eliud Mutonyi], the former Chair of the Mau Mau Central Committee, claimed to have seen two fellow detainees beaten to death at Mariira, and that the guards continued to beat the lifeless victims long after they were dead. Neither accusation is true.

"Elkins [continues Lees], claiming that the specific details were 'sadly familiar', quotes from a letter sent by detainees at Mariira to Colin Legum, The Observer's African Correspondent:

'This Camp… is a place where many wonderful tortures and maltreatments are meted out to us by a South African born European, D E Hardy… The Camp is hidden in a deep valley covered by a forest of wattle trees. No outsiders or people around locally can notice what is going on there. Here is a camp comparable to none–perhaps the Nazi Concentration camps could be better. The Government pays no heed whatsoever, although deaths after severe beatings have been reported

by us. The first death was of a detainee who on 23rd January 1958 was beaten by
warders to death. On 9 June a convict was battered to death. His name is Mwaura
Gathirwa, and three others Kariuki s/o Mwangi, Githutha s/o Wahoga and Irungu
s/o were seriously injured and were rushed to Fort Hall Hospital unconscious.

So far, we have written several letters to the Kenya Government about these
cases and none of our letters have been answered. Nor do we see any improvement
of the situation or action to stop these atrocities. For the first time in the history of
our detention we [have] been denied water, bathing or washing. Here bathing and
washing is restricted to once a week (Saturday). We do not have lights in our huts.
We are issued one shirt and one pair of shorts, and two blankets. The camp being
very cold as it lies within the Kenya highlands, we find the life very hard. We receive
very little medical care. A detainee is not to attend hospital treatment unless he is
on the brim of dying. We get inadequate and very badly cooked food…

The only work we do, which is breaking stones in the quarry, is supervised very
harshly. Everyone is forced to shout songs as he works. The day's work commences
at 6am, till 6pm, and in the evening everyone's voice is completely gone.

In this camp about 50 detainees are cripples, having been beaten, and others
suffering from asthma and poliomyelitis are forced to do heavy duties in the quarry
where they remain the whole day. Their complaints are not considered…

We write this article to you so that the public in the United Kingdom and the
Commonwealth may know how we are treated. Your paper is esteemed and impartial
and is well known all over the world. We therefore hope that you will kindly implore
all your readers to pray for us in our difficult times in our lives.'

"Elkins then asserts that the *'colonial government's spin team shifted into*
overdrive.' She describes the Colonial Secretary's response as 'uncritical' and
his explanations as 'excuses' on the basis that the District Commissioner had
reported that Commandant Hardy was from Derbyshire, not South Africa,
was a sound chap who believed in strict discipline and hard work and had
the attitude of a headmaster of a preparatory school.

"This so-called 'spin' is a truthful account of Hardy. Hardy was not a
South African, did not speak with a South African accent, and was not racist.
He was more jovial than terrifying, a big schoolboy who loved pranks. I
knew him well.

"I know of only one unnatural death at Mariira. That is consistent with
the advice provided to the Colonial Secretary: the other so-called victim
died of natural causes. Nor do I know of seriously injured detainees being
rushed to Fort Hall Hospital. In short, these other claims are also untrue.

"On the day in question [of the one death] I accompanied the Senior Superintendent of Prisons, John Cowan, to inspect a small weir that the detainees had constructed. Also present were my driver, First Class Constable Muli Wambu, and the Camp Commandant, D E Hardy. We had driven into the compound in my Land Rover and had alighted and started walking slowly down the hill towards the weir. Muli drove down beside us and we were followed by the group of detainees. There were sixty-three detainees and seven guards armed only with short bamboo sticks.

"The incident started off as a prank, initiated by two or three detainees only, in the middle of the group. It involved throwing small pebbles at us, initially in good humour. This was a common prank at Mariira, which was strewn with pebbles. It was intended to embarrass the guards in the presence of Cowan, who had arrived in full uniform. One pebble hit Cowan in the back of the neck puncturing his dignity and he turned angrily. So we got back into the Land Rover and drove further down the hill, across the playing field, back up the hill, and parked out of harm's way on the observation platform. We were then able to survey the scene below us.

"Hardy joined the guards to sort out the pebble throwing and on his instructions the guards sounded the alarm. The standard procedure required the detainees to squat down with their hands on their head in orderly ranks. They did so immediately. Thus order was restored and Hardy proceeded to tell the detainees not to be silly in the presence of senior visitors.

"After a minute or so, one detainee in the middle of the group stood up and started to shout at Hardy. Hardy patiently let him go on for several minutes and then instructed a guard to get him to sit down. A guard, a Kikuyu himself, approached the detainee and, when he refused to sit, hit him on the back of the legs. He continued to shout so the guard hit him again on his bottom. The detainee then put his hands on his head, but continued to shout. The guard then hit a third time on his arms. This caused the detainee to wave his arms about and a further blow aimed at the arms hit the detainee on the head instead. He then sat down.

"From our vantage point, the blows did not appear serious and no harm seemed to have been done. Hardy resumed his talk, the detainees were dispersed, we dropped Cowan off, and I returned to my interrogation duties elsewhere.

"I was stunned the following day when my love interest at the time, Sister Jane Arthur, stopped me as I drove past the Fort Hall Hospital and told me that a detainee had died some time after the prank. She was livid as there had been nothing like this previously, and asked me what had happened. She had assisted at the autopsy and told me that the detainee had some bruising on his body and had a rare abnormality to the brain lining, which was deemed the cause of his death. Her account is consistent with that given by the doctor who conducted the autopsy at the inquest."

Unbeknownst to Lees, the Hanslope Park documents confirm the official version of this affair, in CO 6300 170/58: "June 9 disturbance at Maririra – death of one prisoner by misadventure (coroner's verdict) – no evidence of an offence having been committed – 25 unco-operative convicts had been admitted, under the Heaton plan, and ordered into the quarry, where they threw stones, injuring 2 staff; for 3 minutes there was a running fight, as the convicts tried to get the detainees to join in. 3 hours later, 1 convict collapsed and subsequently died – the MO said he had an abnormally thin lining of the brain."

Lees challenges another set of claims which revisionist historians have taken at face value: those made by Victor Shuter (erroneously named "Sluter" in Anderson's book) and investigated in early 1959 by the Director of Public Prosecutions, A P Jack. Shuter made a number of claims about abuses at Mariira and Fort Hall (83 in all according to a note from Baring to Lennox-Boyd, 95 according to a statement in the House of Commons reporting that Jack had concluded that "the allegations are disproved".) The minister making that statement noted that Shuter was "certainly heavily in debt" when he made his claims, and was deemed "of disreputable character". His grocer had obtained a judgment against him in September 1958, and his camp account was in disarray. According to FCO 141/6333, Shuter – who had fled to London – was due to be tried for forgery and false pretences, and only submitted the affidavit listing his allegations in January 1959 when he was about to be surcharged for his grocery debt. He was ordered back to Kenya on July 15 1959, having managed to delay both his flight and publication of the Jack Report (which, incidentally, meant that Jack had to bow out of the disciplinary inquiry into the Hola disaster, which was handled instead by Duncan Fairn). What happened on Shuter's return is not disclosed, but Lees provides a full understanding of the whole farrago, in his statement to the Jack Inquiry in 1959, below, and then in a narrative he sent to me in 2018.

On 17 February 1959 I provided the following Sworn Affidavit to the Jack Inquiry:

"Kenneth Lees states:

I am an Inspector of Police stationed at Traffic Branch, Nairobi Area.

From 13th May 1956, to 2nd December, 1958,[1] I was stationed within Special Branch, Fort Hall, on detachment from Nairobi Headquarters, Detainees Section.

I was not in any way involved with the running of the camps. I was only interested in the people in the camps and as to their movement from one camp to other camps and their eventual release.

The camps which I had an interest in were Fort Hall Reception camp, Kandara Works Camp, Mariira Camp, Kigumo Works Camp, Kangema Works Camp and Kamaguta Works Camp.

The Fort Hall Reception Camp was for receiving persons from outside the district and for sending persons from within the Fort Hall District to hard-core camps. The other camps, except for Mariira, were divisional screening camps, and persons arriving at Fort Hall from those divisions went to their respective divisional camps.

In March 1957, the Commandant of Mariira Works Camp was a Mr D Hardy. His assistant, I cannot recall his name, was discharged, and one Shuter arrived at Mariira. He was not there very long when he was transferred to Kangema, I think. I know an African clerk named Nasson. He was stationed at Mariira Works Camp.

I visited Mariira Works Camp a considerable number of times throughout my tour at Fort Hall. I never saw any indiscriminate punishment or beatings administered to detainees. I never saw Hardy or Nasson give or order corporal punishment to detainees. I have, however, seen detainees who would not get off vehicles hit on the bottom with sticks wielded by prison warders to hurry them up. Hardy and the clerk had been present when this was done. As far as I could see this was more of a 'chivvying up' process rather than ill-treatment of detainees. These persons were new batches of arrivals at the camp. The sticks they used were thin pieces of bamboo, they were certainly not batons. The number of warders I have seen at the lorries on arrival of detainees were 10 to 20.

---

[1] These are the dates of Lees' formal out-posting to Fort Hall. His contract expired on 2 December 1958, but was extended on a one-off basis for six months to enable him to finish up the interrogation work that he was doing. He did not leave Fort Hall in practice until about mid-February, 1959.

I know one A W Shaw very well. He was staff officer in charge of works camps. I cannot recall whether he was present. At Mariira, there were a number of crippled detainees whom we were always trying to stop coming into the camp, as they were an embarrassment in that they could not work in the quarry. I knew a legless detainee who moved around on shortened crutches. I cannot remember his name. He was one of the first cripples to come to the camp. He was also one of the first detainees to change over from Mau Mau and to assist Security Forces in the camp. He was an original propagandist for Mau Mau. This man's legs were both off just above the knees. He used to work in the quarry, sitting down and breaking stone into small pieces. He worked in the quarry from the first day he arrived. This was not from a point of punishment, but from discipline. He was ordered to work in the quarry by Mr Hardy. It is my view that Mr Hardy could not have allowed him to sit in the camp doing nothing. After he changed over to the Security Forces he used to want to go down to the quarry to talk with the other detainees.

At no time did I ever see or hear that as this man was moving about on his crutches they were kicked from under him. As he had changed over to the Security Forces about three months after his arrival, there would have been no point in anyone kicking the crutches from under him. I think that this legless detainee stayed in the camp for about six months, was transferred to Kangema Works Camp, and then released to his home at Ichichi.

I can recall, in May, 1957, or thereabouts, I went round this Mariira Works Camp, and the others, including Kamaguta, together with Dr Junod and Dr Gailland, the delegation of the International Red Cross. We were accompanied by the medical officer, Dr R Y Taylor, the assistant district commissioner, Mr Pollok-Morris and the divisional district officer, and Mr Hardy. The camp was thrown completely open to the delegation. They could go where they liked and speak to whom they wanted. If I remember rightly I stood at the top of a central flight of stairs with, I think, Hardy, while the delegation toured the camp. At this time we had a particularly hard-core batch of detainees arrive only the day before. They were still in handcuffs and refused to come out of the compound. They would not let the prison staff near them to remove the handcuffs.

The delegation went into this compound and saw them. Not to my knowledge were crippled detainees removed from the camp to prevent their being seen by the delegation. I saw the delegation after its tour of the camp. I heard no complaints raised by them of allegations of ill-treatment of detainees. I heard them compliment Mr Hardy on the cleanness of the camp.

I knew Mr Hartley and Mr Irwin, they were at Kamaguta Works Camp and Fort Hall Reception Camp, respectively. I never heard either of these officers threaten detainees that if they raised complaints to visiting bodies they would be beaten.

I visited the Fort Hall Reception Camp a lot and entered the office quite a lot. There was a notice inside the office, hanging on the wall: 'Abandon hope all ye who enter here.' This was printed in English, and as far as I know the majority of the detainees could not read it. It was in the Administrative Office and very few detainees ever went in there, in proportion to the numbers passing through the camp. It was there when I first went to Fort Hall. I have no idea where it came from or when it was put there.

I know a number, three or four, deaf and dumb detainees at the camp generally. I remember two at Kamaguta. I never knew of a deaf and paralysed detainee at Kamaguta. Had there been such a person he would have been in hospital. The camp had no facilities to cope with such a person. I cannot say off-hand whether any of these deaf persons was named Macharia. I knew of no detainee being deaf, who was beaten so badly that he was released by the officer in charge without authority. All detainees were released on the orders of the District Commissioner, through me. Had such a detainee been released without authority I should have known about it, and raised it with the District Commissioner. I know of no case in which Mr Shuter, whilst officer in charge Kamaguta, released a detainee without authority.

During my time at Fort Hall, each camp had its own screening team of about 30 persons subdivided into locational teams. The teams were made up of local elders, a clerk to each team, and probably a rehabilitated detainee wishing to assist the Security Forces.

Everything a man said was recorded, and from this report, together with report on camp conduct and previous reports compiled, I decided whether he was suitable for release or not.

On my recommendation, and if he thought fit, the District Commissioner acted accordingly, either by releasing the detainee or ordering continued detention. No complaints were ever made to me by Kamaguta detainees that they had been beaten at their previous camps.

I have, however, read in their screening reports that according to them, they had been beaten, but from my knowledge of the camps and the people it was all part of Mau Mau *doctrine to allege beatings, and I took these allegations in the statements to be untrue. These statements are on record at Fort Hall. On my tours around the camps, I never saw any of the screeners using violence towards detainees.*

I know that Shuter is the type of chap who, if he found himself in any trouble, and thought it was caused by someone else, would try and get that other person in trouble. Going around, and in my job, I have heard that Shuter was down on his stores and rations, and that Irwin was the responsible officer in his (Shuter's) headquarters, and he obviously thinks the trouble he is in came from Irwin. It was always noticeable that Irwin and Shuter did not get on well together, in their workings.

Now his amplification, nearly 40 years after the event:

"I was one of 94 witnesses, and one of the 28 people about whom Shuter made allegations (7 who had returned to England could not be traced: the rest all denied his claims). Shuter falsely claimed that detainees arriving at Kamaguta from Mariira or Fort Hall reception had complained to me of ill-treatment there, and that I had failed to act on these complaints. No such complaints were made to me, nor is it possible that any such ill-treatment could have occurred without my knowledge of it. He also falsely claimed that detainees with injuries were hidden when outside inspections occurred (as if such a process would have had any chance of success), and that detainees were threatened with punishment if they complained to such visitors: again, false. No doctors, nurses or dressing staff could corroborate his claims of injuries inflicted on detainees.

"I knew Shuter from his time as second-in-command at Mariira, and also at Fort Hall. Although I did not deal with him when he was at Kamaguta, my conclusion from interactions with him was that he was an insignificant and incompetent officer, who made trouble wherever he went. The commandant at Mariira, Hardy, needed better support in a difficult job, and I was glad when Shuter was moved from there. Needless to say, Shuter lied about Hardy as well as about everything else. Unfortunately, I was indirectly responsible for Shuter being assigned to

Hardy, as his previous second-in-command had been caught by me in the only unauthorised punishment I encountered during my tour of duty: half a dozen detainees had been forced to sit with their feet in freezing flowing water. I put a stop to it, reported the officer concerned, told the Assistant District Commissioner that Hardy needed a break, and saw him waiting for a bus to Nairobi later that day. He returned two weeks later, and Shuter was then appointed as the new second-in-command, but Hardy quickly realised he was unsuitable, and had him replaced. He turned up at Fort Hall, answering to Aaron Irwin, but again did not last long, and was sent off to Kamaguta.

"One of the more absurd charges made by Shuter – solemnly re-cycled by Professor Elkins in her book – was that there was a sign on display in Fort Hall saying "Abandon Hope All Ye Who Enter Here", as if to intimidate the detainees. In fact, as I made clear in my affidavit, this sign was put up, presumably as a joke, inside the administrative office: few detainees would ever see the inside of that office, and, in any case, the majority could not read English. That Mr Jack was forced to investigate this trivia was a waste of time in 1959: that an academic historian should take this complaint seriously is, unfortunately, only evidence of her bias and credulity.

"My first encounter with Shuter had occurred when he was transferred to Mariira. I was there with the commandant, Hardy, when a voice called from inside a building asking how many t's there were in the word "battery": to which Hardy replied "three, you fool", only to receive the response "oh, don't be like that". When I asked him whose voice that had been, he said it was a fellow called Shuter they had sent him.

"About a month later, Shuter was transferred to Fort Hall, presumably because Hardy found him inadequate. There was an officer there who befriended him, called Williams: he was the officer responsible for formally charging anyone accused of an offence. In September 1957, I was president of the police mess, responsible for social events, and Williams asked if Shuter could attend the film shows we ran on a Saturday night. I talked to Shuter for a few minutes, which was enough time for him to claim to me that he had been a full lieutenant in the King's African Rifles, having originally worn one "pip" as a second lieutenant, and then having served enough time to earn an automatic second "pip". Then, apparently, a brigadier had noticed his second "pip", and demanded it be removed. Quite why he would want to tell a story about this "demotion" I never understood. As far as I could gather, he never rose higher than the rank of sergeant. How he passed the interview test to become a prison officer is a puzzle I have not solved.

"Now it so happened that my driver, Muli, and I had been involved in a river rescue, saving a young boy (though sadly not all those who were in the vehicle that had crashed into the river), and as well as my receiving a certificate from the Royal Humane Society, the father of the boy – a prominent member of the Asian business community – sent over a large chicken curry lunch for a number of Sundays.[2] On one of these days, Williams drove over to Shuter's quarters to collect him for the lunch, and caught him having sex with his houseboy. He realised that this put Shuter in jeopardy on many fronts: homosexuality was then illegal, also risked catching what we then called "SLIMS" disease (and was later named HIV-AIDS), and exposed him to the risk of blackmail, not least by Mau Mau.

"Soon afterwards, I found Williams in the main sitting room of the mess, holding his head in his hands, and groaning: "what should I do?" He told me the story, and I advised him to treat Shuter as he would anyone else, but I assume he chose to keep quiet, as I heard nothing further. Similarly, Group Captain "Tiger" Shaw told me that Shuter's returns on supplies required were deficient, but not whether anything had been done about it.

"Then, in February 1959, I was asked by Nairobi CID if I would go to the UK to help arrest Shuter, who had fled the jurisdiction in order to escape his debts, and was to be charged with forgery and fraud. It was not convenient for me to go, but I later heard that he had been arrested on a warrant in July 1959. What happened thereafter I do not know.

"What caused Shuter to contact The Observer and then take refuge in London, I also do not know: perhaps further money issues, or possibly the risk of blackmail had made life too difficult – it may even be that his sworn statement to the newspaper was concocted to mollify blackmailers, but that is speculation, though some incidents relating to detainee interviews at Kamaguta after he was transferred there, and how he came to know their contents, raised questions in my mind which were never satisfactorily answered.

---

[2] Ken Lees received letters of congratulation from both the Commissioner of Police (Robert Catling) and the Chief Secretary (Walter Coutts) in connection with this award.

"For instance, Shuter would not have known Macharia's village, or the name of his local chief *[a detail in one of Shuter's many stories]*. Nor would he have known anything about whether or not I recorded claims of beatings, as he was never in my office, and rarely in the camp (like most commandants, he would spend the day with working parties). My assumption was that this kind of allegation would have stemmed from the chief screener at Kamaguta, whom I had reprimanded for failing to bring a released detainee in to see me, after he had complained that the man had been spreading Mau Mau propaganda. He reported that the man had died of pneumonia – a very unlikely story. Unfortunately, as he was one of my best interpreters, I could not afford to dismiss him.

"That Shuter is still being taken seriously by the High Court, sixty years after he was comprehensively discredited, is a mystery in itself.

"Ken Lees October 2018"

That I have included the details of Ken Lees' comments and evidence on Mariira and Shuter at such length is because they give the strongest documentary proof of his relevance to the second court case (see section 12 below). Ken is the most reliable living witness on these matters, and his version of events is substantially preferable to those provided by contemporary historians relying on allegations rather than truth.

Shuter's fate is not disclosed in the documents. In February 1959, Ken Lees returned to Nairobi to complete his tour of duty, and then departed Kenya, never to return, nor to make public until now what he knew about the scale of Mau Mau killings. Meanwhile, the Jack inquiry report, running to 111 pages, with 241 pages of statements, was itself reduced to a footnote as soon as the Hola scandal emerged.

11. Hola

As the detention system wound down towards the end of 1958, the problem of the hard core resisters, who had been sent down the pipeline to Hola, became more urgent; urgency heightened by the prospective transfer from Takwa of 79 detained Mau Mau intellectuals (the ones Askwith felt he had no one of the right intellectual calibre to tackle for rehabilitation purposes). Their arrival was imminent, as Takwa was closing and there was no alternative location. Monkey Johnston insisted that under no circumstances should they be allowed to interact with the existing Hola inmates.

The Minister of Defence and the Commissioner of Police, Cusack and Lewis, visited Hola and concluded that the situation would only worsen – in the sense of the last 200 detainees, mostly recent arrivals, retreating into complete defiance – unless some attempt was made to challenge their resistance ("we must either let them stew and risk the contamination of the convicts and the open camp detainees, or take such action as planned with the risk of someone getting hurt or killed" – a form of words that was to cause Lewis, who wrote them, and the whole administration, acute embarrassment when his note was published by the magistrate investigating the Hola deaths).

A plan of action had been drafted by John Cowan. Given the perceived success of the Mwea operation, it was natural to send Cowan to Hola to advise on what to do. As with Thiba, he recommended that nothing be attempted till the main compound was replaced with four smaller units. He proposed then that small groups of non-co-operators be taken to a nearby agricultural development, and put to work on something as basic as weeding, on the theory that any agreement to work would be a breach in the rigid rejection of the entirety of the detention process (the most fearsome detainees at Hola refused to eat camp food, or allow inspection of their living space, which was described by visiting Red Cross officials as utterly squalid). Cowan concluded that, in extremis, the detainees' hands should be held by warders so as to ensure some "work" was done.

The magistrate who investigated the Hola deaths that occurred when the work scheme was implemented thought that Cowan's idea was neither realistic nor safe, and most likely illegal; but he also concluded that what the Hola Superintendent, Michael Sullivan, actually undertook was a reckless version of the Cowan recommendations. First, Sullivan accepted both the refusal by the director of the local agricultural scheme to allocate a weeding task, and his insistence that spades and other tools be used to dig trenches. Then, Sullivan declined Cowan's offer to send officers from Mwea to help, instead asking for an Assistant Commissioner of Police, only to be told that none was available. For reasons never explained, Cowan's detailed written report to the Police Commissioner on how he expected the operation to proceed (invariably called "the Cowan plan", even though he insisted it was not a plan as such) was never sent to Sullivan. Nonetheless, the Minister of Defence and the Police Commissioner agreed that Sullivan should go ahead when he felt ready to do so, and there was no need to notify the colony's

Security Council of this – even though (as described above) Lewis had warned that the operation might result in injury, or even death.

Cowan's report – handed in just before he departed the colony to take leave in England – provided for small groups of detainees, no larger than 20, one group at a time, to be escorted to the work place, with equivalent numbers of warders, supervised at all times by several European officers. No batons were to be used to enforce compliance. He assumed that any resistance would be encountered inside the camp, where it would be readily contained, as it would not involve more than one group. Instead, Sullivan marched 85 detainees out of the camp towards the irrigation scheme site where 34 co-operative detainees were already at work; the 85 were outnumbered by six platoons of warders armed with batons, rifles, shields and shotguns, but only one European officer was available to oversee the operation (all the rest were engaged that day on other duties). As soon as the detainees realised that they were not, as they had assumed, going to gather wood to heat their huts, but were being sent to dig trenches, disturbances broke out, each of which took several minutes to quell.

Eventually, the party arrived at the irrigation ditches, but only Sullivan and his deputy, Alex Coutts, were – intermittently – available to supervise this highly risky operation (absurdly, two of Sullivan's four European officers were required in court that day as witnesses). At a time when both Sullivan and Coutts were absent, the askaris supervising the detainees – mostly Nandi – started using their batons to beat recalcitrants. Sullivan had instructed Coutts to send a water truck, so that all those working – the co-operators digging trenches close by as well as the 85 and their warders – could refresh themselves. When Coutts returned to the location, at 11.30 am, he found a detainee vomiting large amounts of water, and then collapsing, dead. Soon, another collapsed. Coutts instructed work to cease, and started ferrying apparently injured men back to the camp's medical centre. He told the magistrate that it "looked like an army returning from action, with many wounded, supported by comrades". By mid-afternoon, there were ten dead; another died two days later.

The scale of the disaster was compounded by the shock and confusion displayed by Sullivan and his team. His medical officer could not advise on the cause of death. Post-mortems could only be conducted in Nairobi, and would take days to be completed. Sullivan notified the Mombasa CID, who immediately began an investigation, and asked the local District Officer to arrange an inquest into the deaths, which would be presided over by the Senior Resident Magistrate, William Goudie.

Meanwhile, the local District Commissioner, Willoughby Thompson (who, as a DO in Central Province had been heavily involved in dealing with Mau Mau attacks), arrived at Hola. He was irritated that he had not been forewarned about the operation, and had only now been notified of the calamity, and was not persuaded by Coutts' claim that somehow the water wagon was implicated – why had all the others drinking from it, including guards and officers, not been affected? He sent a telegram to a senior official at the African Affairs ministry in Nairobi, Garland. It seems that he, or others at Hola, also alerted key officials at Defence and Prisons, Small and Campbell. To Garland he signalled, cryptically: "Imperative reps yours flies Hola immediately. Contact Campbell who has also been asked to fly in. Reason on arrival." (The original telegram is in the archives.)

Campbell had already been contacted by Sullivan on the camp wireless, and alerted to four deaths, but Sullivan did not want to speak more openly on an insecure communication system. Campbell confirmed with his superior, Lewis, that he should go, but it is probably putting the status of the three men rather too formally, when they arrived, semi-briefed, the next morning at Hola, as "a sort of Government Commission" (the magistrate's description, and also Thompson's, understandable but inaccurate), though Government House was aware of their journey.

When they reached Hola, at 8.30 am after a two-hour flight, the three men so summoned found a group of camp officers still seemingly in a state of shock. Although it was reported by the Medical Officer, Dr Moyes, that some of the victims had physical injuries, including fractures, the extent of bruising was not yet fully apparent. The "commission" had no time to visit the camp infirmary and so saw none of the injured, let alone the dead bodies. The Assistant Superintendent of Police from Mombasa, O'Dwyer, saw "no obvious signs of death being caused by violence or brutality" (the post-mortem revealed three fractured knee-caps, two fractured forearms, a fractured jaw and a fractured skull amongst seven of the victims, but O'Dwyer's observations the day after the disaster explain why Baring felt able to tell Lennnox-Boyd that "there is not the slightest indication that any force used had any connection with any of the deaths").

The youthful Dr Moyes thought two of the victims might have died of "aspiration pneumonia", and Sullivan and Coutts could still not exclude the water wagon from their thinking. Nor could they admit their gross negligence in leaving these detainees, deemed so highly dangerous, in direct confrontation with their African guards, unsupervised by European officers. Whereas a majority of warders at the Mwea were Kikuyu or Kikuyu-speakers, just 21 out of 225 were at Hola. Most warders – Nandi, Kipsigis, Nyanza, Kamba and Samburu – would probably have feared and despised the detainees, in equal measure.

The Nairobi officials, muddled by the briefings they had received, returned in the afternoon to report to the colony's Governor and cabinet. Making notes was the colonial government's chief press officer, Robert Lindsay, who took it on himself to publish a release blaming contaminated water for the deaths. This attempt to mitigate criticism may have been misguided rather than a deliberate attempt at a cover-up (which would have no chance of success, as the CID investigation and autopsies would inevitably arrive at the true cause of death), but it proved shatteringly counter-productive as soon as the post-mortem results emerged a few days later. All the dead had been severely beaten with batons.

One additional factor that emerged during the inquest triggered further criticism: there were widespread indications of vitamin D deficiency, which raised a question of whether scurvy might have been a contributor to the fatal outcomes (the coroner confirmed that susceptibility to bleeding, which was a characteristic of scurvy, would have amplified the impact of heavy beatings, but was only potentially implicated in one of the deaths). The Hola authorities argued strongly that any dietary problems were self-inflicted, as the hard core non-co-operators insisted on preparing their own food, and rejected ascorbic acid tablets routinely issued to other detainees (it transpired that some warders showed symptoms of scurvy: they were not issued with tablets). This did not stop the Labour opposition at Westminster latching on to the scurvy issue, along with the supposed cover-up and the damning findings of Senior Magistrate Goudie, and ministers were lashed in a series of parliamentary questions and debates.

Famously, a leading Tory backbencher, Enoch Powell, in a brief but decisive intervention, condemned a policy which seemed to provide "African standards in Africa, and perhaps British standards here at home". We must, he concluded "be consistent with ourselves everywhere". (Typically, Elkins, with her tenuous grasp of British political history, repeatedly describes Powell as a "former" Tory MP, who had "resigned from the party" six months earlier:

he had actually resigned as a junior minister 18 months earlier, but was still a Tory MP, remaining so for another 15 years, including two as a cabinet minister. He actually voted with the government when the debate ended. This kind of howler is perplexing in a Pulitzer-winning book.)

Although nearly all Labour speakers in these 1959 debates praised and cited magistrate Goudie's conduct of the inquest and findings ("a remarkable and penetrating analysis," judged Labour front-bencher Frank Soskice), Professor Elkins goes out of her way to criticize him as some kind of stooge, engaged in a cover-up. Perhaps what upset Elkins was how dismissive Goudie was of the closed camp detainees ("hard core fanatics" – "the inner core of the hard core" – "sullen, suspicious and quite obviously entirely fanatical" – "potentially dangerous in the highest degree") and of nearly all the African witnesses called: none was prepared to co-operate with the court, be they detainees or warders. Yet he was just as scathing about the European witnesses, especially those who should have prevented or intervened in the massacre.

The only "witness" Elkins chooses to cite is Paul Mahehu, using an interview given to her 40 years after the event, failing to recognize that he was obviously telling lies in claiming that "well over 500 askaris" were assigned to undertake a deliberate assault. In fact, only 111 warders were available. He claims to have been covered with the brains of someone whose skull had been broken. No such injury was inflicted. He claims that the commandant, Sullivan, asked after each calculated assault how many were dead – first six, then ten. The real problem, as identified by the inquest, was that Sullivan was not there at all during nearly all the beatings, having returned to the camp for over two hours, and only realized when Coutts tracked him down at 12.15 in the camp that there had been any casualties at all.

28 detainees were called as witnesses at the inquest: no one named Paul Mahehu was among them. Some of those who agreed to testify claimed to have been beaten for four continuous hours. Goudie disbelieved them (and not just because he regarded that as highly improbable in 120-degree heat). All the independent witnesses spoke of batons only being used for ten to fifteen minutes. Goudie had also established, in questioning 50 detainees at Hola himself, that no beatings had taken place at any time before March 3rd. In Hola's previous four years, there had been just three deaths, two as a result of dysentery, one caused by "ileus paralitic". Instead of canings as punishment for refusing to work, the Hola commandant simply withdrew

privileges. This tolerance of work evasion was one of the reasons that Cusack and Lewis had asked Cowan to make recommendations as to how to restore control at Hola.

Mahehu claimed to have stayed in the camp clinic for "several weeks", with "scores of others" "watching the eleventh man die"; in fact, 29 of the 30 men hospitalized were treated for minor injuries, one for a more serious injury, none of them stayed for "weeks", and the eleventh victim did not even report sick till nearly two days after the massacre. But Elkins believes Mahehu, word for word. It is hard to know what to make of an historian who is so willing to trust oral testimony, however at variance with the known facts (that said, the Wikipedia entry on Hola, which cites Elkins but also the Mau Mau mouthpiece, Nairobi's "Daily Nation", is even more ridiculous).

She also claims it was Barbara Castle who "exposed" the truth about the water truck: in fact, a government chemist called Kirby had conducted an inspection on March 6th, and reported that there had been no contamination. By the time the final post-mortem was completed, on March 9th, there was nothing left to "expose", except the excruciating incompetence of Sullivan, the role of the Cowan "plan", the inadequacy of Coutts, Moyes and O'Dwyer, the disturbing reluctance to intervene on the part of the irrigation scheme employees and the wall of silence from the warders: Goudie would be the man who would expose all that.

Anderson, too, seems not to have bothered to read the readily available inquest proceedings, and chooses to quote from his own 1999 interview with Willoughby Thompson rather than Thompson's actual testimony at the inquest. In the interview, again 40 years after the event, and when Thompson was 70 years old, he told Anderson that he had seen corpses lying on the ground in front of one of the compounds; but what he actually told Goudie at the inquest was that he had been informed of three deaths by Inspector O'Connor of the local police force, who had been called in by Sullivan, that Dr Moyes had then reported five deaths, with more dying, at which point Thompson had asked the Kilifi police to send a senior CID officer. It was when Superintendent O'Dwyer arrived that Sullivan and Coutts mentioned the water cart.

In the 1999 interview with Anderson, Thompson claimed that they (exactly who he meant by "they" is unspecified) had said "they had thrown lots of water over these chaps, and as a result they had drowned". Nobody

said this to Thompson, nor did he testify to such nonsense at the time;
nor, as Anderson asserts, was this the lie that Nairobi propagated (that
was a different lie, about contaminated water, and – at the time, and again
contrary to Anderson – it was believed, when Baring passed it on to
London, correcting it as soon as the first post-mortems came in). Sadly, this
garbled story was repeated in Thompson's obituary in the Daily Telegraph
when he died in 2018. Anderson also mistakenly describes Thompson as a
District Officer rather than District Commissioner, and the work demanded
of the Hola victims as "hard labour", when it was paid-for ditch-digging,
whose nature and extent the 34 co-operators negotiated directly with the
irrigation scheme managers.

Anderson's conclusion, that "eleven detainees lay dead, clubbed to death
by their African guards while European warders looked on", is simply
careless: there were only two dead initially, four more dying on the way
to hospital, after all work had ceased, four more in hospital that afternoon,
with the eleventh victim dying three days later; and the problem was not
that the European warders looked on, but that they had effectively left the
askaris unsupervised for lengthy periods (what the Fairn inquiry into Hola
later called Sullivan's "crowning folly"). Also – thanks to Sullivan's patchy
Swahili – the warders were under the impression that if the detainees caused
any kind of trouble ("fanya matata"), they were at liberty to beat them
(Sullivan thought "matata" meant violent resistance).

The detainees who did offer testimony were seemingly indifferent to
truth or even consistency. One said that everyone on the work detail agreed
to work; another said that none was willing. All denied any knowledge of
Mau Mau or oathing, one even claiming not to know why he had been
arrested. Giving evidence to the inquest, Provincial Commissioner O'Hagan
(who had previously served in the Mau Mau heartland of Central Province)
disagreed: "It was impossible for the detainees at Hola not to be connected
with Mau Mau. These men at Hola were the inner core of the hard core.
They are fanatics. Most hard core Mau Mau had been responsible for
atrocities, many atrocities. There was a reign of terror and killing of women
and children accompanied by horrible brutalities."

"Not a single prison officer, warder or detainee made any attempt to
tell the truth," said Goudie in his judgment. His strongest condemnation
was for "the blatant lies of all the detainees themselves, whose sole concern
seemed to be to paint the blackest possible picture against the entire

Prison Staff irrespective of how patently impossible, even ridiculous, their evidence sounded". With warders collectively refusing to submit to identity parades, and detainees more interested in frustrating the legal process than securing justice, even to the extent of refusing to identify the dead, Goudie reluctantly concluded that it was impossible to assign blame to any individual for any of the deaths.

When Solicitor-General Conroy chaired a disciplinary tribunal, Sullivan was dismissed, and both Taxi Lewis and Jake Cusack took retirement (one of them early). Coutts was absolved. Griffith-Jones considered prosecuting Sullivan for abetting manslaughter, and even one of the irrigation scheme managers for perjury, but conceded that convictions were unlikely. Cowan was exonerated, while the evidence was insufficient that Campbell, let alone Garland and Small, had deliberately misled the Nairobi meeting (if anything, Lindsay had been more culpable for the "contaminated water" story). Anderson concludes that this was yet another case of the Kenya administration blaming the junior staff: yet, based on the evidence what other option was there? As it turned out, none of those who struck the fatal blows was ever charged, let alone convicted, whilst Sullivan, Lewis and Cusack, as well as (eventually) Baring and Lennox-Boyd at least lost their jobs. Anderson's account of Hola, with its multiple errors, is disappointing in an otherwise authoritative history.

In the archive there is an intriguingly annotated copy of the Goudie verdict. Judging by the asperity of the comments, a minister must have been responsible, probably Cusack, as this is a Ministry of Defence file. In response to Goudie's denunciation of the "Cowan plan", as contemplating the use of illegal force, there is annotated: "coroner's interpretation of the 'Cowan plan' has no more validity than anyone else's" – Goudie "seems not to have fully understood the plan", which (said the note-writer) required only one small group at a time to proceed to the irrigation scheme, with the whole operation being abandoned if the group either failed to obey the order to proceed, or thereafter the order to work. Goudie had "confused" the two orders. As for the finding that Sullivan believed he had "carte blanche" to use "whatever force might be necessary", the note-writer asserts that this is contrary to prison and Emergency regulations, which require any use of force to be proportionate and reasonable, and that only "Mwea-style" force would be used, "which Cowan, in particular, would know".

Likewise, the note-writer criticises the magistrate's reference to Sullivan's call for a Senior Superintendent of Police ("that was not in the plan"). As for Goudie's criticism of the lack of detail in Cowan's proposal with regard to European supervision, the note-writer simply refers to the fact that Cowan had specifically called for "sufficient European staff of all ranks". Goudie noted that there were indeed four European officers in the compound: to which the note-writer's riposte is "but not on site". As for Goudie's comment on the "absence of express orders" to Sullivan, the note-writer drily says of Sullivan: "he was in charge of the operation". The most dismissive note is in relation to Goudie describing Campbell as one of "the Government Committee of Inquiry", and saying that Campbell, Garland and Small "had been sent to Hola as a sort of Government Commission": "nonsense" is the comment.

Where Goudie says "I find it impossible to understand how Mr Campbell could properly report that 'there was no apparent evidence of punitive beating', the annotator impatiently comments "there *was* no *apparent* evidence", and that anyway, none of the three officials looked at any of the bodies. Notably, Thompson did see several bodies, on the day of the disaster, but like O'Dwyer failed to spot any bruising. And the annotator also took exception to Thompson's comments, as highlighted by the magistrate, challenging Campbell's statement that there nothing indicating that the 'compelling exercise' was connected to the deaths: "but did he [ie Thompson] say it was?" Indeed, says the annotator, responding to Goudie's assertion that Campbell "must have known about the previous day's 'compelling exercise'", "of course he did, but compulsion does not include batons and Dr Moyes misled him".

Goudie was critical of Campbell's role in the Government House meeting: was there enough consideration of the role of the water tanker? The annotator says "it was discussed at nauseam" (implying he was there), and of Goudie's reference to Lindsay ("he ought to have studied Campbell's report with the greatest care"), the response is just: "he did".

The subtleties and evasions that had characterized ministerial support for the Mwea system for two years could not survive Goudie's blunt assessment: "beating to compel detainees to work or to punish them for not working was entirely unjustified and illegal". That the Mwea punishments were ostensibly for refusing to obey orders, and not directly related to working, was lost on the magistrate, and completely lost in the parliamentary uproar that followed his verdict. No wonder the anonymous annotator bewailed the abandonment of "the old-fashioned idea that loyal officers are not thrown to parliamentary wolves".

Yet Cusack (if he was the annotator) and Lewis had only themselves to blame for this abandonment. Even their supportive cabinet colleagues struggled to justify Lewis'"hurt or killed" choice of words, especially when the two of them nonetheless agreed between themselves not to involve the Security Council. Perhaps they saw it as just another medium-risk operation in the sorry history of managing detention, which had already claimed a number of lives without putting ministerial careers at risk. The eventual formulation that ministers adopted to explain the gloomy prediction was that such an eventuality was not foreseen as part of the work process, but rather as a potential result of a riot in the compound if one of the groups realised what was intended (and then, it would only be detainees, not warders who greatly outnumbered them, who might be at risk).

This contorted and belated reading of the note persuaded no one on the Labour benches in the House of Commons, and outrage was expressed that both men were allowed simply to retire. Following on from the magistrate's strictures, one MP, Kenneth Robinson, declared that the Cowan plan must have been intrinsically illegal, as even after the 85 detainees had been split into groups of twenty or so, beatings leading to death occurred (omitting the equally valid observation that at least 40 of the 85 had undertaken work for some hours, and that the beatings had been in contravention of Cowan's explicit instructions for no batons to be used, with European officers always in attendance). He also, not having had the benefit of Ken Lees' expansion on his evidence to the Jack inquiry, expressed dismay that the Jack report (which was published in time to play a supporting role in the Hola debacle) should have thought a double amputee suitable for working in a quarry (as Lees explains above, he volunteered for that work). And, inevitably, in Robinson's view, attributing the death of the Mariira detainee to natural causes was clearly all part of a collective cover-up.

By this time, the Labour Party had lost all confidence in the government's Kenya policy, and disbelieved virtually anything ministers said. One of its MPs, Dingle Foot, refused to accept that any detainee was a member of Mau Mau unless he had been convicted in a court – not realising that most of those remaining in detention after 1958 were actually convicts whose sentences had been converted to detention orders.

The Kiambu District Commissioner made available to the inquest the dossiers of the six victims from his district: Foot might have found them instructive reading.

Mwema Kinuthia alias Gichinga Kamau took his first Mau Mau oath in 1949; Batuni (more senior) oath 1953; chair of Muguga War Council and fundraising; "by far the most influential member of the Council"; involved in attacks; arrested 1955; "one of the most difficult cases of hard core fanaticism ever to be received into the camp system";

Ndungu Kibathi, oathed 1952; Batuni oath 1953; third oath (Kindu) 1954; particularly violent; arrested 1955; involved in riots at Athi River and Gatundu;

Kinyanjui Njorege was Secretary Kamandura Committee; oath administrator; arrested 1954; Thiba 1956, organised resistance, sent to Manyani, then back to Thiba; "just wanted to die";

Kiamau Karanja took two oaths in 1953, attended nine oathing ceremonies, murdered, with five others, Githau Gikiriti, who was strangled and dumped in a dam; arrested 1954; made four admissions at Thiba, sent to Kiambu works camp, reneged, sent back;

Karuba Mboro, forest terrorist, leader of 1953 Marigi raid (eight dead, including four children); strangled, with others, Ngugo Mrefu, and threw body in river; strangled resistant girl at Kariobangi; oathed at least twenty; strangled another refusenik on the spot; captured 1958; "mass murderer and irredeemable Mau Mau thug of worst kind";

Kahuthu Kamau took two oaths, including Batuni; arrested 1954 and convicted of Mau Mau membership; sentenced to 7 years hard labour; rioted at Gatundu.

The Hola nightmare did not end with the anti-climax of the verdicts and their consequences. Baring signalled London that he was installing Thompson, the Tana River District Commissioner ("I should give him a meal or a bed," he told colleagues at Government House, once Thompson had steadied the show at Hola) to take charge of Hola ("like we did with Gavaghan at the Mwea"). However, trying now to induce the remaining Hola inmates to take their ascorbic acid tablets, as insisted upon by Lennox-Boyd, the new prison commandant found himself facing a hunger strike which started on May 12th, of which the prime movers were 25 of the Takwa "petitioners" (as the other detainees labelled these inveterate letter writers and campaigners).

Soon there were 144 strikers, with 82 more threatening to join. Forced feeding was deemed too risky, transfers by aircraft to hospital were fraught with danger ("should they be taken to hospital by force there will be riot, repeat riot!" – there is a "possibility of fatalities": this is "not panic but fact," telegraphed a panicky Thompson at 12.45 on May 22nd). With a succession of such hunger strikes planned, involving endless flights to hospital, a full cabinet meeting decided to send all the strikers back to Manyani, and on June 1st – in almost his last ministerial act – Lewis promulgated Operation Nectarus, whereby 52 Hola closed camp inmates were secretly transferred, first to Nairobi and then Langata, in five caged vehicles guarded by 50 warders, 20 armed with rifles; and then on by rail to Manyani. The operational instructions ran to seven pages.

By this date, there were just 133 detainees left at Hola, including 103 "unacceptables" from Kandongu, who could not be sent up the pipeline. The largest group of "unacceptables", 26 in number, was, unsurprisingly, from Kiambu. Hola underwent a name change – to Galole – in October: but its history could be neither deleted nor re-written (after independence, the name change was reversed). Through the last stages of the Emergency, ministers were also unnerved by the apparent recrudescence of Mau Mau in the shape of movements like Kiama Kia Muingi ("overshadowing all other matters" said one police document, reporting 3,000 members, of whom 172 had been arrested and 130 served with GDOs). By June 1959, there were 450 KKM at Aguthi, but just 21 female "intransigents" at Kamiti (compared with 164 two years earlier) and 60 Hola "survivors" now at Senya.

The Fairn Commission recommendations had once again inverted the structure of responsibility, returning the task of rehabilitation back from prisons to a new Special Commissioner (Robert Wilson, replacing Johnston) accountable to the Ministry of African Affairs. Fairn shared Heaton's view that separating detainees from prisoners was an essential pre-condition of a rehabilitation policy: in prison, "convicts formed irredentist Mau Mau cells", and although eventually the more amenable were sent up the pipeline towards filter camps (such as the Mwea), divisional work camps (such as Fort Hall) and eventual release, the hard core were "eddied by their obduracy to the pool of present unmanageable detainees", mostly held in Hola since it had opened in 1955. According to Fairn, the sheer numbers being held had for a long time "largely nullified all efforts at rehabilitation": the scale of detention fostered a level of intransigence "with the remnants of which we are still dealing".

Lennox–Boyd had banned compulsory work whilst awaiting the
Fairn report, despite anguished protests from Nairobi, pointing out that
6,000 recently released detainees had only broken with Mau Mau after
accepting orders to work. Indeed, those currently working at Aguthi
and Kandonga, without the threat of punishment, would "revert to
idleness". Fairn now forbade the use of "shock" treatment (making "no
judgment on the past") for fear of further hardening resistance. Yet as he
found when encountering a solid block of Mau Mau at Senya, he was
met with "hatred and contempt"; "discipline vanished" in the absence of
"punishment for anything"; all of which was "destructive" of detainee
morale and "fatal" for staff morale. At the end of August 1959, officials
reported "an acute loss of discipline at both Manyani and Senya – prison
staff are generally demoralized about the Hola affair – it is impossible to
bring Senya under control".

And there were morale issues with loyalists, too. The Nairobi bureaucracy
recorded in painful detail the process of tracing the families of the Hola
victims in order to dole out the statutory 120 shillings compensation. One
victim, who came from Turkana, had no traceable family. Another had three
wives, and children by each: how to divide the money? However trivial the
amounts, they provoked great bitterness amongst Mau Mau victims and
the family survivors of those who had been killed by Mau Mau: who will
compensate us, they cried?

By March 1960, even with the Emergency having ended two months
earlier, the new Special Commissioner was acknowledging "a complete
breakdown of rehabilitation". The Lancaster House negotiations for
independence only encouraged intransigence amongst the few remaining
in custody ("'uhuru' was just around the corner," as one report put it).
By January 1961, a year after the Emergency's end, there remained just
25 detainees and less than a hundred restrictees (who launched their own
hunger strike, requiring forced feeding). Thirty-three hard core detainees
diagnosed with TB had simply been released; four others were declared
"civil lunatics"; but even those deemed at one time most dangerous were
allowed home, under supervision. The last three Kiambu district works
camp detainees were released in May 1961. Although tensions remained
high in Kikuyuland, there was no return to physical conflict (the recent
bouts of electoral violence in Kenya have been inter-tribal rather than
intra-tribal).

Essentially, the administration (and the International Commission of the Red Cross, in parallel) concluded that there were just three groups of detainees by this stage: politicals, thugs (or gangsters as the ICRC termed them) and psychopaths. With Mau Mau disarmed and dismantled, the thugs could do little harm; perhaps the psychopaths might be offered psychiatric treatment; and the politicals could scarcely be held back now that elections were planned and independence was looming. All the bureaucratic agonizing and detainee suffering could simply be allowed to come to an end.

12. The second verdict

In delivering his lengthily-argued conclusions in the case of Kimathi v FCO, Mr Justice Stewart went out of his way to preface his judgment with a full citation of William Hague's 2013 statement, including this formulation: "many thousands of Mau Mau members were killed while the Mau Mau themselves were responsible for the deaths of over 2,000 people including 200 casualties among the British regiments and police". It is not obvious why he should have thought it necessary to recite this mantra – he clearly had no way of knowing how misleading it was – and it is equally not obvious whether this reference back to the Mutua litigation was prompted by the Crown's presentation of its case. But another aspect of the judgment puzzled me even more.

Four years ago, I was sent a copy of a letter from the Treasury Solicitor (no doubt by someone aware of my published letters and articles on the subject of detention and "excess" deaths during the Kenya Emergency) seeking help in locating potential witnesses for the Crown in the pending Kimathi litigation. The person in the department who wrote the letter was Ms Anju Lohia, and I put her in direct touch with Ken Lees. Subsequently, her team spent some hours talking to him by telephone. He heard nothing further from them, and was not asked to give evidence in London.

It was therefore perplexing to read paragraphs 100, 221, 223 and 224 of the Kimathi judgment. In these, Mr Justice Stewart repeatedly remarked on the dearth of witnesses available to the Crown due to the passage of time. He noted that "it was very rare for a witness to have been the author of a document such that the document could properly be put into context by that witness"; that Ms Lohia, in her tenth (sic) statement on behalf of the Crown, had said she could find no one who had any knowledge of any Test Claimant mistreatment, or "incidence of violence in the community, including Mau Mau reprisals"; that there was no "evidence from people [such as Mr Jack] conducting inquiries into alleged misbehaviour and from those they interviewed at the time and against whom allegations of misconduct have been made, in particular allegations by Mr Shuter"; and that there was "a lack of evidence from this type of witness".

Nothing could be clearer from Ken Lees' experience than that he was indeed one of those against whom Shuter had made allegations, that he knew a great deal about the whole Jack inquiry, that he had made a statement to Jack, that he had given evidence to the inquest into the death at Mariira, and that he had abundant knowledge of the "incidence of violence in the community, including Mau Mau reprisals". Yet he had not been called as a witness, despite the Crown being perfectly aware of his availability.

During the course of the case, I had tried more than once to make contact with Ms Lohia and the solicitor handling the case for the Crown, Andrew Robertson, and had been politely deflected. Reading the judge's words, I wrote to Mr Robertson, and to leading counsel, Guy Mansfield QC, to ask if they were aware that the court may have been misled by Ms Lohia, perhaps inadvertently. I sent them the original statement Ken had made to the Jack inquiry, together with the amplifications printed above. Mr Robertson promptly promised to investigate,

A few days later, he wrote to me to say that counsel and solicitors representing the Crown case had "carefully" considered whether the Court might have been, even inadvertently, misled, and concluded that it was not. He went on to say that all dealings with witnesses were "privileged and confidential", and could not be discussed with me. In any event, the time for service in the proceedings had passed, and he had no intention of re-opening the matter.

Undeterred, I sent all the material directly to the judge, whose reply was both swift and cordial, but essentially made the same points. It was entirely up to the Crown to decide which witnesses to call, such decisions were privileged, and the case was closed. He made no comment on my reference to Ms Lohia, who had, so it seemed to me, failed to tell him about a witness who met several of the key criteria he raised in his judgment. Of course, it may have been only after he delivered his judgment that it would have been apparent to Ms Lohia how Ken Lees would have fitted Mr Justice Stewart's stated requirements in the presentation of witnesses. Even so, the deliberate choice not to call Ken raised some questions in my mind.

After all, if the consideration had been Ken's health, and the question of travelling to England from Australia, it would have been easy to say so. It was certainly true that, in the end, any evidence from Ken would not have affected the outcome, as that was decided on technical legal grounds. Yet the decision not to call Ken was clearly deliberate, and only two further possibilities remain.

The first is that the Crown legal team simply did not believe what Ken had to say. It is the case that various people who have read material based on Ken's claimed experiences have expressed doubts about its veracity. One former member of the Kikuyu Guard thought he was a "Walter Mitty" character. A leading historian doubted if he spent more than a brief time at Fort Hall. However, such doubts cannot be sustained in the light of the documentary and photographic evidence Ken has retained of his years at Fort Hall, nor of the independent evidence of his presence there (such as the Jack Report and the citation for bravery sent by Wally Coutts, the Chief Secretary of the colony). Notably, to re-assure the original co-author of his planned memoir, Ken sought out a justice of the peace and swore an affidavit as to the truthfulness of his account. (Despite five years of co-operation, the two terminated the project after a disagreement over assignation of copyright and recovery of expenses.)

One historian has suggested that, even if these confessions were made, perhaps the detainees invented them, because that is what the mzungu (stupid white man) wanted to hear: rather begging the question as to how different detainees in different camps could make interlocking confessions about the same crimes, and why. As we know from John Pinney's own report to Nairobi, the agreement of Special Branch was required before any detainee could be released: and no one other than Ken Lees has laid claim to playing that role at Fort Hall.

Yet what is indisputable – because it is in the official record – is that Ken Lees served at Fort Hall for the period he claims, was a witness to the Jack inquiry, and gave evidence at the Mariira inquest. Even if he had simply repeated in court what he had told the Jack inquiry sixty years ago, he would have ticked one of Mr Justice Stewart's's stated boxes. A much older witness, Sir Willoughby Thompson (he was knighted when he was appointed Governor of Montserrat), was well into his 90s when he testified, not very helpfully, at the trial (he died shortly afterwards, aged 98).

There is another possible explanation for not calling Ken, and not explaining why he was not called: that his testimony as to the scale of Mau Mau killings (which would inevitably have emerged in the course of giving evidence) might, even so many decades later, prove an embarrassment for the Government. Corfield's terms of reference – the "origins and growth of Mau Mau" – carefully omitted the scale of killings, and he could only tangentially refer to it in his findings. A more honest inquiry would have asked every single District Officer, Chief and Headman in Kikuyuland to assemble a list of known victims, and an estimate of total numbers of those killed, as a key element in the story. But the sheer degree of complacency and indifference displayed by the pre-Emergency administration, if fully exposed to view, could have caused a scandal several multiples of that generated by the Hola killings, even decades later, and especially after compensating thousands of the veterans of the organisation that had carried out those killings.

That key historians continue to ignore or misrepresent what Corfield believed and Ken Lees can confirm allows even today's politicians to evade responsibility. The adoption of the Elkins "moral balance" is consistent with decades of denial and obfuscation. Arguably, the apology and compensation that ended the Mutua litigation were deemed a pragmatic alternative to a full-scale examination of the Emergency and its precursor failures. "Virtue signalling" is a widespread phenomenon these days, with apologies abounding for all kinds of governmental blunders, however many decades in the past.

But if it is true that 10,000, 20,000 or even more Kikuyu were slaughtered by Mau Mau before the British colonial authorities responded, then the whole tenor of historical inquiry into the Emergency would have to change. Capital trials, harsh conditions in detention, even the abuses in the screening camps and the deaths at Hola would need to be viewed in terms of an entirely different "moral balance". Those who fought Mau Mau, or tried by hook or by crook to rehabilitate the tens of thousands of Mau Mau detainees and convicts, knew what they were dealing with: a dangerous, ruthless and brutal insurgency which could have cost tens of thousands more Kikuyu their lives if action, however belated, had not been taken.

That is surely the story that Ken Lees is telling us. How he played his part in helping thousands of Mau Mau shed the burden of their oaths is an important contribution to the history of the Emergency: but the story behind it is of even greater significance.

David Elstein is a TV executive, broadcaster, writer, and radio and TV producer. He was awarded a major scholarship in history at Gonville and Caius College, Cambridge, graduated with double first class honours at the age of 19 in 1964, and was later elected to an Honorary Fellowship of the College. However, his planned DPhil thesis at St Antony's College, Oxford – on the replacement of British by American power in Palestine 1944-7 – had to be abandoned when his supervisor took up a vice-chancellorship at short notice.

He was selected as a general trainee by the BBC in 1964, working as a producer/director on such programmes as "Panorama", "Cause For Concern", "People In Conflict" and "24 Hours", before joining the main commercial network, ITV, to work on "This Week" (of which he was executive producer for four years), "Weekend World" and "The World at War" (of whose 26 episodes he produced three and wrote one). For Channel 4 he created and produced "A Week in Politics", and the Emmy-winning drama "Concealed Enemies" (about the Alger Hiss case). He won a Canadian Gemini award for co-producing the mini-series "Glory Enough For All" (the story of insulin). More recently he has worked as an executive producer on the Oscar-winning Polish film "Ida", and on the 2-hour documentary marking the 80th birthday of Athol Fugard, "Falls The Shadow".

After running his own production companies for four years, he was appointed Director of Programmes at the leading ITV company,

Thames TV, then Head of Programming at BSkyB, and Chief Executive at Channel 5 (which he launched, and took to a valuation of £1 billion). He subsequently served as a non-executive director or chairman of Virgin Media Inc, Sparrowhawk Media, Luther Pendragon, DCD Media plc, Sports Network plc, Screen Digest, the Commercial Radio Companies Association, the National Film and Television School and the British Screen Advisory Council.

He has given more than a dozen public lectures, written scores of articles for newspapers and other publications, and has been a visiting professor at the universities of Oxford, Stirling and Westminster. His Oxford Lectures were published as "The Political Structure of UK Broadcasting 1949-99". He was the lead author of the Broadcasting Policy Group's 2004 report on the future of the BBC entitled "Beyond the Charter". The 2-hour audio dramas he has written and produced, "July 1914: Countdown to War" and "Countdown to Peace: March to November 1918", are distributed by audible.co.uk.

INDEX